THE REGULATION
OF PARALEGALS
Ethics,
Professional Responsibility,
and Other Forms
of Control

THE REGULATION OF PARALEGALS
Ethics, Professional Responsibility, and Other Forms of Control

by

William P. Statsky
Professor of Law
Western State University
College of Law (San Diego)

WEST PUBLISHING COMPANY
St. Paul   New York   Los Angeles   San Francisco

Cover by Paul Konsterlie
Composition by Rolin Graphics

COPYRIGHT © By WEST PUBLISHING COMPANY
50 W. Kellogg Boulevard
P.O. Box 64526
St. Paul, MN 55164-1003

Printed in the United States of America

Library of Congress Cataloging-in-Publication Data

Statsky, William P.
    The regulation of paralegals.

    Includes index.
    1. Legal assistants—United States.   2. Legal
ethics—United States.   1. Title.
KF320.L4S745   1988   174'.3'0973   87-13802
ISBN 0-314-59231-8

Also by William P. Statsky

Case Analysis and Fundamentals of Legal Writing, 2d ed. St. Paul: West Publishing Company, 1984 (with J. Wernet)

Family Law, 2d ed. St. Paul: West Publishing Company, 1984

Inmate Involvement in Prison Legal Services: Roles and Training Options for the Inmate as Paralegal. American Bar Association, Commission on Correctional Facilities and Services, 1974

Introduction to Paralegalism: Perspectives, Problems and Skills, 3d ed. St. Paul: West Publishing Company, 1986

Legal Research and Writing: Some Starting Points, 3d ed. St. Paul: West Publishing Company, 1986

Legal Thesaurus/Dictionary: A Resource for the Writer and Computer Researcher. St. Paul: West Publishing Company, 1985

Legislative Analysis and Drafting, 2d ed. St. Paul: West Publishing Company, 1984

Paralegal Employment: Facts and Strategies for the 1990s, St. Paul: West Publishing Company, 1988

Torts: Personal Injury Litigation. St. Paul: West Publishing Company, 1982

Rights of the Imprisoned: Cases, Materials and Directions. Indianapolis: Bobbs-Merrill Company, 1974 (with R. Singer)

The Legal Paraprofessional as Advocate and Assistant: Roles, Training Concepts and Materials. Center on Social Welfare Policy and Law, 1971 (with P. Lang)

What Have Paralegals Done? A Dictionary of Functions. National Paralegal Institute, 1973

For
Gabriel

CONTENTS

Introduction

A paralegal or legal assistant is a person with legal skills who works under the supervision of a lawyer or who is otherwise authorized to use these skills. The terms "paralegal" and "legal assistant" are often used interchangeably to cover the same position. There is, however, no definition that everyone accepts. No law exists defining the position.

The American Bar Association (ABA) has provided us with the following definition:

> A legal assistant is a person, qualified through education, training or work experience, who is employed or retained by a lawyer, law office, governmental agency, or other entity in a capacity or function which involves the performance, under the ultimate direction and supervision of an attorney, of specifically-designated substantive legal work, which work, for the most part, requires a sufficient knowledge of legal concepts that, absent such assistant, the attorney would perform the task.

This definition, while awkwardly phrased, covers most legal assistants and paralegals in the country today. But not all of them. The definition assumes that legal assistants and paralegals always work under the ultimate supervision of a lawyer. As we shall see in later chapters, this is not so. The ABA would like it to be so, but the reality is otherwise. Hence the definition is incomplete.

The growth of this new career over the last ten years has been dramatic. This development, however, has not been without conflict. A major center of controversy has been the issue of regulation. In this book we will focus on regulation by examining the kinds of controls that exist, why they exist, and what shape the continuing debate will probably take in the future.

THE REGULATION
OF PARALEGALS
Ethics,
Professional Responsibility,
and Other Forms
of Control

Summary

There are seven ways in which the activities of paralegals are or could be regulated:

1. Laws on the unauthorized practice of law and on the *authorized* practice of law by nonlawyers.
2. State licensing of paralegals.
3. Bar regulation of a lawyer's use of paralegals.
4. Regulation of the education of paralegals.
5. Self-regulation by paralegals.
6. The Fair Labor Standards Act.
7. Tort law, e.g., the negligence of paralegals and of lawyers who use them.

1. THE PRACTICE OF LAW

Statutes defining the practice of law apply to paralegals. Criminal prosecution can result from a violation of these statutes. In general, the statutes prohibit nonlawyers from appearing for another in a representative capacity, giving legal advice, and drafting legal documents. A common theme in the literature is that if the activity calls for the exercise of professional judgment, a lawyer is required. But clear definitions of such concepts are often difficult to find. Furthermore, there are some major exceptions to the prohibitions on nonlawyer conduct.

In a limited number of circumstances, nonlawyers are authorized to do what would otherwise constitute the unauthorized practice of law. For example:

- In many states, a real estate broker can draft sales contracts.
- Some lower courts, e.g., Justice of the Peace Court, allow a nonlawyer to represent others before such courts in certain kinds of cases.
- A few states allow paralegals to "appear" in court to request a continuance or a new date for the next hearing in a case.
- An inmate can "practice law" in the institution, e.g., by giving legal advice to, and drafting court documents for, another inmate if the institution does not provide adequate alternative methods of providing legal services.
- Many administrative agencies, particularly at the federal level, allow nonlawyers to represent clients before the agencies.

2. LICENSING OF PARALEGALS

A number of states have considered paralegal licensing statutes. To date, no such statutes have been enacted. There is no license requirement for paralegals in any state. A major objection to licensing is that it will stifle the development of paralegalism and fail to account for the great diversity in the field. The vast majority of paralegals work for lawyers. Since lawyers are licensed and are responsible for what their paralegals do, the argument is that the public does not need the added protection that would come from a separate licensing scheme for paralegals. Yet proposals for mandatory licensing continue to emerge in spite of the fact that organized paralegals (through their associations) and most bar associations feel that licensing is premature.

3. ETHICAL RULES GOVERNING
LAWYERS AND PARALEGALS

Lawyers are regulated by their state bar association and state court system. The rules governing their conduct are found in the canons of ethics and in the ethical opinions that interpret these canons.

No lawyer must belong to the American Bar Association. It is a voluntary national organization. The ABA has its own canons of ethics and ethical opinions that individual states are free to adopt, modify, or reject. For years the canons were found in the ABA Model Code of Professional Responsibility. In 1983 the Model Code was revised. The current document is the ABA Model Rules of Professional Conduct.

No canon of ethics at the state or national level can directly apply to paralegals because the latter cannot be members of bar associations. A paralegal, therefore, cannot be disciplined by a bar association for unethical conduct. But a lawyer can be disciplined for the improper use of paralegals, e.g., the failure to supervise them properly.

Over the years, the bar associations have issued guidelines on the permissible scope of paralegal use by lawyers. But the bar associations have not always agreed on what these boundary lines should be. The following are some of the issues that have been addressed:

- What the nonlawyer employees can be called.
- Whether paralegals can sign their name on letters written on law firm stationery.
- Whether the names of paralegals can be printed on law firm stationery.
- Whether paralegals can have their own business card.
- When paralegals should identify themselves as nonlawyers to the public.
- Whether paralegals can be present at real estate closings when their supervising lawyers are not also present.

Later we will examine how such issues have been resolved.

One ethical responsibility on which there is no disagreement is the obligation of lawyers to ensure that their paralegals preserve the confidences of clients.

4. BAR ASSOCIATION CONTROL OF PARALEGAL EDUCATION

The American Bar Association "approves" paralegal training schools. The approval is voluntary. No school must be ABA-approved, and most schools have decided not to apply for this approval.

Initially, the entity that conducted the approval program was the ABA Committee on Legal Assistants. The Committee made its recommendations on approval to the governing body of the ABA, which made the final decision. More recently, the ABA has established an Approval Commission to administer the approval process. The Commission reports to the Committee on Legal Assistants, which in turn makes its recommendations to the governing body of the ABA.

The ABA has been ambivalent about the propriety of its role in regulating paralegal schools. While no court or law prohibits the ABA from continuing its approval process, the ABA has decided to withdraw from the process in the expectation that its role will eventually be taken over by an independent accrediting entity. It is unclear, however, whether such an entity is feasible.

5. SELF-REGULATION BY PARALEGALS

There are two national paralegal associations: the National Association of Legal Assistants (NALA) and the National Federation of Paralegal Associations (NFPA). There has been considerable disagreement between the two groups on major issues. For example, NALA favors a proposal to allow paralegals to become associate members of the American Bar Association; NFPA opposes it. More significantly, NALA favors the voluntary certification of paralegals and has launched its own certification program through the Certified Legal Assistant examination. NFPA opposes certification at this time. Both NALA and NFPA agree, however, that mandatory state licensing of paralegals should be discouraged.

6. FAIR LABOR STANDARDS ACT (FLSA)

The FLSA requires employers to pay overtime compensation to employees *unless* the employees are employed in an executive, administrative, or professional capacity. Paralegal managers with major responsibility for the supervision of other paralegals would fall within this exception and hence would not be entitled to overtime compensation. The U.S. Department of Labor, which administers the FLSA through its Wage and Hour Division, takes the position that most other paralegals do not fall within the exception and therefore are entitled to overtime compensation.

7. TORT LIABILITY

If a paralegal commits a tort, e.g., negligence, slander, the paralegal is personally liable to the defendant. Under the theory of respondeat superior, the supervising attorney is also liable for the wrong committed by the paralegal if it occurred within the scope of employment. Most attorneys have malpractice insurance that covers their employees.

Before examining each of these categories of regulation in detail, we need to define the terminology involved in any system of control:

> *Accreditation* is the process by which an organization evaluates and recognizes a program of study (or an institution) as meeting certain predetermined qualifications or standards.

Certification is the process by which a nongovernmental organization grants recognition to an individual who has met certain predetermined qualifications specified by that organization.

Licensure is the process by which an agency of government grants permission to persons meeting predetermined qualifications to engage in a given occupation and/or to use a particular title.

Registration is the process by which qualified individuals are listed on an official roster maintained by a governmental agency or by a nongovernmental organization.[1]

Approval means the recognition that comes from accreditation, certification, licensure, or registration. As we will see, the American Bar Association uses the word "approval" as a substitute for "accreditation" of paralegal education programs.

Code is any set of rules regulating conduct.

Guideline is suggested conduct that will help an applicant obtain accreditation, certification, licensure, registration, or approval.

Regulation is any governmental or nongovernmental method of controlling conduct.

Unfortunately, the distinctions made in the above definitions are often blurred in discussions of the topic.

---

[1] National Commission on Accrediting, *Study of Accrediting of Selected Health Educational Programs,* Part II, Staff Working Papers, p. ii (Feb. 1982).

2

The Unauthorized and the Authorized Practice of Law

(a) DEFINING THE PRACTICE OF LAW

Every state has laws on who can be a lawyer and on the unauthorized practice of law. In most states it is a *crime* to practice law illegally. For example:

> **Alaska Stat. Ann. 08.08.230 (1968).** Any person not an active member of the Alaska Bar who engages in the private practice of law or represents himself as entitled to engage in the private practice of law in the state. . . is guilty of a misdemeanor and upon conviction is punishable by a fine of not more than $1,000, or by imprisonment for not more than one year, or by both.

Normally such rules do not apply when a citizen is acting as his/her own lawyer. The regulation is aimed at people who represent others. It is not a crime to represent yourself in a criminal case or in a civil case such as one growing out of an automobile accident.

What is the practice of law? Most definitions are extremely broad. Examine, for example, the following Louisiana statute:

> **La. Rev. Stat. 37:212 (1964).** "Practice of law" defined.—The practice of law is defined as follows:
> (1) In a representative capacity, the appearance as an advocate, or the drawing of papers, pleadings or documents, or the performance of any act, in connection with proceedings, pending or prospective, before any court of record in this state; or

6

(2) For a consideration, reward, or pecuniary benefit, present or anticipated, direct or indirect,
  (a) the advising or counseling of another as to secular law, or
  (b) in behalf of another, the drawing or procuring, or the assisting
      in the drawing or procuring of a paper, document, or instru-
      ment affecting or relating to secular rights, or
  (c) the doing of any act, in behalf of another, tending to obtain or se-
      cure for the other the prevention or the redress of a wrong or
      the enforcement or establishment of a right.

Problems arise, however, in the application of such broad definitions, as you will see in doing the following assignment.

ASSIGNMENT 1

Below you will find excerpts of three opinions from Massachusetts
(*Opinion of the Justices*), West Virginia (*Earley*), and New York (*Winder*).
Assume that the above Louisiana statute (section 37:212) was in effect
in Massachusetts, West Virginia, and New York.

1. Is the *Opinion of the Justices* consistent with section 37:212? Could
   the "gratuitous furnishing of legal aid to the poor" violate section
   37:212? Explain your answer.
2. Is *Earley* consistent with section 37:212? Would *Earley* have
   reached a different result if the West Virginia court was applying
   section 37:212? Explain your answer.
3. Is *Winder* consistent with section 37:212? Would *Winder* have
   reached a different result if the New York court was applying section 37:212? Explain your answer.

Opinion of Justices to the Senate
Supreme Judicial Court of Massachusetts, 1935.
289 Mass. 607, 194 N.E. 313.

The gratuitous furnishing of legal aid to the poor and unfortunate
without means in the pursuit of any civil remedy, as a matter of charity,
the search of records of real estate to ascertain what may there be disclosed without giving opinion or advice as to the legal effect of what is
found, the work of an accountant dissociated from legal advice, do not
constitute the practice of law. There may be other kindred pursuits of
the same character. All these activities, however, lie close to the border
line and may easily become or be accompanied by practice of the law.
The giving of advice as to investments in stocks, bonds and other securi-
ties in real or personal property, and in making tax returns falls within
the same category.

West Virginia State Bar et al. v. Earley
Supreme Court of Appeals of West Virginia, 1959.
144 W. Va. 504, 109 S.E.2d 420.

The courts in numerous decisions in different jurisdictions have undertaken to define and designate what constitutes the practice of law; but it is generally recognized that it is extremely difficult, perhaps impossible, to formulate a precise and completely comprehensive definition of the practice of law or to prescribe limits to the scope of that activity. It is clear, however, that a licensed attorney at law in the practice of his profession generally engages in three principal types of professional activity. These types are legal advice and instructions to clients to inform them of their rights and obligations; preparation for clients of documents requiring knowledge of legal principles which is not possessed by an ordinary layman; and appearance for clients before public tribunals, which possess the power and authority to determine rights of life, liberty and property according to law, in order to assist in the proper interpretation and enforcement of law.

. . .

Section 14, Article 1, Chapter 23, Code, 1931, provides that the State Compensation Commissioner shall prepare and furnish blank forms of applications for benefits, notices to employers, proofs of injury or death, of medical attendance, of employment and wage earnings and other proofs, and that it is the duty of employers to keep on hand a sufficient supply of such blanks at all times. The completion of such blank forms does not require any knowledge and skill beyond that possessed by the ordinarily experienced and intelligent layman, and a layman may properly complete and file such forms in behalf of another person as employer, employee, claimant or beneficiary without engaging in the practice of law. In Shortz v. Farrell, 327 Pa. 81, 193 A. 20, the court said that preparation and filing of pleadings in connection with a workmen's compensation claim do not constitute practice of law for the reason that they are executed on forms prepared by the Workmen's Compensation Board, are elementary in character, and do not rise to the dignity of pleadings as that term is understood in judicial proceedings. A natural person who appears in his own behalf as claimant, litigant, or party in interest in courts or other duly constituted agencies or tribunals does not engage in the unauthorized practice of law. Natural persons may manage, prosecute, or defend their own actions, suits and proceedings and defend prosecutions against themselves except when the public welfare demands otherwise, and such activity does not constitute the practice of law.

The justification for excluding from the practice of law persons who are not admitted to the bar and for limiting and restricting such practice to licensed members of the legal profession is not the protection of the members of the bar from competition or the creation of a monopoly for the members of the legal profession, but is instead the protection of the public from being advised and represented in legal matters by unqualified and undisciplined persons over whom the judicial department of the government could exercise slight or no control.

The admission to membership in the legal profession is a privilege granted in the interest of the public to those who are morally fit and mentally qualified for the sole purpose of protecting the unwary and the ignorant from injury at the hands of persons unskilled or unlearned in the law. The licensing of lawyers is not designed to give rise to a professional monopoly but instead to serve the public right to protection against unlearned and unskilled advice and service in relation to legal matters. The reason for the requirement that the practice of law be engaged in only by duly licensed practitioners of the law is to establish and maintain a legal standard by which the rights of persons may not be jeopardized or sacrificed by counsel and advice of unlicensed and incompetent persons who give or attempt to give legal advice, prepare documents and pleadings, file and prosecute proceedings and examine witnesses in courts or other tribunals. It is essential to the administration of justice and the proper protection of society that unlicensed persons be not permitted to prey upon the public by engaging in the practice of law.

The reason laymen are forbidden to engage in the practice of law is that it is detrimental to the public interest for them to represent themselves to the public that they are qualified to do so when in fact they are not so qualified.

State v. Winder
Supreme Court, Appellate Division, Fourth Dept. of New York, 1973.
348 N.Y.S.2d 270.

MEMORANDUM:

The Divorce Yourself Kit offered for sale by defendant, a layman, purports to offer forms and instructions in law and procedure in certain areas of matrimonial law and the judicial process. In Matter of New York Co. Lawyers' Ass'n v. Dacey, 28 A.D.2d 161, 283 N.Y.S.2d 984, rev'd, on the dissenting opinion in the Appellate Division, 21 N.Y.2d 694, 287 N.Y.S.2d 422, 234 N.E.2d 459, the court dealt with the publishing of a book "How to Avoid Probate!" consisting of 55 pages of text and 310 pages of forms. In the dissenting opinion adopted by the Court of Appeals, Justice Stevens, analyzing the pertinent rules of law, stated at page 173, 283 N.Y.S.2d at page 997: "It cannot be claimed that the publication of a legal text which purports to say what the law is amounts to legal practice. And the mere fact that the principles or rules stated in the text may be accepted by a particular reader as a solution to his problem does not affect this. . . . Apparently it is urged that the conjoining of these two, that is, the text and the forms, with advice as to how the forms should be filled out, constitutes the unlawful practice of law. But that is the situation with many approved and accepted texts. Dacey's book is sold to the public at large. There is no personal contact or relationship with a particular individual. Nor does there exist that relation of confidence and trust so necessary to the status of attorney and client. This is the essential of legal practice—the representation and the advising of a particular person in a particular situation." "At most the book assumes to offer general advice on common problems, and does not purport to give personal advice on a specific problem peculiar to a designated or readily identified person."

Similarly [in the case now before us] the defendant's publication does not purport "to give personal advice on a specific problem peculiar to a designated or readily identified person," and because of the absence of the essential element of "legal practice—the representation and the advising of a particular person in a particular situation" in the publication and sale of the kits, such publication and sale did not constitute the unlawful practice of law in violation of Sec. 478 of the Judiciary Law and was improperly enjoined by the judgment appealed from. There being no legal impediment under the statute to the sale of the kit, there was no proper basis for [1] the injunction against defendant maintaining an office for the purpose of selling to persons seeking a divorce, separation, annulment or separation agreement any printed material or writings relating to matrimonial law or [2] the prohibition . . . against defendant having an interest in any publishing house publishing his manuscript on divorce and against his having any personal contact with any prospective purchaser. The record does fully support, however, the finding of the court that for the charge of $75 or $100 for the kit, the defendant gave legal advice in the course of personal contacts concerning particular problems which might arise in the preparation and presentation of the purchaser's asserted matrimonial cause of action or pursuit of other legal remedies and assistance in the preparation of necessary documents. [The injunction as to] conduct constituting the practice of law, particularly with reference to the giving of advice and counsel by the defendant relating to specific problems of particular individuals in connection with a divorce, separation, . . . should be affirmed.

Judgment unanimously modified. . . .

ASSIGNMENT 2

Rewrite section 37:212 (p. 6) so that it is fully consistent with the *Opinion of the Justices, Earley* and *Winder.* Draft the statute so that it is clear that what these cases authorize is reflected in your new statute. You can add to the statute as now written, take away from it, or change it in any way so that it is in harmony with what the three cases say about what is or is not the practice of law.

ASSIGNMENT 3

Why did the *Earley* case say that there must be regulation of the practice of law? Can you think of an opposing argument? What is a more cynical argument for why lawyers want to control who does or does not practice law? Do you agree with this cynical view?

NOTE ON DEFINING
THE PRACTICE OF LAW

The American Bar Association has taken the position that it is neither "necessary nor desirable" to try to define the practice of law. ABA, Model Code of Professional Responsibility, EC 3-5:

> It is neither necessary nor desirable to attempt the formulation of a single, specific definition of what constitutes the practice of law. Functionally, the practice of law relates to the rendition of services for others that call for the professional judgment of a lawyer. The essence of the professional judgment of the lawyer is his educated ability to relate the general body and philosophy of law to a specific legal problem of a client; and thus, the public interest will be better served if only lawyers are permitted to act in matters involving professional judgment. Where this professional judgment is not involved, non-lawyers, such as court clerks, police officers, abstracters, and many governmental employees, may engage in occupations that require a special knowledge of law in certain areas. But the services of a lawyer are essential in the public interest whenever the exercise of professional legal judgment is required.

ASSIGNMENT 4

Do you think that it is strange that someone can be convicted of a crime for engaging in what the ABA has said is neither "necessary nor desirable" to define?

ASSIGNMENT 5

(a) What is the definition of the practice of law in your state? Try to find a definition in a statute and in a court opinion. To find a statute, go to the state code for your state. To find a case, look for case summaries under relevant statutes within your state code. Also check the digest for your state. A digest is a set of books that contain small-paragraph summaries of court opinions.

(b) Are you practicing law in your state if you tell a neighbor how to fight a traffic ticket in court?

ROSEMARY FURMAN: FOLK HERO

Rosemary Furman, a former legal secretary, believes that you should be able to solve simple legal problems without hiring a lawyer. Hence she established the Northside Secretarial Service in Jacksonville, Florida. She compiled and sold packets of legal forms (for $50) on divorce, name changes, and adoptions. The price included her assistance and advice in filling out and filing the forms. The Florida Bar Association and the Florida courts moved against her with a vengeance for practicing law illegally. She was convicted and sentenced to 30 days in jail.

Widespread support for Ms. Furman developed. Her case soon became a cause célèbre for those seeking increased access to the legal system for the poor and the middle class.[2] Many were outraged at the legal profession and the judiciary for its treatment of Ms. Furman.

---

[2] Peoples & Wertz, *Update: Unauthorized Practice of Law*, 9 National Paralegal Reporter 1 (National Federation of Paralegal Associations, No. 4, Feb. 1985).

The CBS program, "60 Minutes," covered the case. Warner Brothers is considering a docudrama on the story. An editorial in the Gainesville Sun said, "Throw Rosemary Furman in Jail? Surely not after the woman forced the Florida Bar and the judiciary to confront its responsibility to the poor. Anything less than a 'thank you' note would indeed show genuine vindictiveness on the part of the legal profession" (Nov. 4, 1984). There were, however, other views. An editorial in USA Today said, "If she can give legal advice, so can charlatans, frauds, and rip-off artists" (Feb. 2, 1984).

The events in the Rosemary Furman story are as follows:

- 1978 & 1979: the Florida Bar Association takes Rosemary Furman to court, alleging that she is practicing law without a license.
- 1979: the Florida Supreme Court rules against her. She is enjoined from engaging in the unauthorized practice of law.
- 1982: the Florida Bar Association again brings a complaint against her business, alleging that she was continuing the unauthorized practice of law.
- 1983: Duval County Circuit Judge A.C. Soud, Jr. finds her in contempt of court for violating the 1979 order. The judge makes this decision in a nonjury hearing. She is then ordered to serve 30 days in jail.
- 1984: the United States Supreme Court refuses to hear the case. This had the effect of allowing the state jail sentence to stand. The Court was not persuaded by the argument that she should have been granted a jury trial of her peers rather than be judged solely by a legal profession (lawyers and judges) that was biased against her.
- Her attorneys ask the Florida Supreme Court to vacate the jail sentence if she agrees to close her business.
- The Florida Bar Association tells the Florida Supreme Court that the jail term was a fitting punishment and should be served.
- November 13, 1984: the Florida Supreme Court orders her to serve the jail sentence for practicing law without a license. (451 So.2d 808)
- November 27, 1984: Rosemary Furman is granted clemency from the 30 day jail term by Florida Governor Bob Graham and his Clemency Board. She does not have to go to jail.
- Furman and her attorneys announce that they will work on a constitutional amendment that will define the practice of law to make it easier for citizens to avoid a dependency on attorneys in civil cases. Says Ms. Furman, "I have only begun to fight."

NOTE ON "TREATIES" BETWEEN THE BAR AND COMPETITIVE GROUPS

There are a number of occupations that engage in activities that constitute or that border on the practice of law, e.g., the drafting of a sales contract by a real estate broker. Traditionally the legal profession has tried to place restrictions on such activities. Lawyers, however, have not been successful in prohibiting them altogether. Legislatures and the public would not stand for it. The delicate relationship between the legal profession and these occupations has been handled through negotiations where the participants attempt to identify the boundary lines of permitted conduct by these occupations.

YEGGE, R., MOORE, W., HOLME, H., NEW CAREERS IN LAW "Inter-Occupational Treaties" pp. 19, 20 (1969). In some areas, attorneys have attempted to reconcile their differences with ancillary occupations through negotiations. The American Bar Association has negotiated nine "statements of principles" with different groups. In general, each statement provides for a conference committee consisting of lawyers and members of the other group to meet to determine the areas in which attorneys and the other practitioners can cooperate, and to discuss problem areas. The conference committee may also issue additional statements clarifying the statement of principles or discussing certain practices.

Implied in ratification of a statement of principles is bar recognition of the legitimacy of the ancillary occupation and some of its law-related activities. The statements of principles thus recognize the complementarity of the occupations, which include claims adjusters (passed in 1939), banks with trust functions (passed in 1941), publishers (passed in 1941), realtors (passed in 1943), life insurance agents (passed in 1948), accountants (passed in 1951), collection agencies (passed in 1955), social workers (passed in 1965), and architects (passed in 1968). The American Bar Association also instituted a conference with casualty insurers in 1962, . . . Some state and local bar associations have also negotiated agreements with ancillary occupations.

[On the antitrust implications of such agreements or treaties, see p. 105.]

There is a reason to doubt the effectiveness of treaty negotiation:

> Most of the conferences meet at least once a year, but one or two are relatively inactive. In disposing of complaints, the conferences rely on persuasion rather than sanctions. Presumably the various associations of

laymen that are parties to the agreements have the power to punish violators by expelling them from association membership, but seemingly there have been no such expulsions. Nor would this be much of a sanction, as association membership is rarely essential to engaging in a trade or profession. And this sanction leaves beyond control those who are not association members, a sizable group in most occupations.[3]

In addition to these negotiated "treaties," some states have enacted legislation that authorizes activities by certain occupations that would otherwise constitute the unauthorized practice of law. For example:

Ga. Code Ann. § 9-401 (Supp. 1970). §9-401 . . . . Provided that, a title insurance company may prepare such papers as it thinks proper, or necessary, in connection with a title which it proposes to insure, in order, in its opinion, for it to be willing to insure such title, where no charge is made by it for such papers.

Utah Code Ann. 1968, 61-2-20. §61-2-20. Rights and privileges of real estate salesmen—brokers.—It is expressly provided that a real estate salesman shall have the right to fill out and complete forms of legal documents necessary to any real estate transaction to which the said broker is a party as principal or agent, and which forms have been approved by the commission and the attorney general of the state of Utah. Such forms shall include a closing real estate contract, a short-form lease, and a bill of sale of personal property.

Tenn. Code Ann. §62-1325 (1955). §62-1325. Licensed Real Estate Brokers may draw contracts to option, buy, sell, or lease real property.

(b) THE AUTHORIZED PRACTICE OF LAW

Examine the following phrase closely: unauthorized practice of law by nonlawyers. If there is such a thing as the *un*authorized practice of law, then, by implication, there must be an *authorized* practice of law. And indeed there is. The treaties and statutes discussed above are examples of this. Lawyers are not the only members of our society who are permitted to practice law. There are designated areas where

---

[3] Johnstone, Q., & Hopson, D., Lawyers and their Work: An Analysis of the Legal Profession in the United States and England, 185 (1967).

nonlawyers are authorized to practice law. Occasionally there are attempts to call what they do something other than the practice of law, but as we will see, these attempts conflict with reality since the nonlawyers are doing what lawyers do within the sphere of the special authorization. All the special authorizations to be discussed below have been vigorously opposed by lawyers at one time or another on the ground that the authorizations conflict with the privileged domain of lawyers. Lawyers are not always this blunt in stating their opposition. Their objections are couched in terms of the "protection of the public," but in large measure, the opposition has its roots in territorial or turf protection. Lawyers are not above engaging in battles for economic self-preservation.

Several reasons account for the fact that lawyers have lost some of the arguments against permitting special authorization to nonlawyers to practice law. First, lawyers are sometimes distrusted. Second, lawyers have failed to meet a demonstrable need for legal services in particular categories of cases.

The public image of a lawyer is sometimes said to be that of a fighter, someone who will pursue an issue to the bitter end. While this trait may place the lawyer in a favorable light in the eyes of the client for whom s/he is doing battle, many feel that the aggressive inclination of the lawyer can be counterproductive. Administrative agencies, for example, are often suspicious of the involvement of lawyers. They are viewed as combatants who want to turn every agency decision into an adversarial proceeding. Courtroom gymnastics and "gimmicks" are often seen as the primary mode of operation of the lawyer. The lawyer is argumentative to a fault. This image of the lawyer as someone who complicates matters is best summed up by an old accountant's joke that taxation becomes more and more complex in direct proportion to attempts by lawyers to *simplify* the tax law. Whether or not this view of the lawyer is correct, it has accounted for some erosion of the legal profession's monopoly over the practice of law.

The unavailability of lawyers has also produced this result. A vast segment of our population has legal complaints that are never touched by lawyers. This, in part, is due to the fact that most of these complaints do not involve enough money to attract lawyers.

We now turn to a fuller exploration of these themes under the following headings:

(i) Court "representation" by nonlawyers.

(ii) Attempted restrictions on the activities of the "jailhouse lawyer" and the broader policy considerations raised by such restrictions.

(iii) Agency representation by nonlawyers.

(i) Court Representation

As we have seen, a paralegal, or anyone else, is usually allowed to represent himself/herself in court (p. 6). In very limited situations, paralegals are also authorized to appear in court on behalf of someone else. This occurs mainly in some Justice of the Peace and Magistrate Courts in a number of states where even the judges often do not have to be lawyers.

> **Idaho Code Ann. §3-104 (Sup. 1969).** . . . any person may appear and act in a magistrate's division of a district court as representative of any party to a proceeding therein so long as the claim does not total more than $300, and so long as . . . he shall do so without making a charge or collecting a fee therefor.

> **Mont. Rev. Code Ann. §93-2008 (1964).** If any person practices law in any court, except a justice's court or a police court without having a license as attorney and counselor, he is guilty of a contempt of court.

The Oregon Small Claims Court specifies that there can be an agent representing a party, but does not specify that this agent must be an attorney:

> **Or. Rev. State. 55.020 (1965).** Actions in the small claims departments shall be deemed commenced by the plaintiff appearing in person or by agent. . . .

On Indian Reservations in the Midwest, there are Tribal Courts that have jurisdiction over certain civil and criminal actions where both parties are Indian. Nonlawyer Indian advocates represent the parties at these proceedings, and in some instances, non-Indian lawyers are specifically excluded.

Many Juvenile Courts in the country are very informal in their procedures. Nonlawyer probation officers, for example, often speak of behalf of or against the youngster involved in a juvenile delinquency petition. Their involvement frequently amounts to the assumption of an advocate's role before the judge. In a recent case involving the termination of parental rights in North Carolina, the United States Supreme Court noted the role of nonlawyers in termination hearings:

> In fact, . . . the North Carolina Departments of Social Services are themselves sometimes represented at termination hearings by social workers instead of by lawyers.

Lassiter v. Dept. of Social Services, 452 U.S. 18, 29, 101 S.Ct. 2153, 2161, 68 L.Ed.2d 640, 651 (1981). See also the footnote in Justice Douglas' opinion in the *Hackin* case on the extensive legal advocacy role of social workers (p. 32). Some criminal courts authorize diversion programs for certain types of defendants. For example, an employment or drug rehabilitation program may be available in lieu of criminal prosecution. Nonlawyer representatives of these programs interview prospective candidates from among the accused and sometimes go before the judge to argue that the individual should be diverted into their program.

It is well known that lawyers waste a good deal of pre-trial time traveling to court and waiting around simply to give documents to the judge and to set dates for the various stages of pre-trial and trial proceedings. Another problem is that a lawyer may have to be in two different courtrooms at the same time on a particular day. For example, the time spent at an early morning hearing may be unexpectedly extended so that the lawyer cannot appear at a previously scheduled mid-morning proceeding in another courtroom on a different case. In such situations, wouldn't it be helpful if the lawyer's paralegal could "appear" in court for the limited purpose of delivering papers to the judge, asking for a new date, or presenting some other message? *In most states, such activity is strictly prohibited.*

On August 16, 1982, a Kentucky paralegal learned about this prohibition in a dramatic way. Her attorney was involved in a trial at the Jefferson Circuit Court. He asked the paralegal to go to another courtroom during "Motion Hour" where lawyers make motions or schedule future proceedings on a case. He told her to ask for a hearing date on another case that he had pending. She did so. When the case was called during "Motion Hour," she rose, identified herself as the lawyer's paralegal, and gave the message to the judge, asking for the hearing date. Opposing counsel was outraged. He verbally assaulted the paralegal in the courtroom and filed a motion to hold the paralegal and her lawyer in contempt of court for the unauthorized practice of law. When a hearing was later held on this motion, members of a local paralegal association packed the courtroom. Tensions were high. Eventually, when the contempt motion was denied, the audience broke out into loud applause. "Apparently the judge concluded that [the paralegal] had rendered no service involving legal knowledge or advice, but had merely transmitted to the court [the lawyer's] message regarding disposition of the motion, that is, she had been performing a function that was administrative, not legal, in nature." C. Winter, "No Contempt in Kentucky," 7 *National Paralegal Reporter* 8 (No 2, Winter, 1982).

About twenty years earlier, a celebrated Illinois case took a position similar to that of this Kentucky court. *It must be stressed, however, that this position remains a minority view within the courts of the country.* The Illinois case is People v. Alexander, 53 Ill. App. 2d 299, 202 N.E.2d 841 (1964). In this opinion, the defendant was an unlicensed law clerk who appeared before the court to state that his employing attorney could not be present in court at the moment because he was trying a case elsewhere. On behalf of his employer, the law clerk requested a continuance. The defendant's actions were challenged. It was argued that any appearance by a layperson before a court in which s/he gives information as to the availability of counsel or the status of litigation constitutes the unauthorized practice of law. The Illinois court took the unique position that this was not the practice of law. The reasoning of the court was as follows:

In the case of People ex rel. Illinois State Bar Ass'n v. People's Stock Yards State Bank, 344 Ill. 462, at page 476, 176 N.E. 901, at page 907, wherein a bank was prosecuted for the unauthorized practice of law, the following quotation is relied upon:

"*According to the generally understood definition of the practice of law in this country, it embraces the preparation of pleadings, and other papers incident to actions and special proceedings, and the management of such actions and proceedings on behalf of clients before judges and courts * * *.*"

Since this statement relates to the appearance and management of proceedings in court on behalf of a client, we do not believe it can be applied to a situation where a clerk hired by a law firm presents information to the court on behalf of his employer.

We agree with the trial judge that clerks should not be permitted to make motions or participate in other proceedings which can be considered as "managing" the litigation. However, if apprising the court of an employer's engagement or inability to be present constitutes the making of a motion, we must hold that clerks may make such motions for continuances without being guilty of the unauthorized practice of law. Certainly with the large volume of cases appearing on the trial calls these days, it is imperative that this practice be followed.

In Toth v. Samuel Phillipson & Co., 250 Ill. App. 247 (1928) the court said at page 250:

"*It is well known in this country where numerous trial courts are sitting at the same time the exigencies of such a situation require that trial attorneys be represented by their clerical force to respond to some of the calls, and that the court acts upon their response the same as if the attorneys of record themselves appeared in person.*"

After that opinion was handed down, the number of judges was substantially increased in the former Circuit and Superior Courts and the problem of answering court calls has at least doubled. We cannot add to the heavy burden of lawyers who in addition to responding to trial calls must answer pre-trial calls and motion calls—all held in the morning—by insisting that a lawyer must personally appear to present to a court a motion for a continuance on grounds of engagement or inability to appear because of illness or other unexpected circumstances. To reduce the backlog, trial lawyers should be kept busy actually trying lawsuits and not answering court calls. 202 N.E.2d at 843ff.

Again, it must be remembered that most states would *not* agree with Kentucky and Illinois. Most states would prohibit nonlawyers from doing what was authorized in these two states. Fortunately, however, there are at least a few additional states that have begun to move in the direction of the minority view.

The Allen County Bar Association of Indiana has taken the bold move of permitting paralegals to perform what hitherto had been considered lawyer functions in court. A paralegal, under rule 3 of the program (see text of rule below), is authorized:

- To "take" default judgments.
- To set pre-trial conferences, uncontested divorces, and all hearing dates.
- To file motions for dismissal.
- Etc.

The paralegal, however, still cannot communicate directly with judges in performing these tasks.

The vast majority of lawyers in the country would be amazed to learn what is going on in Allen County. Once the shock subsides, however, these lawyers will probably see the wisdom and common sense of what Allen County has done, and begin to think of ways to try it themselves.

The rules of the Allen County program are as follows:

PARALEGAL RULES OF PRACTICE

1. Generally, a legal assistant employee shall be limited to the performance of tasks which do not require the exercising of legal discretion or judgment that affects the legal right of any person.
2. All persons employed as legal assistants shall be registered [see form below] by their employer law firm with the Allen County Circuit and Superior Court Administrator and the Clerk of the Allen Superior and Circuit Courts. Said law firm shall, by affidavit, state that it shall

be bound and liable for the actions of its legal assistant employee, and that any and all actions or statements made by such personnel shall be strictly and completely supervised by his employer member of the Bar. All documents the legal assistant presents or files must contain the attorney's signature, either as an attorney for the petitioning party, or a statement affixed indicating that the documents were prepared by said attorney. Each law firm shall certify in writing that the legal assistant employee is qualified in each field in which they will act with the Courts (probate, dissolution of marriage, collection, etc.). A copy of such statement and certification shall be given to such legal assistant and shall be carried by such person whenever activity with the Courts is pursued by such person. There shall be one legal assistant certified by each law office desiring same, but [an] alternate shall be allowed in case of illness, vacation or unavailability. However, in those instances where a single law firm has more than one full time legal assistant, each of whom operate in separate specialized areas, a certification can be had by more than one person, showing that such person's specialization on a full time basis is limited to one specific area. Otherwise, there should be a limit of one person certified as a legal assistant per law firm.

3. Such employee shall be limited to the following acts:

    (a) Such employee may take default judgments upon the filing of an affidavit in each case stating the amount of damages and that proper service was obtained sworn to by affidavit. Caveat: The legal assistant shall not make the affidavits. (Circuit Court will require attorneys to make Default Judgments.)

    (b) Such employee shall have authority to set Pre-Trial Conferences, Uncontested Divorces, and all other hearing dates.

    (c) Such employee shall have authority to obtain trust account deposits at the Allen County Clerk's Office but only in the name of his employer firm.

    (d) Such employee shall have authority to file stipulations or motions for dismissal.

    (e) Such an employee shall have the authority to do all filing of documents and papers with the Clerk of the Allen Superior Courts and Circuit Court where such documents and papers are not to be given to anyone authorized to affix a judge's signature or issue Court orders.

    (f) Notwithstanding the limitations of subparagraph (e) above, such employee shall have the authority to obtain from the law clerk the signature stamp of the judge on non-discretionary standard orders and notices, such as notice of hearing, and orders to appear and to answer interrogatories on the filing of a Verified Motion for Proceedings Supplemental.

Note: Standard orders which depart from the usual format, restraining orders, suit and support orders, bench warrants, and body attachments must be secured by an attorney.

(g) Such employee is not to negotiate with opposing litigants within the Courthouse nor confer with a judge on legal matters. Matters requiring communications with a judge, require an attorney.

(h) Where circumstances permit, attorneys shall take precedence over such employees in dealings with courts and clerks.

STATEMENT OF CERTIFICATION

This is to certify that _____

is employed by the law firm of _____

_____. Said law firm binds itself and takes full responsibility and liability for the actions of its legal assistant employee above-named and that any and all actions or statements made by such personnel shall be strictly and completely supervised by a member of the Bar of the State of Indiana. This is to certify that the above-mentioned legal assistant is qualified to assist an attorney in the _____ area of law.

LAW FIRM OF: _____

BY: _____

STATE OF INDIANA, COUNTY OF ALLEN, SS:

Subscribed and sworn to before me, a Notary Public in and for said County and State, this _____day _____, 19_____.

_____
Notary Public

Note again that the above program does not allow the paralegal to talk directly with a judge in performing the authorized tasks. ("Matters requiring communications with a judge, require an attorney.") Why such a restriction? Wouldn't it make sense to allow paralegal-judge communication on some procedural matters that are of a routine nature? No, would be the response of most bar associations.

Yes, however, is the refreshing response of several county bar associations in the state of Washington. In these counties, paralegals are allowed to "present" certain orders to judges. Hence the paralegal deals directly with the judge; there is no prohibition against communicating with the judge. The program works as follows:

WHAT THE PARALEGAL IS ALLOWED TO DO:

1. Present agreed and/or ex parte orders (i.e., involving one party only) to Superior Court Judges and to Commissioners based solely on the documents presented and the records in the file.
2. Check out court files from the Clerk of the Court.
3. Use the county law library.

QUALIFICATIONS OF PARALEGAL:

1. The paralegal must be duly registered by the county bar association according to the criteria listed below.
2. The paralegal must be sponsored by a county attorney who is the supervisor of the paralegal. The attorney cannot sponsor more than one paralegal.
3. The paralegal must be currently employed six months or longer by a county law firm, or by a city, county, or state administrative agency or corporation under the direct supervision of an attorney.
4. Seventy-five percent of the paralegal's work time must be devoted to legal assistant (non-clerical) work, consisting of the performance of tasks under the direct supervision of a lawyer, which tasks shall not include the giving of legal advice, the quoting of legal fees, or the appearance in court in contested matters.
5. The paralegal must have obtained (a) a degree or certificate of completion from a legal assistant program of at least two years' duration, or (b) a substantially equivalent college education and/or work experience in the legal field that is deemed adequate by the Legal Assistant Committee of the county bar association.

Among the bar associations participating in this registration program are the Tacoma-Pierce County Bar Association and the Seattle-King County Bar Association. It is anticipated that other counties will adopt a similar program in the state. In Tacoma-Pierce County, the sponsoring attorney must file the following affidavit:

AFFIDAVIT OF SUPERVISING ATTORNEY

STATE OF WASHINGTON   )
) ss.
County of Pierce   )

_____hereby certifies as follows:

(1)   I am an active member of the Washington State Bar Association. I am with a Pierce County law firm, or a city, county or state administrative agency or corporation.

(2)   I am presently engaged in the active practice of law with

_____

(Name of Firm or Organization)
with office at this address:

_____

_____

(3)   I agree to act as the responsible attorney for

_____

as a legal assistant and will furnish such information and reports regarding his or her practice as a legal assistant as may be prescribed by the Board of Trustees of the Tacoma-Pierce County Bar Association.

(4)   The applicant, if approved, shall be the only legal assistant for whom I am the supervising attorney.

(5)   My legal assistant is trained by experience and/or special education to carry on investigative and information gathering matters, use independent judgment and deal with clients in a professional and ethical manner under my supervision and control and to whom the legal assistant is responsible at all times. I will faithfully supervise and direct his/her work and will be responsible for his/her professional conduct.

(6)   I agree to see that the applicant surrenders his/her registration card upon change of employment of if he/she for any other reason no longer qualifies for registration.

_____

SUBSCRIBED AND SWORN to before me this ____ day of
_____, 19___.

_____

NOTARY PUBLIC in and for the State of Washington, residing at

_____

NOTE ON REFORM OF
THE UNAUTHORIZED-PRACTICE-
OF-LAW-RULES

Again, the *authorized* practice of law by nonlawyers described above is quite limited. But there have been calls for reform. For example, the National Federation of Paralegal Associations "supports and encourages new interpretations as to what constitutes the practice of law," p. 112. Others have been more direct in seeking radical reform. The Chairman of the Legal Services Corporation has said that the time has come for a full-scale deregulation of the legal profession. We will examine his position at the end of this book, p. 142, after we have explored the other dimensions of regulation that exist today.

(ii) The Jailhouse Lawyer

A jailhouse lawyer is a nonlawyer who helps fellow prisoners with their legal problems. Some prisons attempted to prevent the jailhouse lawyer from providing this legal assistance even though no meaningful alternatives for such assistance were provided by the prisons. This prohibition, however, was struck down by the United States Supreme Court in *Johnson v. Avery* in 1969. The basis of the opinion was that without the jailhouse lawyer, prisoners may not have access to the courts. The concurring opinion of Justice Douglas has become one of the most widely quoted and influential statements in the field of paralegalism.

Johnson v. Avery
Supreme Court of the United States, 1969.
393 U.S. 483, 89 S.Ct. 747, 21 L.Ed.2d 718

. . .

Mr. Justice DOUGLAS, concurring.

While I join the opinion of the Court [in striking down the prohibition on the activities of jailhouse lawyers] I add a few words in emphasis of the important thesis of the case.

The increasing complexities of our governmental apparatus at both the local and the federal levels have made it difficult for a person to process a claim or even to make a complaint. Social security is a virtual maze; the hierarchy that governs urban housing is often so intricate that it takes an expert to know what agency has jurisdiction over a particular complaint; the office to call or official to see for noise abatement, for a broken sewer line, or a fallen tree is a mystery to many in our metropolitan areas.

A person who has a claim assertable in faraway Washington, D.C., is even more helpless, as evidenced by the increasing tendency of constituents to rely on their congressional delegation to identify, press, and process their claims.

We think of claims as grist for the mill of the lawyers. But it is becoming abundantly clear that more and more of the effort in ferreting out the basis of claims and the agencies responsible for them and in preparing the almost endless paperwork for their prosecution is work for laymen. There are not enough lawyers to manage or supervise all of these affairs; and much of the basic work done requires no special legal talent. *Yet there is a closed-shop philosophy in the legal profession that cuts down drastically active roles for laymen. That traditional, closed-shop attitude is utterly out of place in the modern world where claims pile high and much of the work of tracing and pursuing them requires the patience and wisdom of a layman rather than the legal skills of a member of the bar.* [Emphasis added.]

"If poverty lawyers are overwhelmed, some of the work can be delegated to sub-professionals. New York law permits senior law students to practice law under certain supervised conditions. Approval must first be granted by the appellate division. A rung or two lower on the legal profession's ladder are laymen legal technicians, comparable to nurses and lab assistants in the medical profession. Large law firms employ them, and there seems to be no reason why they cannot be used in legal services programs to relieve attorneys for more professional tasks." Samore, Legal Services for the Poor, 32 Albany L.Rev. 509, 515-516 (1968).

The plight of a man in prison may in these respects be even more acute than the plight of a person on the outside. He may need collateral proceedings to test the legality of his detention or relief against management of the parole system or against defective detainers lodged against him which create burdens in the nature of his incarcerated status. He may have grievances of a civil nature against those outside the prison. His imprisonment may give his wife grounds for divorce and be a factor in determining the custody of his children; and he may have pressing social security, workmen's compensation, or veterans' claims.

While the demand for legal counsel in prison is heavy, the supply is light. For private matters of a civil nature, legal counsel for the indigent in prison is almost nonexistent. Even for criminal proceedings, it is sparse. While a few States have post-conviction statutes providing such counsel, most States do not. Some states like California do appoint counsel to represent the indigent prisoner in his collateral hearings, once he succeeds in making out a prima facie case. But as a result, counsel is not on hand for preparation of the papers or for the initial decision that the prisoner's claim has substance.

NOTES

1. The *Johnson* opinion stressed that the prison provided *no* alternative to the jailhouse lawyer. If alternatives had been available, the inmate would not be allowed to practice law. In Williams v. U.S. Dept of Justice, 433 F.2d 958 (5th Cir. 1970), the court held that the presence

of law students in the prison could be an alternative, but only if it is demonstrated that the students are meeting the need for inmate legal services. If the inmates had to wait a considerable period of time, for example, before they could be interviewed by the law students, then no alternative existed and the jailhouse lawyer could not be prevented from helping other inmates.

2. In Gilmore v. Lynch, 319 F.Supp. 105 (N.D.Cal.1970), affirmed by the United States Supreme Court in Younger v. Gilmore, 404 U.S. 15 (1971), the court held that California either had to satisfy the legal needs of its prisoners or expand the prison law library to include more comprehensive law books. See also *Bounds v. Smith,* p. 223.

3. How far can the rationale of *Johnson* be extended? Suppose for example, it is demonstrated that many claimants before state administrative agencies are not receiving legal services because attorneys cannot be afforded. Would the *Johnson* opinion permit paralegal representation before such agencies even if the latter prohibited it? What is the difference between an inmate's right to have access to the courts and *anyone's* right to complain to an agency? How do you think Justice Douglas would handle the case if it came before him?

Statsky, W. and Lang, P., The Legal Paraprofessional as Advocate and Assistant: Roles, Training Concepts and Materials, pp. 49-50 (1971): "Although the *Johnson* case is admittedly narrow in scope, it does nevertheless, give aid and comfort to the view that whenever lawyers are unavailable for whatever reason, society will sanction alternative systems for the delivery of legal services. The paramount consideration will not be ethics nor the exclusivity of the right to practice law, but rather it will be the facilitation of access routes to the grievance machinery set up for the resolution of claims. If lawyers are not available to assist the citizenry with these claims, then the question arises as to whether skilled nonlawyers represent a viable alternative. The inevitability of this question becomes clear when we listen to the statistics on the demand for the services of a lawyer. Estimates have been made to the effect that if every lawyer devoted full time to the legal needs of the poor, there would still be significant shortage of lawyers for the poor. If the legal needs of the middle class are added, the legal service manpower shortage becomes overwhelming."

See also, Statsky, W., Inmate Involvement in Prison Legal Services: Roles and Training Options for the Inmate as Paralegal (American Bar Association, Commission on Correctional Facilities and Services, Resource Center on Correctional Law and Legal Services, 1974).

Two other important Supreme Court cases in this area need to be considered:

Procunier v. Martinez
Supreme Court of the United States, 1974.
416 U.S. 396, 94 S.Ct. 1800, 1814, 40 L.Ed.2d 244.

. . .

The District Court also enjoined continued enforcement of Administrative Rule MV-IV-02, which provides in pertinent part:

"Investigators for an attorney-of-record will be confined to not more than two. Such investigators must be licensed by the State or must be members of the State Bar. Designation must be made in writing by the Attorney."

By restricting access to prisoners to members of the bar and licensed private investigators, this regulation imposed an absolute ban on the use by attorneys of law students and legal paraprofessionals to interview inmate clients. In fact attorneys could not even delegate to such persons the task of obtaining prisoners' signatures on legal documents. The District Court reasoned that this rule constituted an unjustifiable restriction on the right of access to the courts. We agree.

The constitutional guarantee of due process of law has as a corollary the requirement that prisoners be afforded access to the courts in order to challenge unlawful convictions and to seek redress for violations of their constitutional rights. This means that inmates must have a reasonable opportunity to seek and receive the assistance of attorneys. Regulations and practices that unjustifiably obstruct the availability of professional representation or other aspects of the right of access to the courts are invalid. Ex parte Hull, 312 U.S. 546, 61 S.Ct. 640, 85 L.Ed. 1034 (1941).

The District Court found that the rule restricting attorney-client interviews to members of the bar and licensed private investigators inhibited adequate professional representation of indigent inmates. The remoteness of many California penal institutions makes a personal visit to an inmate client a time-consuming undertaking. The court reasoned that the ban against the use of law students or other paraprofessionals for attorney-client interviews would deter some lawyers from representing prisoners who could not afford to pay for their traveling time or that of licensed private investigators. And those lawyers who agreed to do so would waste time that might be employed more efficaciously in working on the inmates' legal problems. Allowing law students and paraprofessionals to interview inmates might well reduce the cost of legal representation for prisoners. The District Court therefore concluded that the regulation imposed a substantial burden on the right of access to the courts.

[Handwritten annotations at top: "Inmates have a right to assistance, assistance could be a law library or someone trained in the law."]

[Handwritten: "Legal Asst. under Attorney has right to communicate w/ prisoners."]

Bounds v. Smith

430 U.S. 817, 97 S.Ct. 1491, 52 L.Ed.2d (1977).

[In this opinion the Supreme Court is again concerned with the need of prisoners to have access to the courts and the use of nonlawyers in helping to provide that assistance. The Court held that prisons must assist inmates in the preparation and filing of meaningful legal papers by providing the inmates with adequate law libraries or adequate assistance from persons trained in the law. The Court rejected the claim that nonlawyer inmates were ill-equipped to use the "tools of the trade of the legal profession." In the Court's experience, nonlawyer petitioners are capable of using law books to file cases raising claims that are "serious and legitimate" whether or not such petitioners win the cases. In outlining the options available to a prison, the Court specifically referred to paralegals:]

It should be noted that while adequate law libraries are one constitutionally acceptable method to assure meaningful access to the courts, our decision here, . . . , does not foreclose alternative means to achieve that goal. Nearly half the States and the District of Columbia provide some degree of professional or quasi-professional legal assistance to prisoners. . . . Such programs take many imaginative forms and may have a number of advantages over libraries alone. Among the alternatives are the training of inmates as para-legal assistants to work under lawyers' supervision, the use of paraprofessionals and law students, either as volunteers or in formal clinical programs, the organization of volunteer attorneys through bar associations or other groups, the hiring of lawyers on a part-time consultant basis, and the use of full-time staff attorneys, working either in new prison legal assistance organizations or as part of public defender or legal services offices.

Finally, the right of an inmate to assist a fellow inmate in legal matters does *not* extend to representing the inmate in court. Guajardo v. Luna, 432 F.2d 1324 (5th Cir. 1970.) Nor can a nonlawyer represent an inmate in court even if this nonlawyer is not an inmate him/herself. This latter point was decided by the United States Supreme Court in Hackin v. Arizona, 389 U.S. 143 (1967). Justice Douglas vigorously dissented from the majority opinion in *Hackin.* He made the following telling observations, id. at 144ff:

Rights protected by the First Amendment include advocacy and petition for redress of grievances and the Fourteenth Amendment ensures equal justice for the poor in both criminal and civil actions. But to millions of Americans who are indigent and ignorant—and often members of minority groups—these rights are meaningless. They are helpless to assert their rights under the law without assistance. They suffer discrimination in housing and employment, are victimized by shady consumer sales practices, evicted from their homes at the whim of the landlord, denied welfare payments, and endure domestic strife without hope of the legal remedies of divorce, maintenance, or child custody decrees.

If true equal protection of the laws is to be realized an indigent must be able to obtain assistance when he suffers a denial of his rights. Today, this goal is only a goal. Outside the area of criminal proceedings covered by our decisions in Gideon v. Wainwright, 372 U.S. 335, and Douglas v. California, 372 U.S. 353, counsel is seldom available to the indigent. As this Court has recognized, there is a dearth of lawyers who are willing, voluntarily, to take on unprofitable and unpopular causes.

Some States, aware of the acute shortage of lawyers to help the indigent, have utilized the abilities of qualified law students to advise indigents and even to represent them in court in limited circumstances. But where this practice is not sanctioned by law, the student advocate for the poor may be subjected to criminal penalty under broadly drafted statutes prohibiting unauthorized practice of law.

There is emerging, particularly in the ghetto areas of our cities, a type of organization styled to bring a new brand of legal assistance to the indigent. These groups, funded in part by the federal Office of Economic Opportunity, characteristically establish neighborhood offices where the poor can come for assistance. They attempt to dispense services on a comprehensive integrated scale, using lawyers, social workers, members of health professions, and other nonlawyer aides. These new and flexible approaches to giving legal aid to the poor recognize that the problems of indigents—although of the type for which an attorney has traditionally been consulted—are too immense to be solved solely by members of the bar. The supply of lawyer manpower is not nearly large enough.* But the necessary involvement of lay persons in these programs threatens their success.

The so-called "legal" problem of the poor is often an unidentified strand in a complex of social, economic, psychological and psychiatric problems. Identification of the "legal" problem at times is for the expert. But even a "lay" person can often perform that function and mark the path that leads to the school board, the school principal, the welfare agency, the Veterans Administration, the police review board, or the

---

* See Cahn & Cahn, What Price Justice: The Civilian Perspective Revisited, 41 Notre Dame Law 927 (1966). "Finally, with respect to manpower, we have created an artificial shortage by refusing to learn from the medical and other professions and to develop technicians, nonprofessionals and lawyer-aides—manpower roles to carry out such functions as: "informal advocate, technical, counsellor, sympathetic listener, investigator, researcher, form writer, etc." (P. 934.) "[T]he possibility of advancing the cause of justice through increasing lay involvement in fact finding, adjudication and arbitration, should not be sacrificed a priori out of fear of abuse." (P. 951).

urban renewal agency.‡ If he neither solicits nor obtains a fee for his services, why should he not be free to act? Full-fledged representation in a battle before a court or agency requires professional skills that laymen lack; and therefore the client suffers, perhaps grievously, if he is not represented by a lawyer. But in the intermediate zone where the local pastor, the social worker, or best friend** commonly operates, is there not room for accommodation? Dean Charles E. Ares recently said:

> "... [T]he *structure* of the legal profession is middle class in its assumptions. We assume that the lawyer can sit quietly in his office awaiting the knock on the door by a client who has discovered that he has a legal problem and has found the way to the lawyer's office.... This assumption is not valid for the great mass of people who live in poverty in the United States.... The ways in which this structure can be changed open exciting and interesting prospects." Poverty, Civil Liberties, and Civil Rights: A Symposium, 41 N.Y.U.L.Rev. 328, 346 (1966).

Moreover, what the poor need, as much as our corporate grants, is protection before they get into trouble and confront a crisis. This means "political leadership" for the "minority poor." Id., at 351. Lawyers will play a role in that movement; but so will laymen. The line that marks the area into which the layman may not step except at his peril is not clear.

Legal representation connotes a magic it often does not possess—as for example, the commitment procedure in Texas, where, by one report, 66 seconds are given to a case, the lawyer usually not even knowing his client and earning a nice fee for passive participation. Weihofen, Mental Health Services for the Poor, 54 Calif.L.Rev. 920, 938-939 (1966). If justice is the goal, why need a layman be barred here?

---

‡ See Frankel, Experiments in Serving the Indigent, in National Conference on Law and Poverty Proceedings 69, 75–76 (1965): "[W]e lawyers must certainly confront constructively the idea that what we have traditionally regarded as legal business cannot permanently be so regarded. The needs of the poor for services in matters that are somehow legal appear pretty clearly to be enormous. Among those needs are many kinds of matters that are narrow, that are specialized, and can be routinized. Matters related to housing, to workmen's compensation, to consumer problems are a few that one could name.... [W]e should attempt to create a class of legal technicians who can handle, under lawyers' supervision, some of the problems that have thus far seemed to us to be exclusively the province of the lawyer. I think we have an important creative function to perform in trying to mark out these areas where lawyers are not really needed."

See Paulsen, The Law Schools and the War on Poverty, in National Conference on Law and Poverty Proceedings 77, 81 (1965): "Services to the poor will undoubtedly call for advocacy and advice by lay persons as well as lawyers. A lawyer's time is costly. Not every problem thrown up by legal arrangements requires the skill and costly time of a law-trained person. We can, perhaps, expect the creation of advice centers operated by laymen not unlike Britain's Citizen's Advice Bureaus."

** In habeas corpus proceedings, "the practice of a next friend applying for a writ is ancient and fully accepted." United States v. Houston, 273 F. 915, 916 (C.A.2d Cir.).

Broadly phrased unauthorized-practice-of-law statutes such as that at issue here could make criminal many of the activities regularly done by social workers who assist the poor in obtaining welfare and attempt to help them solve domestic problems.‡‡ Such statutes would also tend to deter programs in which experienced welfare recipients represent other, less articulate, recipients before local welfare departments.

As this Court's decisions indicate, state provisions regulating the legal profession will not be permitted to act as obstacles to the rights of persons to petition the courts and other legal agencies for redress. . . . Certainly the States have a strong interest in preventing legally untrained shysters who pose as attorneys from milking the public for pecuniary gain. But it is arguable whether this policy should support a prohibition against charitable efforts of nonlawyers to help the poor. It may well be that until the goal of free *legal* assistance to the indigent in all areas of the law is achieved, the poor are not harmed by well-meaning, charitable assistance of laymen. On the contrary, for the majority of indigents, who are not so fortunate to be served by neighborhood legal offices, lay assistance may be the only hope for achieving equal justice at this time.

(iii) Agency Representation

A considerable number of administrative agencies will permit a paralegal or other nonlawyer to represent clients at the agency. These individuals are usually called agents, practitioners, or representatives. They engage in informal advocacy for their clients at the agency, or formal advocacy including full control of the case in an adversarial administrative hearing. The major issues are often economic, statistical, or scientific, but legal issues are also involved. It is clear that in conducting an agency hearing, the nonlawyer can be practicing law in a manner that is remarkably similar to a lawyer's representation of a client in court.

‡‡ "Social workers in public assistance may already be *required* to practice law as substantially as if they were in a courtroom. In making an initial determination of an applicant's eligibility, the public assistance worker must complete the applicant's financial statement. 'Every question, or nearly every question, on the financial statement, is a legal question. When the social worker advises, or even discusses the questions or answers, he may very likely be giving legal advice.' The private social worker who advises an applicant that he should apply, how to apply, what to answer and how to appeal if the application is rejected is also giving 'legal' advice. When he argues with the public worker on behalf of the applicant, he is giving representation. When and if he goes to a hearing on behalf of the applicant, he is surely engaging in advocacy." [Sparer, Thorkelson & Weiss, "The Lay Advocate," 43 U. of Detroit L.J. 493, 499–500 (1966) Ed.]

For federal agencies, Congress has passed a statute, the Administrative Procedure Act, that gives each federal agency the power to decide for itself whether only lawyers can represent clients before it:

> **Administrative Procedure Act 5 U.S.C.A. § 555 (1967).** (b) A person compelled to appear in person before an agency is entitled to be accompanied, represented, and advised by counsel or, if permitted by the agency, by other qualified representative. . . .

See the chart on p. 183 on paralegal representation in federal agencies.

When an agency decides to use this power to permit nonlawyer representation, it can simply allow anyone to act as the agent or representative of another before the agency, or it can establish elaborate qualifications or standards of admission to practice before it. If the agency takes the latter course, its qualification or standards could include a specialized test to demonstrate competency in the subject matter regulated by the agency, minimum educational or experience requirements, registration or enrollment on the agency's approved roster of representatives, and an agreement to abide by designated ethical rules of practice—a violation of which could result in suspension and "disbarment."

The United States Patent Office has established criteria for individuals to practice (as "registered agents") before this agency in drafting and filing applications for patents, searching legal opinions on patentability, etc.[4] In 1982, there were approximately 12,000 registered agents who had met this criteria at the agency. Of this number, about 1,900 (or 15.8 percent) were nonlawyers. At the Interstate Commerce Commission, close to 10,000 nonlawyer "practitioners" have been authorized to represent clients at ICC proceedings that often involve issues such as rate increases and service extensions for railroads and other transportation carriers.[5] Perhaps the largest use of nonlawyers in federal agencies is at the Internal Revenue Service within the Treasury Department.[6] Any certified public accountant is authorized to practice before the IRS. There are over 190,000 members of the American Institute of Certified Public Accountants, most of whom are not lawyers. In addition, thousands of other nonlawyers (called

---

[4] 37 C.F.R. 1.341–1.348 (1983).

[5] 49 C.F.R. 1103.1–1103.5 (1983).

[6] 31 C.F.R. 10.3–10.75 (1983); 20 U.S.C. 1242 (1975).

"enrolled agents" or "enrolled actuaries") have acquired the authority to practice.[7]

While these numbers are impressive, it is not true that extensive numbers of nonlawyers actually use the authority that they have. A recent study by the American Bar Association of thirty-three federal administrative agencies reached the following conclusion: "We found that the overwhelming majority of agencies studied permit nonlawyer representation in both adversarial and nonadversarial proceedings. However, most of them seem to encounter lay practice very infrequently (in less than 5 percent of adjudications), while only a few encounter lay practice as often as lawyer practice. Thus, although universally permitted, lay practice before federal agencies rarely occurs."[8]

One agency where nonlawyer representation is fairly high (about 15 percent) is the Social Security Administration. Paralegals are frequently appointed by clients (see form on p. 35) to represent them before the agency. In 1983 a study was conducted that compared the success of clients at hearings based upon the kind of representation they received. The results were as follows:

- 59 percent of clients were successful when they were represented by lawyers.
- 54.5 percent of clients were successful when they were represented by nonlawyers.
- 43.7 percent of clients were successful when they were represented by themselves.[9]

Fees can be charged by lawyers or paralegals for these services, but the fee must be specifically approved (see form on p. 37) by the agency. This is not to say, however, that lawyers and paralegals are treated alike. If a lawyer successfully represents a claimant, the agency will deduct up to 25 percent of the claimant's award, which will be paid directly to the attorney to cover fees. On the other hand, if a paralegal successfully represents a claimant, the paralegal must collect the fee

---

[7] Rose, J., *Representation by Non-Lawyers in Federal Administrative Agency Proceedings: An Expanded Role* (Administrative Conference of the United States, 1984); Vom Baur, "The Practice of Non-Lawyers before Administrative Agencies," 15 *Fed. Bar Journal* 99 (1955).

[8] *Report of 1984 Survey of Nonlawyer Practice Before Federal Administrative Agencies* (ABA Standing Committee on Lawyers' Responsibility for Client Protection, Oct. 19, 1984).

[9] *Participant Involvement in Request for Hearing Cases for Fiscal 1983*, Table 6, DSS/OHA (May, 1984).

directly from the client since the agency will not deduct anything from the award.[10]

DEPARTMENT OF
HEALTH AND HUMAN SERVICES
SOCIAL SECURITY ADMINISTRATION
APPOINTMENT OF REPRESENTATIVE

I appoint _____
(Print or Type Name and Address of Representative)

to act as my representative in connection with my claim under Titles II, XVI or XVIII of the Social Security Act and/or Title IV of the Federal Coal Mine Health and Safety Act based on the social security record of

NAME	SOCIAL SECURITY NUMBER

I authorize my representative to make or give any request or notice; present or elicit evidence; obtain information; and receive any notice in connection with my claim wholly in my stead.

Date _____   Signature _____
(Claimant)

Address _____

ACCEPTANCE OF APPOINTMENT

I, _____, hereby accept the above appointment. I certify that I have not been suspended or prohibited from practice before the Social Security Administration; that I am not, as an officer or employee of the United States, disqualified from acting as the claimant's representative; and that I will not charge or receive a fee for the representation unless it has been authorized in accordance with the laws and regulations referred to on the reverse side hereof. In the event that I decide not to charge or collect a fee for the representation I will notify the Social Security Administration.

I am _____
(Attorney, union representative, relative, law student, etc.)   *

Date _____   Signature _____
(Representative)

Address _____

Form SSA-1696-U3 (8-77) (Formerly SSA-1696)

---

[10] 42 U.S.C. 406 (1975).

At the *state* level, most states have established a similar system for authorizing nonlawyers to provide representation at many, but by no means all, state agencies. For example:

> **Cal. Unemployment Insurance Code § 1957 (1956).** Any individual claiming benefits in any proceedings before the Appeals Board or its authorized representative may be represented by counsel or agent but no such counsel or agent shall charge or receive for such services more than an amount approved by the Appeals Board. Any person who violates any provision of this section shall for such violation be fined not less than fifty dollars ($50) nor more than five hundred dollars ($500) or be imprisoned not more than six months or both.

> **Minn.Stat.Ann. § 290.52 (1962) [State Income Tax Dept. Ed.].** § 290.52 . . . The commissioner may prescribe rules and regulations governing the recognition of agents, attorneys, or other persons representing claimants before the commissioner, and may require of such persons, agents, and attorneys, before being recognized as representatives of claimants, that they shall show that they are of good character and in good repute, possessed of the necessary qualifications to enable them to render such claimants valuable services, and otherwise competent to advise and assist such claimants in the presentation of their case. Such commissioner may, after due notice and opportunity for hearing, suspend and disbar from further practice before him, any such person, agent, or attorney, shown to be incompetent, disreputable, or who refuses to comply with the said rules and regulations, . . .

ASSIGNMENT 6

Make a list of every state and local administrative agency in your state. Have a class discussion in which students identify as many state and local agencies as they can. The total number of agencies will then be divided by the number of students in the class so that each student will be assigned the same number of agencies. For your agencies, find out whether nonlawyers can represent citizens before those agencies. What are the requirements, if any, to provide this representation informally (e.g., calling or writing the agency on behalf of someone else) or formally (e.g., representing someone else at an agency hearing). Check your state statutes. Check the regulations of the agency. If possible, call the agency to ask what their policy is and whether they can refer you to any statutes or regulations on the policy.

DEPARTMENT OF HEALTH, EDUCATION, AND WELFARE SOCIAL SECURITY ADMINISTRATION	Form Approved OMB No. 72-R0832

PETITION TO OBTAIN APPROVAL OF A FEE FOR REPRESENTING A CLAIMANT BEFORE THE SOCIAL SECURITY ADMINISTRATION.	DO NOT WRITE IN THIS SPACE

No fee may be approved unless the information requested by this form has been received. (20 CFR 404.975 and 976)

I request approval to charge a fee of $ _____for services

performed as a representative of _____

in a claim before the Social Security Administration.

TYPE OF CLAIM

1. Circle claim involved (DIB; RIB; B/L; SSI.)

2. Hearings Case:

Yes _____ No _____

ENTER THE NAME AND ADDRESS OF THE PERSON ON WHOSE SOCIAL SECURITY RECORD CLAIM IS BASED	ENTER THE SOCIAL SECURITY NUMBER OF PERSON ON WHOSE RECORD CLAIM IS BASED

THE INFORMATION BELOW IS FURNISHED IN SUPPORT OF THIS PETITION

1. My services as a representative began *(mo., day, yr.)* _____ and ended *(mo., day, yr.)* _____

2. Itemization of Services Rendered *(Do not include services in connection with court proceedings)*

DATE (Mo., Day Yr.)	*(Itemize each meeting, conference, item of correspondence, telephone call, and each activity engaged in, such as research, preparation of a brief, attendance at a hearing, travel, etc., related to your services as representative in this case.)*	TIME SPENT (To nearest quarter hour)
	If more space is needed, attach separate sheet. **TOTAL HOURS**	

3. Did you render any services relating to this matter before any State or Federal court? ☐ Yes ☐ No
If "Yes," what fee did you or will you charge for services in connection with the court proceedings? $

4. Have you and your client tentatively agreend upon a fee for your services? ☐ Yes ☐ No
If "Yes," please specify the amount (or the agreed-upon formula). $

5. Have you received, or do you expect to receive, any payment for your representa- ☐ Yes ☐ No
tion other than the fee indicated above, such as reimbursement for expenses you incurred?
If "Yes," itemize below. (Where funds have been received and held in escrow, e.g., as a retainer, indicate the amount followed by the word "escrow.")

	$
	$
	$
TOTAL	$

I certify that the above information is true and correct to the best of my knowledge and belief. I further certify that I have furnished a copy of this petition and any attachments to the person(s) for whom the above services were performed.

SIGNATURE OF PETITIONER	DATE	ADDRESS

FIRM WITH WHICH ASSOCIATED, IF ANY	TELEPHONE NO. AND AREA CODE

FORM SSA-1560-U4 (10-78)

As indicated earlier, many lawyers have not been happy with the authorization given nonlawyers to practice law such as within administrative agencies. Bitter campaigns have been launched against it by the bar association.

If the agency permitting nonlawyer representation is a *federal* agency, its authorization takes precedence over any *state* laws that would prohibit it. This principle was established by *Sperry v. State of Florida ex rel the Florida Bar,* 373 U.S. 379, 83 S.Ct. 1322, 10 L.Ed.2d 428 (1963). The case involved a nonlawyer who was authorized to represent clients before the United States Patent Office. The Florida Bar claimed that the nonlawyer was violating the state practice-of-law statutes. The United States Supreme Court ruled that the Supremacy Clause of the U.S. Constitution gave federal laws supremacy over conflicting state laws. The Court also said:

[handwritten margin note: now lawyers have practiced in the past]

> Examination of the development of practice before the Patent Office and its governmental regulation reveals that: (1) nonlawyers have practiced before the Office from its inception, with the express approval of the Patent Office and to the knowledge of Congress; (2) during prolonged congressional study of unethical practices before the Patent Office, the right of nonlawyer agents to practice before the Office went unquestioned, and there was no suggestion that abuses might be curbed by state regulation; (3) despite protests of the bar, Congress in enacting the Administrative Procedure Act refused to limit the right to practice before the administrative agencies to lawyers; and (4) the Patent Office has defended the value of nonlawyer practitioners while taking steps to protect the interests which a State has in prohibiting unauthorized practice of law. We find implicit in this history congressional (and administrative) recognition that registration in the Patent Office confers a right to practice before the Office without regard to whether the State within which the practice is conducted would otherwise prohibit such conduct.
>
> Moreover, the extent to which specialized lay practitioners should be allowed to practice before some 40-odd federal administrative agencies, including the Patent Office, received continuing attention both in and out of Congress during the period prior to 1952. The Attorney General's Committee on Administrative Procedure which, in 1941, studied the need for procedural reform in the administrative agencies, reported that "[e]specially among lawyers' organizations there has been manifest a sentiment in recent years that only members of the bar should be admitted to practice before administrative agencies. The Committee doubts that a sweeping interdiction of nonlawyer practitioners would be wise. . . ."

[handwritten margin note: The committee doubts prohibiting nonlawyers would be wise]

Suppose, however, that a *state* agency permits nonlawyer representation. Can this be challenged by the bar? The issue may depend on who has the *power* to regulate the practice of law in a particular state. If the state legislature has this power, then the agency authorization of nonlawyer representation is valid since the agency is under the jurisdiction and control of the legislature. So long as the nonlawyer representation is based on a statute of the legislature, it is valid. If, however, the state judiciary has the power to control the practice of law in a state, then the courts may be able to invalidate any nonlawyer representation that is authorized by the agency.

Even though it may be quite legal for a paralegal to represent citizens before administrative agencies, there is a need to distinguish between paralegals who provide this representation on their own, and paralegals who do it within the employ of lawyers. There should be *no* distinction. Some lawyers, however, feel that law firms should not allow their paralegals to engage in any agency representation even if the agency authorizes it. Contrast the following two views within the report of the Pennsylvania Professional Guidance Committee and the Unauthorized Practice of Law Committee on paralegal use:

Majority View

Paralegals may represent claimants not only before federal agencies, but also before state agencies whose federal funding source requires these agencies to meet federal statutory requirements as a condition of federal aid. In AFDC (42 U.S.C. 601 *et seq.*), Medicaid (42 U.S.C. 1396a *et seq.*), WIN (42 U.S.C. 602 and 639), Food Stamp (7 U.S.C. 2011 *et seq.*) and Unemployment Compensation (42 U.S.C. 402) programs, federal law provides that if state programs fail to comply with federal requirements, federal assistance to the state shall be terminated. States that deny paralegals access to due process hearings before such agencies when their presence is requested by claimants, and allowed by federal statute run the risk of forfeiting federal benefits. . . .

[I]f lawyers are prohibited from employing paralegals to represent claimants at administrative hearings, the lawyer in most cases, would find this type of representation economically unfeasible. While an attorney may wish to provide the public with this type of representation, because most claims involve small amounts of money or are concerned with non-monetary benefits, he may find this type of service to represent a loss in income. If the lawyer employs, trains and supervises paralegals who may provide such representation, the public will be assured of competent representation at a price it can afford and which is feasible from the lawyer's perspective. The public, therefore, would be provided with quality representation under the supervision of a lawyer, and would be discouraged from approaching unsupervised, unaffiliated laymen. The result is the provision of more services, more economically, to those persons seeking assistance at administrative agency hearings.

If paralegals are well trained and well supervised, the public should be protected because attorneys have a real stake in ensuring that paralegals provide the best possible representation.

Minority View

By permitting paralegals to appear before administrative agencies of record, [the] principles of control by the attorney [and the restrictions against paralegals holding themselves out to the public] as experts in legal matters, etc., are abandoned. In an administrative hearing of record, the attorney does not have the opportunity to review and correct the error of the non-lawyer. The client can suffer permanent damage to his legal position through errors of omission or commission by the paralegal.

Would any client want to be represented by a paralegal if his lawyer properly described to him the risks of non-lawyer representation in such a hearing? Would the client be adequately protected by relying on the malpractice liability [insurance] of the lawyer for actions of his paralegal in the hearing? I believe the answers to be in the negative.

The only justification for the use of paralegals in administrative hearings is an economic one. There has been no factual presentations beyond the bare conclusion that lawyers are not available at reasonable cost for rendering these services.

ASSIGNMENT 7

Which side is correct, the majority or minority view? Why? Which view do you think Justice Douglas would adopt? Why?

3

State Licensing
of Paralegals

Many occupations are licensed: electricians, brokers, nurses, etc. What about paralegals? To date, *no* state has required licensing for paralegals. This is not to say, however, that efforts to license paralegals have not been tried, nor that licensing will not eventually come. The proposals of several states will be examined: California, Michigan, Arizona, and Oregon. Read this material carefully since it is highly likely that in the not-too-distant future you will be asked to comment on similar proposals for your state.

The California legislature once considered passing the "Certified Attorney Assistant Statute," which would have permitted the California Bar to set up a certification system for paralegals. It was, in effect, a licensing scheme. The statute did not pass. There was vigorous opposition from many paralegals who objected to lawyer domination in the system of control.

In 1977 the Michigan state legislature considered, but did not enact, the Legal Assistant Act, which would "regulate the practice of legal assistants" and "provide a system to certify legal assistants." This again was a licensure proposal since it would have the sanction of the government. The highlights of the proposed bill were as follows:

- A Commission on Legal Assistants would be established within the state Department of Education.
- Nine members of the Commission would be appointed by the government subject to confirmation by the state Senate. The nine members would be as follows:
  1 from the state bar of Michigan
  1 representing the public

2 teachers of paralegals (one teacher must be an attorney; the other one must not be an attorney)
1 practicing attorney in Michigan
3 legal assistants with not less than one year of experience as a legal assistant
1 legal assistant student

- Commission members will be paid on a per diem basis and will be expected to meet at least eight times a year.

- The Commission shall establish the requirements for certification of legal assistants; the requirements will deal with the "education, training and experience" of legal assistants.

- The Commission "shall develop and make public guidelines on the appropriate delegation of functions to and supervision of legal assistants according to the level of education, training, or experience of legal assistants. The guidelines shall not be binding, but shall serve to explain how the commission's training criteria coincides with the expectations of attorneys relative to the delegation to and supervision of legal assistants."

- "A person shall not act as a legal assistant, hold himself out as a legal assistant, or use the title or designation indicating he is a legal assistant except as authorized by this act. . . ."

- To be certified, a person must be eighteen years of age or older, be a "graduate of an approved program; or be a licensed, certified, registered, approved, or other legally recognized legal assistant in another state with qualifications substantially equivalent to those established by the commission; or have the education, training, or experience prescribed by this act or the rules of the commission as determined by an examination or evaluation authorized by the commission, . . ."

- "To determine whether an applicant for initial certification has the appropriate level of skill and knowledge as required by this act, the commission shall require the applicant to submit to an examination which shall include those subjects the general knowledge of which is commonly and generally required of a graduate of an accredited legal assistants program in the United States. The commission may waive the examination requirement for graduates of approved programs where such applicants have taken a national examination and achieved a score acceptable to the commission as demonstrating the level of skill and knowledge required by this act. The commission also may waive the examination for applicants who are licensed, certified, registered, approved, or otherwise legally recognized as a legal assistant in another state, when the commission determines that the other state has qualifications, including completion of a national or state approved examination for legal assistants, that are substantially equivalent to those established by this act. For the purpose of this section, the commission shall not, in any case, preclude applicants from taking an examination because of a lack of specific previous education, training, or experience."

- Someone who fails the examination cannot retake it more than three times.
- Certification, once granted, is not perpetual. The Commission must make "determinations of continuing competence," e.g., by retesting, "not less than once every 4 years."
- A person who has been certified "shall publicly display the current certificate" in that "person's place of practice, if feasible, and shall have available for inspection a pocket card" issued by the state "containing the essential information of the certification."
- A legal assistant "shall not undertake or represent that he is qualified to undertake provision of a legal service which he knows or reasonably should know to be outside his competence or lawfully prohibited."
- A legal assistant "shall perform legal functions only under the supervision of an attorney, and only when those functions are within the scope of practice of the supervising attorney and are delegated by the supervising attorney." "A legal assistant shall perform legal functions only in those settings approved by the supervising attorney."
- A legal assistant "is the agent of the supervising attorney. Communications made to a legal assistant which would be privileged communications if made to the supervising attorney shall be considered privileged communications to the legal assistant and the supervising attorney to the same extent as if the communications were made to the supervising attorney."
- "A person who practices or holds himself out as a legal assistant without approval is guilty of a felony punishable by a fine of not less than $1,000.00 or more than $5,000.00, or imprisonment for not more than 1 year, or both."
- The Commission shall also award "accreditation to qualified institutions offering programs for the training of legal assistants." This shall be done "to determine whether graduates of the programs, who may apply for certification in this state, meet the requirements established for legal assistants pursuant to this act. . . ." The Commission shall consider "and may use where appropriate the criteria established by professional associations, educational accrediting bodies, or government agencies." "The standards for educational and training programs shall be designed to determine that each legal assistant has the necessary knowledge and skill to perform in a competent manner with due regard for the complexity attendant to activities in which a legal assistant engages."

Arizona considered, but did not pass, the following licensing legislation:

State of Arizona
House of Representatives
Thirty-seventh Legislature
First Regular Session
1985

H. B. **2299**

1 Be it enacted by the Legislature of the State of Arizona:
2 Section 1. Purpose
3 The purpose of this act is to protect the paralegal profession
4 and the public by providing for the licensing and regulation of
5 paralegals.
6 Sec. 2. Title 32, Arizona Revised Statutes, is amended by add-
7 ing chapter 31, to read:
8 CHAPTER 31 PARALEGALS
9 ARTICLE 1. GENERAL PROVISIONS
10 32-3101. Definitions
11 IN THIS CHAPTER, UNLESS THE CONTEXT OTHER-
12 WISE REQUIRES:
13 1. "BOARD" MEANS THE BOARD OF PARALEGALS.
14 2. "PARALEGAL" MEANS A PERSON LICENSED PURSUANT
15 TO THIS CHAPTER.
16 3. "PARALEGAL PRACTICE" MEANS ANY OF THE FOLLOW-
17 ING IF DONE ON A REGULAR BASIS FOR A LICENSED
18 ATTORNEY:
19 (a) CONDUCTING INTERVIEWS WITH CLIENTS TO GATH-
20 ER BACKGROUND INFORMATION.
21 (b) CONDUCTING CASE AND STATUTE RESEARCH AND
22 WRITING AN ANALYSIS OR SYNOPSIS OF THE RESEARCH.
23 (c) DRAFTING INTERROGATORIES.
24 (d) PREPARING PLEADINGS.
25 (e) INTERVIEWING AND PREPARING WITNESSES FOR DEPO-
26 SITIONS, CROSS-EXAMINATION AND COURT
27 APPEARANCES.
28 (f) CONDUCTING BUSINESS WITH THE POLICE, ATTOR-
29 NEYS, GOVERNMENT OFFICIALS AND AGENCIES AND ALL
30 LEVELS OF COURTS.
31 (g) PREPARING DRAFTS OF TRIAL MOTIONS, COM-
32 PLAINTS, WILLS, LEASES, CORPORATION FORMATIONS,
33 FICTITIOUS NAME PAPERS, PARTNERSHIP AGREEMENTS,
34 CONTRACTS OR APPELLATE BRIEFS.
35 (h) WORKING CLOSELY WITH ATTORNEYS DURING TRIAL
36 BY KEEPING MATERIAL ORGANIZED AND MAKING NOTES
37 DURING EXAMINATION AND CROSS-EXAMINATION OF
38 WITNESSES.
39 (i) REPRESENTING ATTORNEYS' CLIENTS IN ADMINISTRA-
40 TION PROCEEDINGS SUCH AS SOCIAL SECURITY HEARINGS,
41 UNEMPLOYMENT COMPENSATION HEARINGS OR JUSTICE
42 OF THE PEACE HEARINGS.
43 (j) REVIEWING, ORGANIZING AND DIGESTING DEPOSI-
44 TION AND TRIAL TRANSCRIPTS.
45 32-3102. Board of paralegals; appointment;
46 qualifications; terms
47 A. A BOARD OF PARALEGALS IS ESTABLISHED CONSIST-
48 ING OF THE FOLLOWING FIVE MEMBERS APPOINTED BY
49 THE GOVERNOR:

1. ONE PARALEGAL WHO HAS BEEN ACTIVELY PRACTIC-
ING IN THIS STATE FOR AT LEAST THREE YEARS.
   2. TWO PERSONS WHO ARE PARALEGAL EDUCATORS.
   3. TWO PUBLIC MEMBERS PREFERABLY ONE OF WHOM IS A
LICENSED ATTORNEY.
   B. THE TERMS OF OFFICE OF BOARD MEMBERS ARE FIVE
YEARS. MEMBERS SHALL NOT SERVE MORE THAN TWO CON-
SECUTIVE TERMS.
   C. THE GOVERNOR MAY REMOVE A BOARD MEMBER FOR
NEGLECT OF DUTY, MALFEASANCE OR MISFEASANCE.
   32-3103. Organization; meetings; compensation
   A. THE BOARD SHALL ANNUALLY ELECT A CHAIRMAN,
VICE-CHAIRMAN AND SECRETARY-TREASURER FROM ITS
MEMBERSHIP.
   B. THE BOARD MAY HOLD MEETINGS AT TIMES AND PLAC-
ES IT DESIGNATES.
   C. A MAJORITY OF THE MEMBERS OF THE BOARD CONSTI-
TUTES A QUORUM.
   D. MEMBERS OF THE BOARD ARE ELIGIBLE TO RECEIVE
COMPENSATION AS DETERMINED PURSUANT TO SECTION
38-611 FOR EACH DAY OF ACTUAL SERVICE IN THE BUSINESS
OF THE BOARD.
   32-3104. Powers and duties
   A. THE BOARD SHALL:
   1. MAKE AND ADOPT RULES WHICH ARE NECESSARY OR
PROPER FOR THE ADMINISTRATION OF THIS CHAPTER, IN-
CLUDING REQUIREMENTS FOR PARALEGAL EDUCATION.
   2. ADMINISTER AND ENFORCE THE PROVISIONS OF THIS
CHAPTER AND RULES ADOPTED PURSUANT TO THIS
CHAPTER.
   3. MAINTAIN A RECORD OF ITS ACTS AND PROCEEDINGS,
INCLUDING ISSUANCE, REFUSAL, RENEWAL, SUSPENSION
AND REVOCATION OF LICENSES, AND A RECORD OF THE
NAME, ADDRESS AND LICENSE DATE OF EACH LICENSEE.
   4. KEEP THE RECORDS OF THE BOARD OPEN TO PUBLIC IN-
SPECTION AT ALL REASONABLE TIMES.
   5. FURNISH A COPY OF ITS RULES TO ANY PERSON ON
REQUEST.
   6. HAVE A SEAL, THE IMPRINT OF WHICH SHALL BE USED
TO EVIDENCE ITS OFFICIAL ACTS.
   B. THE BOARD MAY EMPLOY AN EXECUTIVE DIRECTOR
WHO HAS BEEN A PARALEGAL FOR AT LEAST THREE YEARS
PRECEDING EMPLOYMENT AND OTHER PERMANENT OR
TEMPORARY PERSONNEL IT DEEMS NECESSARY. THE
BOARD SHALL COMPENSATE ITS EXECUTIVE DIRECTOR
AND OTHER PERMANENT AND TEMPORARY PERSONNEL AS
DETERMINED PURSUANT TO SECTION 38-611.
   32-3105. Board of paralegals fund
   A. A BOARD OF PARALEGALS FUND IS ESTABLISHED. BE-
FORE THE END OF EACH CALENDAR MONTH, ALL MONIES
FROM WHATEVER SOURCE WHICH COME INTO THE POSSES-
SION OF THE BOARD SHALL BE TRANSMITTED TO THE

1   STATE TREASURER WHO SHALL DEPOSIT TEN PER CENT OF
2   SUCH MONIES IN THE STATE GENERAL FUND AND TRANS-
3   FER THE REMAINING NINETY PER CENT TO THE BOARD OF
4   PARALEGALS FUND.
5   B. MONIES DEPOSITED IN THE BOARD OF PARALEGALS
6   FUND ARE SUBJECT TO SECTION 35-143.01.
7   ARTICLE 2. LICENSURE
8   32-3111. Paralegal license; application; qualifications;
9   reciprocity
10   A. AN APPLICANT FOR A PARALEGAL LICENSE SHALL FILE
11 THE FOLLOWING WITH THE BOARD:
12   1. A WRITTEN APPLICATION ON A FORM PRESCRIBED BY
13 THE BOARD.
14   2. EVIDENCE SATISFACTORY TO THE BOARD THAT THE
15 APPLICANT POSSESSES THE NECESSARY QUALIFICATIONS
16 AND EDUCATION.
17   B. EACH APPLICANT SHALL:
18   1. BE AT LEAST EIGHTEEN YEARS OF AGE.
19   2. HAVE COMPLETED AND RECEIVED APPROPRIATE CRED-
20 ITS FOR HIGH SCHOOL EDUCATION OR ITS EQUIVALENT AS
21 PRESCRIBED BY THE BOARD IN ITS RULES.
22   3. PASS AN EXAMINATION GIVEN UNDER THE DIRECTION
23 OF THE BOARD.
24   4. PAY THE PRESCRIBED FEE.
25   C. AN APPLICANT WHO HOLDS A VALID LICENSE FOR PAR-
26 ALEGAL PRACTICE ISSUED BY ANOTHER STATE WHICH
27 HAS, IN THE OPINION OF THE BOARD, LICENSURE REQUIRE-
28 MENTS THAT ARE SUBSTANTIALLY EQUIVALENT TO THE
29 REQUIREMENTS OF THIS STATE AND WHICH GRANTS SIMI-
30 LAR RECIPROCAL PRIVILEGES TO PARALEGALS LICENSED
31 BY THIS STATE AND WHO HAS AT LEAST ONE YEAR'S EXPE-
32 RIENCE AS A LICENSED PARALEGAL IS EXEMPT FROM SUB-
33 SECTION B, PARAGRAPH 3.
34   32-3112. Examinations
35   A. EXAMINATIONS SHALL BE GIVEN AT LEAST EVERY
36 THREE MONTHS AT TIMES AND PLACES DETERMINED BY
37 THE BOARD.
38   B. EXAMINATIONS SHALL CONTAIN A WRITTEN PART
39 AND MAY INCLUDE ORAL QUESTIONS.
40   C. EXAMINATIONS SHALL TEST THE APPLICANT'S
41 KNOWLEDGE OF PARALEGAL PRACTICE.
42   D. A PASSING GRADE ON AN EXAMINATION IS A SCORE OF
43 SEVENTY-FIVE PER CENT OR BETTER ON BOTH THE WRIT-
44 TEN AND ORAL PARTS OF THE EXAMINATION.
45   E. IF AN APPLICANT WHO IS ELIGIBLE TO TAKE AN EXAMI-
46 NATION FAILS TO DO SO AT EITHER OF THE NEXT TWO
47 SCHEDULED EXAMINATIONS, THE APPLICATION IS DEEM-
48 ED TO BE CANCELLED AND THE APPLICATION FEE IS
49 FORFEITED.
50   F. IF AN APPLICANT FAILS AN EXAMINATION HE IS ENTI-
51 TLED TO A REEXAMINATION.
52   G. IF AN APPLICANT FAILS EITHER PART OF THE EXAMI-

1 NATION HE SHALL ONLY RETAKE THE PART OF THE EXAMI-
2 NATION HE FAILED.
3   H. AN APPLICANT DESIRING TO BE REEXAMINED SHALL
4 APPLY TO THE BOARD ON FORMS IT PRESCRIBES AND FUR-
5 NISHES AND PAY THE PRESCRIBED REEXAMINATION FEE.
6   32-3113. Fees; penalty
7   A. THE BOARD SHALL ESTABLISH AND COLLECT FEES,
8 NOT TO EXCEED THE FOLLOWING AMOUNTS:
9   1. PARALEGAL EXAMINATION, TWO HUNDRED
10 DOLLARS.
11   2. PARALEGAL LICENSE, ONE HUNDRED DOLLARS.
12   3. PARALEGAL LICENSE BY RECIPROCITY, TWO HUNDRED
13 DOLLARS.
14   4. REEXAMINATION, FIFTY DOLLARS.
15   B. A DUPLICATE LICENSE SHALL BE ISSUED TO REPLACE A
16 LOST LICENSE IF A LICENSEE FILES A VERIFIED STATEMENT
17 AS TO ITS LOSS AND PAYS A TWENTY DOLLAR FEE. EACH
18 DUPLICATE LICENSE ISSUED SHALL HAVE THE WORD "DU-
19 PLICATE" STAMPED ACROSS THE FACE.
20   C. IF THE BOARD RECEIVES AN INSUFFICIENT FUND
21 CHECK, IT MAY CHARGE A TEN DOLLAR PENALTY FEE.
22   ARTICLE 3. REGULATION
23   32-3121. Disciplinary action
24   THE BOARD MAY TAKE ANY ONE OR A COMBINATION OF
25 THE FOLLOWING DISCIPLINARY ACTIONS:
26   1. REVOKE A LICENSE.
27   2. SUSPEND A LICENSE.
28   3. IMPOSE A CIVIL PENALTY IN AN AMOUNT NOT TO EX-
29 CEED FIVE HUNDRED DOLLARS.
30   4. IMPOSE PROBATION REQUIREMENTS BEST ADAPTED
31 TO PROTECT THE PUBLIC SAFETY, HEALTH AND WELFARE
32 INCLUDING   REQUIREMENTS   FOR   RESTITUTION
33 PAYMENTS.
34   5. ISSUE A LETTER OF CONCERN.
35   32-3122. Grounds for refusal to issue or renew
36   a license or disciplinary action
37   THE BOARD MAY TAKE DISCIPLINARY ACTION OR REFUSE
38 TO ISSUE OR RENEW A LICENSE FOR ANY OF THE FOLLOW-
39 ING CAUSES:
40   1. MALPRACTICE OR INCOMPETENCY.
41   2. ADVERTISING BY MEANS OF KNOWN FALSE OR DECEP-
42 TIVE STATEMENTS.
43   3. ADVERTISING, PRACTICING OR ATTEMPTING TO PRAC-
44 TICE UNDER A NAME OTHER THAN THE ONE IN WHICH THE
45 LICENSE IS ISSUED.
46   32-3124. Unlawful acts; violation; classification
47   A. A PERSON SHALL NOT:
48   1. PRACTICE OR ATTEMPT PARALEGAL PRACTICE WITH-
49 OUT A CURRENT LICENSE ISSUED PURSUANT TO THIS
50 CHAPTER.
51   2. DISPLAY A SIGN OR IN ANY WAY ADVERTISE OR HOLD
52 ONESELF OUT AS A PARALEGAL OR AS BEING ENGAGED IN

1 THE PARALEGAL PRACTICE WITHOUT BEING LICENSED
2 PURSUANT TO THIS CHAPTER.
3   3. KNOWINGLY MAKE A FALSE STATEMENT ON AN APPLI-
4 CATION FOR A LICENSE PURSUANT TO THIS CHAPTER.
5   4. PERMIT AN EMPLOYEE OR ANOTHER PERSON UNDER
6 HIS SUPERVISION OR CONTROL TO ENGAGE IN PARALEGAL
7 PRACTICE WITHOUT A LICENSE ISSUED PURSUANT TO
8 THIS CHAPTER.
9   5. OBTAIN OR ATTEMPT TO OBTAIN A LICENSE BY THE
10 USE OF MONEY OTHER THAN THE PRESCRIBED FEES OR ANY
11 OTHER   THING   OF   VALUE   OR   BY   FRAUDULENT
12 MISREPRESENTATION.
13   6. VIOLATE ANY PROVISION OF THIS CHAPTER OR ANY
14 RULE ADOPTED PURSUANT TO THIS CHAPTER.
15   B. A PERSON WHO VIOLATES THIS SECTION IS GUILTY OF
16 A CLASS 2 MISDEMEANOR.
17   32-3125. Injunctions
18   THE BOARD, THE ATTORNEY GENERAL, A COUNTY AT-
19 TORNEY OR ANY OTHER PERSON MAY APPLY TO THE SUPE-
20 RIOR COURT IN THE COUNTY IN WHICH ACTS OR PRACTIC-
21 ES OF ANY PERSON WHICH CONSTITUTE A VIOLATION OF
22 THIS CHAPTER OR THE RULES ADOPTED PURSUANT TO
23 THIS CHAPTER ARE ALLEGED TO HAVE OCCURRED FOR AN
24 ORDER ENJOINING THOSE ACTS OR PRACTICES.

ASSIGNMENT 8 *CLASS Discussion*

As we have seen, lawyers will seek criminal prosecution against nonlawyers for engaging in the unauthorized practice of law. If licensing comes for paralegals, should criminal prosecution be used to enforce the licensing law? Note that the above Arizona license bill makes it a "misdemeanor" to violate its provisions. Is this, in effect, the creation of a new crime—the unauthorized practice of para-law? See *Legal Assistant Today,* p. 8 (Jan/Feb, 1987).

In 1975, the Oregon Bar Association actually launched a certification program that it later abandoned. It administered an examination to candidates who had been graduated from a paralegal school and had some practical experience. Very little interest was generated by the process and it was discontinued in 1980. In 1985 another Oregon proposal surfaced. The Legislative Counsel Committee of the Oregon State Legislature drafted a licensing (referred to as a "registration") program. The future of this proposed legislation is unclear.

Most licensing proposals are primarily restrictive in that they focus on what paralegals *cannot* do. One recent proposal surprisingly goes the other way. The Santa Monica Bar Association has asked the California State Bar Association and the California state legislature to enact a program that would require paralegals in the state to be licensed by a board within the California Department of Consumer Affairs. The board, to be appointed by the Governor, would consist of five legal assistants, one active legal assistant educator, two members of the Bar with experience in the use of legal assistants, and one member of the public at large. An oral or "practical" examination would be a condition of obtaining the license. The board would also approve paralegal schools and set minimal educational requirements for paralegals applying for a license. Among the functions that a licensed paralegal would be able to perform under the supervision of a lawyer are the following:

1. Make court appearances in ex parte matters;
2. Make court appearances for continuances;
3. Make court appearances for status and trial setting conferences;
4. Appear at judgment debtor examinations; and
5. Make court appearances in uncontested probate matters.

As of the present time, the fate of this proposal is uncertain. The chances of passage, however, are slim.

A number of bar associations have specifically rejected proposals to license or certify paralegals. The following excerpts from bar reports give some of the reasons why:

 North Carolina State Bar, *Report of Special Committee on Paralegals,* p. 3 (1980)

Several states have considered the possibility of adopting a licensing statute for paralegals, but none has done so. It is doubtful that the concept of proper lay assistance to lawyers is now well enough or uniformly enough understood for the terms of a licensing statute to find a proper consensus. Licensing itself is subject to great public and legislative concern at present. So long as the work accomplished by nonlawyers for lawyers is properly supervised and reviewed by a licensed and responsible attorney, there would seem to be no need for a further echelon of licensing for the public's protection. Furthermore, licensing might be more dangerous than helpful to the public. The apparent stamp of approval of a license possibly could give the impression to the public that a person having such a license is qualified to deal directly with and give legal advice to the public. Although the Committee would not attempt to close the door on licensing of paralegals in the future if circumstances change and if, for example, the use of independent, non-lawyer employee paralegals were to become widespread, present conditions, at least, do not call for any program of licensing for paralegals.

 Illinois State Bar Association, *Report on the Joint Study Committee on Attorney Assistants,* p. 6 (6/21/77)

Our Joint Committee arose because there was a suggestion that attorney assistants be licensed. After due consideration we recommend no program of licensure or certification of attorney assistants or other lay personnel.

We are opposed to licensure because the standards on which licensure are to be based are difficult or impossible to formulate. Furthermore, we have started with a premise that precedes this conclusion; to wit: no delegation of any task to an attorney assistant shall diminish the responsibility of the attorney for the services rendered. We believe that any program which purports to say who is "licensed" and who is "not licensed" creates a standard which will diminish the attorney's responsibility. It furthermore may exclude from useful and desirable employment people who, under the supervision and control of an attorney, may perform useful tasks but who may not meet the standards of licensure involved.

We are further opposed to licensure because of the danger that it poses to the public. If a group of persons appears to be authorized to perform tasks directly for the public, without the intervening control of an attorney, it would be humanly inevitable that many of the licensed persons would try to deal directly with the public. We think these risks would be substantially increased by licensure.

Only one state, Oregon, has experimented with state-certification of paralegals, although several bars have studied the possibility. Oregon's program was started in 1975, but it was discontinued in January, 1980. One of the two national organizations of paralegals (National Association of Legal Assistants) has a program of certification by that organization, but the other (National Federation of Paralegal Associations) does not. The latter's position, as well as the position of the American Bar Association, is that certification programs are premature, and possibly stifling, in a field that is growing and constantly undergoing changes. The Committee agrees and is of the view that such factors as (a) the range of services that can be classified as "paralegal," (b) the numerous methods by which intelligent and responsible persons can attain the skills through which to perform these services, and (c) the possible detriment to efficient and competent (but specialized) employees who could not be pigeonholed into any workable certification program, additionally tend to make a certification program of any sort unwise. We would leave the possible sponsorship of any such program to the future, when the developing occupation of paralegalism has matured.

ASSIGNMENT 9

How would you characterize the opposition to licensure and certification expressed in the above excerpts from the bar reports? Do you think there is a conflict of interest in lawyers making these judgments about paralegal control? Explain.

ASSIGNMENT 10

Evaluate the following observation: "The emerging professions and the more established professions have frequently sought greater regulation of their occupational group. They are often motivated, despite the obligatory language on protection of the public interest, to do so in efforts to establish their 'territorial imperative' or to establish barrier(s) to entry into the profession and thereby enhance their economic self-interest." Sapadin, "A Comparison of the Growth and Development of the Physician Assistant and the Legal Assistant," Journal of the American Association for Paralegal Education: *Retrospective 1983*, p. 142 (1983).

_____

The American Bar Association does not favor the licensing of paralegals. In 1986, however, an ABA Commission on Professionalism cautiously suggested "limited licensing of paralegals" and "paraprofessionals" to handle simple legal matters such as some real estate closings, the drafting of simple wills, and performing certain tax work. The report of the Commission stated that this proposal could help reduce the cost of legal services:

> "No doubt, many wills and real estate closings require the service of a lawyer. However, it can no longer be claimed that lawyers have the exclusive possession of the esoteric knowledge required and are therefore the only ones able to advise clients on any matter concerning the law." "Professionalism Declining?" *American Bar Association Journal*, p. 19 (Oct. 1, 1986).

This position of the Commission "drew the ire" of other ABA members and is unlikely to be given serious consideration anytime soon. And again, the ABA has formally gone on record as opposing licensing of paralegals. This, however, will not prevent continued suggestions in the direction of licensure—even within the ABA itself.

_____

Will paralegals one day be licensed? It is, of course, difficult to predict. While there is considerable opposition from the vast majority of paralegals, paralegal associations, and bar associations to licensing legislation, proposals for such legislation continue to emerge with alarming regularity. It is not uncommon for licensing proposals to be before three or four state legislatures every year.

It is anticipated that one of them will eventually pass in spite of the organized opposition against it. How will this occur? A possible scenario is as follows: One day, while working on a case, a paralegal in some state makes a serious and damaging mistake, e.g., an act of negligence (p. 138). Or the paralegal leads a court to believe that s/he is an attorney in an appearance before the court. The blunder is given a great deal of publicity and is blown out of proportion. Cries are heard for regulation: "There otta be a law!" A licensing statute is quickly drafted and enacted with little opportunity for public comment.

Paralegal associations have a vast array of arguments against licensing. But are they ready for the day when everyone wakes up to discover that licensing legislation squeaked through a particular state legislature?

There are two strategies that can be taken. The first is to continue to oppose all efforts at licensing. Have monitors keep a watchful eye on every legislature in the country. When a proposal emerges, bombard the legislature with reasons why it should be defeated. Thus far, this has been the strategy of the opponents and it has been successful. There is no licensing requirement today in any state. A second strategy is for paralegals to design a licensing proposal of their own, one they can live with. Paralegals can continue their organized opposition to licensing, but when an unacceptable lawyer-written proposal has a serious chance of passage in a given legislature, the paralegals produce their own substitute and lobby for its passage.

There are paralegals who oppose the second strategy since the very existence of a paralegal proposal would lead some to believe that paralegals favor licensing. This indeed is a danger. But a choice must be made. If licensing will eventually come, would paralegals rather have their own program or one forced on them? According to Laurie P. Roselle, former president of the National Federation of Paralegal Associations:

> Where we go from here is an issue we must grapple with now before someone decides for us where we go.[11]

---

[11] Roselle, *President's Column,* 9 National Paralegal Reporter 1 (Nat'l. Federation of Paralegal Associations, no. 5, April, 1985).

**What to do when the
Legislature Proposes Legislation
to Regulate Paralegals**

1. Obtain a copy of the proposed legislation or bill as soon as possible. If you know the name of the legislator sponsoring the bill, write or call him/her directly. Otherwise contact the office of the Speaker of the House, Speaker of the Assembly, President of the Senate, etc. Ask how you can locate the proposed bill.
2. Find out the exact technical status of the bill. Has it been formally introduced? Has it been assigned to a committee? What is the next scheduled formal event on the bill?
3. Immediately inform the sponsoring legislator(s) and the relevant committee(s) that you want an opportunity to comment on the bill. Find out if hearings are going to be scheduled on the bill. Make known your interest in participating in such hearings. Your goal is to slow the process down so that the bill is not rushed into enactment. Be particularly alert to the possibility that the paralegal bill may be buried in proposed legislation on a large number of related or unrelated topics. Again, there is a real danger that the bill will get through relatively unnoticed.
4. Determine why the paralegal bill is being proposed. What is the *public* reason given for the proposal of the bill? More important, what is the underlying *real* reason for the proposal? Perhaps some small group or special interest is seeking a special privilege in a law-related field, e.g., real estate agents. Yet the language of the bill they are proposing may be so broad that paralegals will be adversely affected.
5. Alert your local paralegal association. It needs to be mobilized in order to express an organized position on the bill. Contact the major national paralegal associations: NFPA and NALA (p. 110). Do they know about the proposed legislation? Have they taken a position? They need to be activated.
6. If your local bar association has a paralegal committee, seek its support.
7. Launch a letter-writing campaign. Make sure that large numbers of paralegals in the area know about the bill and how to express their opinion to the legislature.
8. Ask local paralegal schools to take a position.

Keep in mind that we are talking about mandatory *licensing* by the state, not voluntary *certification* by entities such as paralegal associations. The certification debate will be covered later (p. 114).

4

Ethical Rules Governing Lawyers and the Lawyer's Use of Paralegals

In order to understand how bar associations control a lawyer's use of paralegals, we must understand the controls that the bar associations place on lawyers themselves. The following topics will be covered:

1. Introduction to bar associations and the canons or rules of ethics governing lawyers.
2. The American Bar Association and paralegals.
3. State and local bar associations and paralegals.
4. The attorney-client privilege, confidentiality, and special ethical problems facing the paralegal who switches jobs and the free-lance paralegal.
5. Doing legal research on an ethical issue.

1. INTRODUCTION TO BAR ASSOCIATIONS AND CANONS OR RULES OF ETHICS GOVERNING LAWYERS

Lawyers are regulated by their state bar association under the authority and supervision of the state's highest court. The regulations take the form of canons of ethics, the violation of which can lead to sanctions such as suspension and disbarment. To discipline a lawyer for such violations, a committee of the bar association will usually conduct a hearing on the case and make a preliminary decision. The result can be appealed to a designated state court, which will make the final decision on whether sanctions are to be imposed. (See Appendix D, p. 174, for a summary of how the system works in your state.) The bar associations often write ethical opinions that interpret and apply the canons.

As we will see, one of the canons covers the lawyer's use of paralegals. This canon is the major source of a paralegal's authority to work in a law office. In essence, a lawyer must supervise the paralegal and see to it that the paralegal does not engage in the unauthorized practice of law.

The canons apply to lawyers and not directly to paralegals. Since paralegals cannot be full members of a bar association (p. 107), the canons do not directly control or regulate paralegals. No paralegal can be disciplined by a bar association for unethical conduct. It is the *lawyer* who will be disciplined for what the paralegal (or other nonlawyer) does within the employ of the lawyer. Other kinds of sanctions can be applied to paralegals, e.g., criminal prosecution for the unauthorized practice of law (p. 6) or a negligence claim (p. 138). Bar sanctions govern only lawyers.

The American Bar Association is a *voluntary* association of lawyers. No lawyer is required to be a member of the ABA. One of the major roles of the ABA is to write ethical rules and issue opinions interpreting these rules. The rules and opinions are *not* binding on state and local bar associations. Since, however, the ABA is a respected body, its rules and opinions have been very influential. In fact, most state and local bar associations have adopted all or some of the ABA ethical positions. They are not required to do so, but they seldom ignore what the ABA has said. If you read the ethical rules and opinions of state and local bar associations, you will find that they are often either taken entirely from the ABA positions or adapted from these positions.

Two important sets of ethical rules should be distinguished:

- *ABA Model Code of Professional Responsibility.*
- *ABA Model Rules of Professional Conduct.*

The Model Code is the older of the two documents. It consists of three main parts. First, the nine canons of the Code. The canons are statements of axiomatic norms expressing in general terms the standards of professional conduct expected of lawyers. Second, the disciplinary rules for each of the nine canons. The disciplinary rules (abbreviated "DR") are mandatory statements of the minimum conduct below which no lawyer can fall without being subject to disciplinary action. Third, the ethical considerations for each of the nine canons. The ethical considerations (abbreviated "EC") are aspirational in character and represent the objectives toward which every member of the profession should strive.

The Model Rules, on the other hand, were adopted by the ABA in 1983. They are a revision of the Model Code. Some of the changes are significant while others are minor. The Model Rules consist of eight rules plus commentary on their application.

While the Model Rules represent the current position of the ABA, you must still be aware of the Model Code. As indicated, many states closely examine the ABA ethical positions and decide whether to adopt, modify, or reject them for their own state. All states have been examining the relatively recent Model Rules. An individual state may decide to adopt some of the Model Rules, keep some of the older Model Code, and add items that are in neither ABA document.

Before covering what the ABA and state bar associations have said about the use of paralegals by lawyers, we need to examine the content of the ABA Model Code and Model Rules. You should know what ethical obligations are imposed on lawyers so that you can help your employing lawyers avoid charges of ethical improprieties. Some states strongly urge lawyers to provide their paralegals with training on these ethical obligations. The ABA mandates that lawyers should give their paralegals "appropriate instruction" on the "ethical aspects" of the practice of law (p. 64). In Kentucky, the paralegal has an obligation "to refrain from conduct which would involve the lawyer in a violation" of the canons of ethics (p. 72). Hence paralegals need to understand the ethical standards imposed on the legal profession. Here we will focus on the positions of the ABA. Later we will examine the research steps that you would take to find the specific canons of your state.

THE ETHICAL OBLIGATIONS OF LAWYERS: A SUMMARY OF THE ABA MODEL CODE AND THE ABA MODEL RULES

(At the beginning of each topic you will find summaries of specific canons or standards. All "Rules" are from the ABA Model Rules; all references to "DR" or "EC" are from the Model Code.)

In this summary, we will cover the following topics:
(a) Competence
(b) Criminal Conduct and Fraud by the Client
(c) Candor and Honesty by the Lawyer
(d) Communication with Client
(e) Fees
(f) Confidentiality of Information
(g) Conflict of Interest
(h) Gifts from Clients
(i) Property of the Client
(j) Withdrawal of a Lawyer from a Case

(k)   Frivolous Claims
(l)   Communication with Opposing Party
(m)   Advertising
(n)   Solicitation
(o)   Reporting Professional Misconduct
(p)   The Appearance of Impropriety
(q)   Paralegals and Other Nonlawyers

(a) Competence

> *Rule 1.1. A lawyer shall provide competent representation to a client.*
>
> *Rule 1.3. A lawyer shall act with reasonable diligence and promptness in representing a client.*
>
> *Rule 3.2. A lawyer shall make reasonable efforts to expedite litigation.*
>
> *DR 6-101(A)(1). A lawyer should not handle a matter which s/he knows or should know that s/he is not competent to handle without becoming associated with a lawyer who is competent to handle it.*
>
> *DR 6-101(A)(3). A lawyer shall not neglect a legal matter entrusted to him/her.*

A lawyer must have the skills needed to practice law, e.g., analyze precedent, evaluate evidence, draft legal documents. For special legal problems, the lawyer must conduct legal research and, where needed, seek the help of more experienced lawyers. It would be unethical for a lawyer to have a large caseload when each case cannot be handled competently. It would be unethical for a lawyer to proceed with a case without adequate preparation.

Also, unreasonable procrastination is unethical. Undue delay must be avoided.

(b) Criminal Conduct and Fraud by the Client

> *Rule 1.2(d). A lawyer shall not counsel a client to engage, or assist a client, in conduct that the lawyer knows is criminal or fraudulent.*
>
> *DR 7-102(A)(7). A lawyer shall not counsel or assist his/her client in conduct that the lawyer knows to be illegal or fraudulent.*

It is unethical for a lawyer to tell a client how to commit a crime or a fraudulent act, e.g., to cheat on an income tax return, to fabricate evidence, or to destroy evidence that must be preserved.

(c) Candor and Honesty by the Lawyer

> *Rule 3.3. A lawyer shall not knowingly make a false statement of material fact or law to a tribunal, knowingly offer false evidence, or knowingly fail to disclose material facts to a tribunal when disclosure is necessary to avoid assisting the client commit fraud or a crime. If the lawyer knows of legal authority that is against his/her client, the lawyer must disclose this authority to the tribunal if it is not offered by opposing counsel.*

> *Rule 3.4. A lawyer shall not unlawfully obstruct another party's access to evidence.*

> *DR 7-102, DR 7-109.*

A lawyer can be zealous in the representation of his/her client. But this cannot include deception on the part of the lawyer by making false statements or offering false or perjured testimony. Also, if the lawyer's legal research has uncovered cases, statutes, or other authority in the jurisdiction that go *against* his/her client, the lawyer must tell the tribunal about this authority if it is not raised by the other side.

(d) Communication with Client

> *Rule 1.4. A lawyer shall keep a client reasonably informed about the status of the case and promptly comply with the client's reasonable requests for information.*

> *EC 9-2. A lawyer should fully and promptly inform the client of material developments in the matters being handled for the client.*

Studies have shown that one of the most common client complaints against lawyers is the failure of the lawyer to communicate with the client about the status of the case.

(e) Fees

> *Rule 1.5. A lawyer's fee shall be reasonable. Information about the fee should be communicated to the client, preferably in writing, before or within a reasonable time after commencing the representation. The reasonableness of a fee depends on factors such as the amount of time and skill required, the fees customarily charged in the locality for similar legal services, the expe-*

*rience, reputation, and ability of the lawyer, etc. Contingent
fees (i.e., where the existence of a fee or its amount is dependent
on the outcome of the case) are prohibited in criminal cases or
in domestic relations cases where the fee is contingent upon the
securing of a divorce or upon the amount of alimony, support,
or property settlement obtained. A lawyer shall not split a fee
with a lawyer who is not a member of the same firm unless certain conditions are met, e.g., the client does not object.*
DR 2-106(A)(B)(C); DR 107(A); EC 2-17; EC 2-19; EC 2-20.

(f) Confidentiality of Information

*Rule 1.6. A lawyer shall not reveal information relating to repre-
sentation of a client unless the client consents. An exception is
made if the lawyer reasonably believes that the revelation is
necessary to prevent the client from committing a criminal act
that is likely to result in imminent death or substantial bodily
harm.*

*Rule 1.8(b). A lawyer shall not use information relating to repre-
sentation of a client to the disadvantage of the client unless the
client consents.*

*DR 4-101. A lawyer shall not knowingly reveal a confidence or se-
cret of a client unless the client consents. A confidence is information protected by the attorney-client privilege. A secret is
any other information gained in the professional relationship
that the client requested to be kept private or that would likely
be detrimental to the client if disclosed. A lawyer, however,
may reveal the client's intention to commit a crime and the information necessary to prevent the crime.*

Without the principle of confidentiality, clients would be
discouraged from communicating fully and frankly with a lawyer, particularly as to embarrassing or legally damaging matters.
It would be unethical for a lawyer to disclose client communications even if the lawyer is called as a witness in court, unless the
exceptions apply.

For more on confidentiality, see p. 81.

(g) Conflict of Interest

*Rule 1.7. A lawyer shall not represent a client if it would be directly
adverse to another client unless each client consents and the
lawyer reasonably believes that this other client will not be adversely affected.*

> *Rule 1.10. If a lawyer is disqualified from representing a client because of Rule 1.7, all other lawyers in the same firm are also disqualified.*
>
> *DR 5-105. A lawyer shall decline a case if s/he cannot devote his/ her independent professional judgment on behalf of the client, or if accepting the case will likely involve representing differing interests. An exception exists if both clients, whom the lawyer seeks to represent, consent and it is obvious that the lawyer can adequately represent the interests of each.*

A client is entitled to a lawyer's undivided loyalty. Assume that a lawyer represents Mary *and* Pat in a fraud case against each other. How can the lawyer be loyal to both? Mary and Pat have adverse interests. For the lawyer to try to represent both would be a conflict of interest. Similarly, a lawyer cannot represent John in a contract case against Bill and *also* represent Fred in a negligence suit against John. Here the subject matter in the two suits is not the same. Yet the lawyer is being asked to use all his/her professional resources to defeat John in the negligence case and all of his/her professional resources to see that John wins in the contract case. The lawyer's loyalty to John is diminished. For example, in the lawyer's office, the lawyer may find out information that could be used against John in the negligence case. There is a conflict of interest.

In the above case, suppose that the lawyer was a member of a law firm of twenty other lawyers. Could one lawyer in the firm represent John in the contract case, and *another* lawyer in the same firm represent Fred in the negligence case against John? No. A firm of lawyers is essentially *one* lawyer for purposes of the rules governing loyalty to the client. John is entitled to the undivided loyalty of every member of the firm that represents him. If the firm represents John in one case, it is disqualified from representing John's adversary in the other case.

An example of one of the rare instances in which it might be ethical for a lawyer to represent *both* parties would be a divorce case in which both the husband and wife want the divorce, there are no children, no support issues, and no property division involved. If the husband and wife make an informed decision to allow the same lawyer to represent both of them, the multiple representation is allowed in many states. In such a case, there is very little likelihood that the parties will have any adverse interests.

(h) Gifts from Clients

> *Rule 1.8(c). A lawyer shall not prepare a document for a client, e.g., a will, in which the client gives the lawyer a substantial gift unless the lawyer is related to the client. The prohibition also applies if the gift is given to a close relative or spouse of the lawyer.*
>
> *EC 5-5. If a lawyer accepts a gift from the client, the lawyer is peculiarly susceptible to the charge that s/he unduly influenced the client in making the gift.*

This is another example of a conflict of interest. Whose interest is the lawyer protecting when s/he prepares the legal document that resulted in the gift? The donor or the donee?

(i) Property of the client

> *Rule 1.15. A lawyer shall hold property of clients separate from the lawyer's own property. Funds shall be kept in a separate account in the state where the lawyer's office is situated. Complete records shall be kept. The client shall be promptly notified if other funds are received.*
>
> *DR 9-102.*

(j) Withdrawal of the Lawyer from a Case

> *Rule 1.16. A lawyer must withdraw from a case (a) if the client demands that the lawyer engage in conduct that is illegal or unethical, (b) if the lawyer's physical or mental condition materially impairs his/her ability to represent the client, or (c) if the client fires the lawyer.*
>
> *DR 2-110. A lawyer shall withdraw if (a) it is obvious that the client's objective is merely to harass or maliciously injure someone, (b) continuing will result in a violation of the canons of ethics, (c) the lawyer's physical or mental condition makes it unreasonably difficult to represent the client effectively, or (d) the client fires the lawyer.*

A client always has a right to discharge a lawyer with or without giving any reasons, subject to an obligation to pay fees for services already rendered. There are times when a lawyer must have the permission of the court to withdraw, e.g., when the lawyer was initially appointed or assigned by the court to represent the client.

(k) Frivolous Claims

> *Rule 3.1. A lawyer shall not bring frivolous cases.*
> *Rule 3.4. A lawyer shall not make a frivolous discovery request. During a trial, a lawyer shall not allude to matters that the lawyer does not reasonably believe are relevant or supportable by admissible evidence.*
> *Rule 4.4. In representing a client, a lawyer shall not use means that have no substantial purpose other than to embarrass, delay, or burden a third person.*
> *DR 7-102(A)(2). A lawyer shall not knowingly advance a claim or defense that is unwarranted under existing law unless a good faith argument can be made for a change in the existing law.*

If a client asks a lawyer to violate these rules, the lawyer must withdraw from the case.

(l) Communication with Opposing Party

> *Rule 4.2. A lawyer should not communicate with the opposing party on a case unless the latter's lawyer consents. If this party is unrepresented, a lawyer shall not give him/her the impression that the lawyer is disinterested in the case (e.g., neutral). No legal advice should be given other than to obtain separate counsel.*
> *DR 7-104.*

The main concern here is that the lawyer might try to take undue advantage of the unrepresented party.

(m) Advertising

> *Rule 7.1; 7.2. A lawyer shall not make false or misleading statements about his/her services. Advertising is permitted through a telephone directory, legal directory, newspaper, other periodical, radio, TV, and other public media.*
> *DR 2-101. A lawyer may publish or broadcast certain information about his/her legal services in designated areas, e.g., name, address, field of practice, associations, information about fees.*

For more on advertising, see p. 99.

(n) Solicitation

> *Rule 7.3. A lawyer may not solicit legal business from a specific prospective client with whom the lawyer has no family or prior professional relationship when a significant motive for the*

lawyer's doing so is the lawyer's pecuniary (i.e., monetary or financial) gain. This prohibition does not forbid the use of letters or advertising circulars distributed generally.

DR 2-104(A). A lawyer who has given in-person unsolicited advice to a layperson that s/he should obtain counsel or take legal action, shall not accept employment resulting from that advice. An exception exists when the layperson is a close friend, relative, or former client (if the advice is germane to the former employment).

(o) Reporting Professional Misconduct

Rule 8.3. A lawyer having knowledge that another lawyer has committed a violation of these ethical rules that raises a substantial question as to that lawyer's honesty, trustworthiness, or fitness, shall inform the appropriate professional authority. DR 1-103.

(p) The Appearance of Impropriety

DR 9-101. A lawyer must avoid even the appearance of professional impropriety.

Under this provision, a lawyer can be disciplined even if no ethical rules are actually violated. It is unethical for a lawyer to act in such a way that *appears* ethically improper.

(q) Paralegals and Other Nonlawyers

See discussion below.

---

2. THE AMERICAN BAR ASSOCIATION AND PARALEGALS

Both the Model Code and the Model Rules of the ABA (p. 55) have provisions that are relevant to a lawyer's use of paralegals.

The ABA Model Code of Professional Responsibility provides as follows:

DR 3-101(A). A lawyer shall not aid a nonlawyer in the unauthorized practice of law.

EC 3-6. A lawyer often delegates tasks to clerks, secretaries, and other lay persons. Such delegation is proper if the lawyer maintains a direct relationship with his/her client, supervises the delegated work, and has complete professional responsibility for the work product. This delegation enables a lawyer to render legal services more economically and efficiently.

A 1967 opinion elaborates on these standards:

American Bar Association, Formal Opinion 316 (1967). A lawyer can employ lay secretaries, lay investigators, lay detectives, lay researchers, accountants, lay scriveners, non-lawyer draftsmen or non-lawyer researchers. In fact, he may employ non-lawyers to do any task for him except counsel clients about law matters, engage directly in the practice of law, appear in court or appear in formal proceedings a part of the judicial process, so long as it is he who takes the work and vouches for it to the client and becomes responsible for it to the client. In other words, we do not limit the kind of assistance that a lawyer can acquire in any way to persons who are admitted to the Bar, so long as the non-lawyers do not do things that lawyers may not do or do the things that lawyers only may do.

The more recent ABA Model Rules of Professional Conduct provides as follows:

Rule 5.3. Responsibilities Regarding Nonlawyer Assistants

With respect to a nonlawyer employed or retained by or associated with a lawyer:

(a) a partner in a law firm shall make reasonable efforts to ensure that the firm has in effect measures giving reasonable assurance that the person's conduct is compatible with the professional obligations of the lawyer;

(b) a lawyer having direct supervisory authority over the nonlawyer shall make reasonable efforts to ensure that the person's conduct is compatible with the professional obligations of the lawyer; and

(c) a lawyer shall be responsible for conduct of such a person that would be a violation of the Rules of Professional Conduct if engaged in by a lawyer if:

(1) the lawyer orders or ratifies the conduct involved; or

(2) the lawyer is a partner in the law firm in which the person is employed, or has direct supervisory authority over the person, and knows of the conduct at a time when its consequences can be avoided or mitigated but fails to take reasonable remedial action.

COMMENT:

Lawyers generally employ assistants in their practice, including secretaries, investigators, law student interns, and paraprofessionals. Such assistants, whether employees or independent contractors, act for the lawyer in rendition of the lawyer's professional services. A lawyer should give such assistants appropriate instruction and supervision concerning the ethical aspects of their employment, particularly regarding the obligation not to disclose information relating to representation of the client, and should be responsible for their work product. The measures employed in supervising nonlawyers should take account of the fact that they do not have legal training and are not subject to professional discipline.

Both the Model Code and the Model Rules are somewhat general in their coverage of paralegals. The paramount theme appears to be the necessity of supervision of the paralegal. We shall examine this and related themes later (p. 77). For now we turn to the more specific provisions of the state and local bar associations on paralegal use.

3. STATE AND LOCAL BAR ASSOCIATIONS AND PARALEGALS

SUMMARY OF SPECIFIC ETHICAL PROBLEMS
(See also the opinions of bar associations on paralegal use in Appendix B, p. 159.)

1. *Can the titles "paralegal," "legal assistant," "legal technician," etc., be used?*

Yes. Almost all states accept this terminology. Years ago there were several bar associations that were afraid that the terminology might be confusing to members of the public who might think that the person is a lawyer. Given the greater use of paralegals today, this is no longer perceived as a serious danger.

2. *Can a paralegal sign letters using his/her own name on law firm stationery, e.g., to a client, to opposing counsel?*

Most states say yes, so long as the nonlawyer status of the paralegal is clear when s/he signs the letter and the letter does not give legal advice or involve the application of legal knowledge. A minority of states, however, say that paralegals can sign only non-routine letters, e.g., to law firm vendors.

3. *Can a paralegal's name be printed at the top of the stationery of a law firm?*

The states are split on this question. There was a time when most states prohibited the printing of a nonlawyer's name on law firm stationery. It was felt that this would offend the dignity of the profession and give the impression that the firm was advertising itself. Since *Bates v. State Bar of Arizona*, 433 U.S. 350 (1970), which held that the bar could not prohibit all forms of lawyer advertising, a number of states have allowed a paralegal's name to be printed on law firm stationery. Other states, however, have continued the prohibition.

For an example of the stationery of a well-known lawyer, Melvin Belli—who allows paralegal names to be printed on law firm stationery—see Appendix C, p. 173.

4. *Can a paralegal have his/her own business card on which the name of the law firm is also printed?*

Yes, in most states. The nonlawyer status of the paralegal must be clear on the card and the law firm must have approved the format and content of the card. The card must not be used to solicit business for the firm.

It is unethical for a lawyer or paralegal to stir up legal business. Lawyers can engage in dignified and truthful advertising, but cannot "ambulance chase," e.g., hand a business card to someone who has just had an automobile accident when the person has not asked for any legal help.

5. *In oral communications with those outside the office, must the paralegal make clear early in the conversation that s/he is not an attorney?*

Yes, unless the paralegal's nonlawyer status is already known to the outside individual with whom the paralegal is dealing. No one must be misled into thinking the paralegal is an attorney.

6. *Can the name and title of a paralegal be printed on the door of the law firm?*

The few states that have considered this question have concluded that it is improper for a lawyer to allow this.

7. *Can a paralegal's name be listed on any pleading, brief, or other document presented to a court?*

The few states that have considered this question have split. Some say no, since only an attorney's name may appear. Others say yes, if the paralegal's name is mentioned in a footnote and his/her nonlawyer status is clear.

It is anticipated that restrictions on the mention of a paralegal's name on such documents will soon disappear. In fact, a paralegal's role in litigation is given formal recognition in some court opinions printed in the reporter volumes that contain the full text of the court opinions. Traditionally, opinions in these volumes list the names of the lawyers who litigated the case. When paralegals have had a major role in the preparation of the briefs submitted to the appellate court, the names of these paralegals are sometimes printed along with the names of the lawyers involved. Here is an example of a paralegal listed along with the lawyers who litigated the case found in the opinion of *United States v. Cooke,* 625 F.2d 19 (4th Cir. 1980) written by the United States Court of Appeals for the Fourth Circuit:

> Thomas J. Keith, Winston-Salem, N.C., for appellant.

> David B. Smith, Asst. U.S. Atty. (H.M. Michaux, Jr., U.S. Atty., Durham, N.C., Becky M. Strickland, Paralegal Specialist on brief), for appellee.

> Before HALL and PHILLIPS, Circuit Judges, and HOFFMAN, Senior District Judge.

> PER CURIAM:. . .

For another example from the Court of Appeals of Oregon, see *Nelson v. Adult and Family Services Division,* 42 Or.App. 865, 601 P.2d 899 (Or.App. 1979).

8. *Can a paralegal and a lawyer form a partnership?*

No, if any part of the partnership involves the practice of law.

9. *Can a paralegal and a lawyer share fees?*

No. This would be the equivalent of the paralegal having a partnership interest in the firm.

10. *Can a paralegal participate in a retirement program of the law firm even though the program is based in whole or in part on a profit sharing arrangement?*

Yes. An exception is made to allow the paralegal to have this kind of financial interest in the firm.

11. *Can a paralegal tell someone outside the firm what s/he learns about a case while working at the firm?*

No. Doing so would be one of the most serious mistakes a paralegal could make. Clients have a right to have information about their cases kept confidential. See also p. 59. Later, we will examine this issue in greater detail when we discuss the free-lance paralegal and the ethical problems involved when a paralegal switches jobs, p. 81.

12. *Can a paralegal communicate with the client of the opposing side?*

No, unless opposing counsel gives permission for such communication.

13. *Can a paralegal communicate with opposing counsel?*

Most states would allow this so long as the paralegal's nonlawyer status is clear and the communication is routine.

14. Can a paralegal represent clients at administrative hearings?

Yes, if the agency gives specific authorization for such representation (p. 32). This authorization would also cover giving the client legal advice and drafting documents for the client pertaining to the agency matter.

15. Can an inmate give legal assistance to another inmate?

Yes, if the prison does not provide any adequate alternatives for inmates to receive legal help. This does not, however, include the right of one inmate to represent another inmate in court (p. 29).

16. Can a paralegal appear in court?

In some lower courts, e.g., small claims court, justice of the peace court, paralegals can represent clients (p. 17). A few states authorize paralegals to set dates on cases and perform similar routine or administrative functions (p. 20).

17. Can a paralegal attend a real estate closing in the absence of a supervising attorney?

Most states allow this so long as the paralegal does not give legal advice or engage in negotiations. Some states, however, forbid the paralegal's attendance unless the attorney is also present (p. 160).

18. Can a paralegal prepare and draft legal documents?

Yes, so long as the supervising attorney approves the documents. The oversight of the attorney must be such that the document loses its separate identity as a document of the paralegal; it must merge into and become the document of the attorney.

19. Can a paralegal ask questions at a deposition?

No. This would constitute the unauthorized practice of law.

20. Can a paralegal interview clients without an attorney being present?

Yes, so long as the attorney has given the paralegal instructions for the interview and is generally supervising the paralegal.

Many states have written ethical opinions specifically on paralegal use. Several of these opinions are printed in Appendix B (p. 159). Some states have also prepared reports that contain guidelines in this area.

Kentucky has adopted comprehensive (and liberal) rules on paralegal use. They are found within the Paralegal Code, which has been
officially approved by the Supreme Court of Kentucky and incorporated within Rule 3 of the Court. The Paralegal Code is reprinted
below in full. First, however, we need to examine a controversial part
of the Code: Sub-Rule 2.

> *Sub-Rule 2*
> *For purposes of this rule, the unauthorized practice of law shall not in-*
> *clude any service rendered involving legal knowledge or legal advice,*
> *whether representation, counsel or advocacy in or out of court, rendered*
> *in respect to the acts, duties, obligation, liabilities or business relations*
> *of the one requiring services where:*
> A. *The client understands that the paralegal is not a lawyer;*
> B. *The lawyer supervises the paralegal in the performance of his du-*
>   *ties; and*
> C. *The lawyer remains fully responsible for such representation, in-*
>   *cluding all actions taken or not taken in connection therewith by the*
>   *paralegal to the same extent as if such representation had been fur-*
>   *nished entirely by the lawyer and all such actions had been taken or*
>   *not taken directly by the lawyer.*

Read this rule slowly three or four times. It is a fascinating statement.
By studying it carefully, we not only can gain insight into the paralegal
role, but also can learn a great deal about legal analysis and
interpretation.

Arguably, there are two possible interpretations of Sub-Rule 2.
Do you agree?

Broad Interpretation.   Three conditions are laid out in the rule: understanding, supervision, and responsibility. (A) The client must *understand* that the paralegal is a nonlawyer; (B) the lawyer must *supervise* the paralegal; and (C) the lawyer must be fully *responsible* for what
the paralegal does. If these three conditions are met, the paralegal can
do just about anything. Compliance with the three conditions will prevent the paralegal from being charged with the unauthorized practice
of law.

Under this interpretation, the rule constitutes a major *expansion*
of paralegal responsibilities.

For example, a paralegal can give legal advice to a client on a
divorce case—so long as the client knows that the paralegal is not a
lawyer, the lawyer is supervising the client, and the lawyer is
responsible for the advice given by the paralegal. Perhaps the main
problem here would be the supervision condition. As we will see,
however, supervision does not necessarily mean that the lawyer must
be standing over the shoulder of the paralegal everytime the latter
does something (p. 77). Supervision can mean general supervision,

e.g., providing guidelines for the paralegal. The paralegal could be giving the client legal advice within the framework of these guidelines.

Another example: a paralegal under Sub-Rule 2 could conduct a deposition of a witness. A deposition is a pretrial proceeding in which a person is questioned as part of a trial preparation strategy. While normally it would be considered the unauthorized practice of law for a paralegal to conduct a deposition, the activity is arguably permitted in Kentucky under this broad interpretation of Sub-Rule 2 if the three conditions can be met. Assume that the client of the office where the paralegal works knows that the paralegal conducting the deposition is not a lawyer; assume also that the lawyer has trained the paralegal to depose witnesses and has provided clear directions on how this particular deposition should be conducted by the paralegal; and finally assume that the lawyer is ultimately responsible for whatever the paralegal does in the deposition. The three conditions, therefore, are met.

Sub-Rule 2 says that paralegals will not be charged with the unauthorized practice of law simply because they render legal advice, engage in representation, counsel, or advocacy in or out of court—so long as the three conditions are met.

Narrow Interpretation.   The rule does *not* add any new authorized tasks to the paralegal role. It simply clarifies what we already know.

The critical word is in the second line of the rule: "involving." The word means *connected with* or *pertaining to.* There is a major difference, for example, between (a) giving legal advice and (b) engaging in an activity *involving* legal advice. The rule simply says that the latter is permitted; it does not authorize the former. A paralegal can engage in an activity "involving" legal advice without actually being the person who gives the advice. For example, the paralegal interviews the client to collect facts and does legal research in the library on these facts. The *lawyer* eventually gives legal advice to the client based in part on the interview and research conducted by the paralegal. Sub-Rule 2 is telling us that paralegal activities such as interviewing and research are not prohibited simply because they are part of a process leading to (i.e., "involving") legal advice.

So too, the rule does not authorize paralegals to conduct depositions or to engage in other advocacy and representation roles in or out of court. The lawyer is still the one who is solely authorized to perform these functions. To argue otherwise is to come close to abolishing any meaningful distinction between a paralegal and a lawyer. Again, all Sub-Rule 2 does is make clear that the paralegal is not acting illegally simply because he or she is assigned responsibilities "involving" advocacy and representation *so long as the paralegal is acting in the traditional capacity as assistant to a lawyer.* There is a distinction between being an advocate oneself, and engaging in activities that assist someone else (the lawyer) to act as an advocate. Sub-Rule 2 simply says that the latter is not the authorized practice of law; it does not authorize the paralegal to do the former.

ASSIGNMENT 11

Which interpretation of Sub-Rule 2 is correct? If the narrow interpretation is correct, what does it add? Why was the rule needed?

Here now is the *entire* Kentucky Paralegal Code of which the controversial Sub-Rule 2 is a part.

KENTUCKY PARALEGAL CODE

RULE 3.700 Provisions Relating to Paralegals

Preliminary Statement

The availability of legal services to the public at a price it can afford is a goal to which the Bar is committed, and one which finds support in Canons 2 and 8 of the Code of Professional Responsibility. The employment of paralegals furnishes a means by which lawyers may expand the public's opportunity for utilization of their services at a reduced cost.

For purposes of this Rule, a paralegal is a person under the supervision and direction of a licensed lawyer, who may apply knowledge of law and legal procedures in rendering direct assistance to lawyers engaged in legal research; design, develop or plan modifications or new procedures, techniques, services, processes or applications; prepare or interpret legal documents and write detailed procedures for practicing in certain fields of law; select, compile and use technical information from such references as digests, encyclopedias or practice manuals; and analyze and follow procedural problems that involve independent decisions.

Purpose

Rapid growth in the employment of paralegals increases the desirability and necessity of establishing guidelines for the utilization of paralegals by the legal community. This Rule is not intended to stifle the proper development and expansion of paralegal services, but to provide guidance and ensure growth in accordance with the Code of Professional Responsibility, statutes, court rules and decisions, rules and regulations of administrative agencies, and opinions rendered by Committees on Professional Ethics and Unauthorized Practice of Law.

While the responsibility for compliance with standards of professional conduct rests with members of the Bar, a paralegal should understand those standards. It is, therefore, incumbent upon the lawyer employing a paralegal to inform him of the restraints and responsibilities incident to the job and supervise the manner in which the work is completed. However, the paralegal does have an independent obligation to refrain from illegal conduct. Additionally, and notwithstanding the fact that the Code of Professional Responsibility is not binding upon lay persons, the very nature of a paralegal's employment imposes an obligation to refrain from conduct which would involve the lawyer in a violation of the Code.

Sub-Rule 1
A lawyer shall ensure that a paralegal in his employment does not engage in the unauthorized practice of law.

Commentary

The Kentucky Constitution, Section 109, creates one Court of Justice for the Commonwealth. Section 116 empowers the Kentucky Supreme Court to promulgate rules of practice and procedure for the Court of Justice. In addition, the Supreme Court has statutory authority to govern the conduct and activity of members of the Bar. KRS 21A. 160.

Pursuant to constitutional and statutory authority, the Kentucky Supreme Court has adopted rules which govern the unauthorized practice of law. SCR 3.020 defines the practice of law in general and descriptive terms. SCR 3.470 provides that any attorney who aids another in the unauthorized practice of law shall be guilty of unprofessional conduct. SCR 3.460 delineates the procedure to be followed when a person or entity "not having the right to practice law" engages in the practice of law.

As of January 1, 1978, the American Bar Association Code of Professional Responsibility was accepted as a sound statement of professional conduct for members of the Kentucky Bar Association, with the exception of provisions which conflict with *Bates v. St. Bar of Arizona.* [See p. 65.].

Canon 3 of the Code of Professional Responsibility provides that "A lawyer should assist in preventing the unauthorized practice of law." Further, "A lawyer shall not aid a non-lawyer in the unauthorized practice of law." DR 3-101(A). The rationale of this Sub-rule may be found in EC 3-1 through EC 3-6 of the [ABA] Code of Professional Responsibility.

The foregoing authorities demonstrate that paralegals cannot, any more than any other person or entity, engage in the unauthorized practice of law. Members of the Bar who employ paralegals incur a professional responsibility to ensure that their paralegal employees do not transgress the rules governing the practice of law contained in these authorities and thereby involve their employers in violations of their own professional responsibilities. A lawyer may, however, allow a paralegal to perform services involving the practice of law, providing that such services comply with the requirements of Sub-rule 2 and Sub-rule 3.

Sub-Rule 2

For purposes of this rule, the unauthorized practice of law shall not include any service rendered involving legal knowledge or legal advice, whether representation, counsel or advocacy in or out of court, rendered in respect to the acts, duties, obligation, liabilities or business relations of the one requiring services where:

A. *The client understands that the paralegal is not a lawyer;*

B. *The lawyer supervises the paralegal in the performance of his duties; and*

C. *The lawyer remains fully responsible for such representation, including all actions taken or not taken in connection therewith by the paralegal to the same extent as if such representation had been furnished entirely by the lawyer and all such actions had been taken or not taken directly by the lawyer.*

Commentary

The Code of Professional Responsibility, in particular EC 3-6, recognizes the value of utilizing the services of paralegals under certain conditions:

> "A lawyer often delegates tasks to clerks, secretaries, and other lay persons. Such delegation is proper if the lawyer maintains a direct relationship with his client, supervises the delegated work, and has complete professional responsibility for the work product. This delegation enables a lawyer to render legal services more economically and efficiently."

Maintaining a "direct relationship" with the client does not preclude a paralegal from meeting with the client nor does it mandate regular and frequent meetings between the lawyer and client. However, when it appears that consultation between the lawyer and the client is necessary, the lawyer should talk directly to the client.

Sub-Rule 3

For purposes of this rule, the unauthorized practice of law shall not include representation before any administrative tribunal or court where such service or representation is rendered pursuant to a court rule or decision, statute, or administrative rule or regulation, which authorizes such practice by nonlawyers.

Commentary

Notwithstanding the restrictions imposed upon nonlawyers with respect to engaging in the practice of law, exceptions exist by virtue of statute, administrative rule or regulation, or court rule or decision. Under certain circumstances, lay representation of parties does not constitute the unauthorized practice of law. For example, the Federal Administrative Procedure Act, Title 5, U.S.C. Section 555(b) authorizes federal administrative agencies to permit nonlawyers to represent parties in proceedings before the agencies [p. 33]. Such lay representation is also provided for in statutes and regulations governing administrative proceedings involving the Public Assistance (AFDC), Medicaid, and Food Stamp Programs. See, 42 U.S.C. Section 601, Section 602 (1977); 42 U.S.C. Section 1396 (1977); 7 U.S.C. Section 2019 (1977); and the implementing regulations, 45 C.F.R. Section 205.10(a), and 7 C.F.R. Section 271.1(a)(1) (1977). [See a more complete list in Appendix E, p. 183.]

The Kentucky Department of Human Resources has implemented these federal regulations. Lay representation is specifically provided for in regulations governing hearings and appeals in certain programs. 904 KAR 2:055, Section 1–12.

The United States Supreme Court has held that federal law controls the administration of federal grant-in-aid programs. *See, King v. Smith,* 392 U.S. 309, 332-333 (1968); *Rosado v. Wyman,* U.S. 397, 421–422 (1970). Additionally, the Court has held that in federally regulated areas, federal statutes and regulations prevail over a state's power to define and regulate the practice of law. *See, Sperry v. Florida,* 373 U.S. 379, 385 (1963); and *Keller v. State Bar of Wisconsin,* 374 U.S. 102 (1963), citing *Sperry* [p. 38].

Sub-Rule 4

A lawyer shall instruct a paralegal employee to preserve the confidences and secrets of a client and shall exercise care that the paralegal does so.

Commentary

This Sub-rule reiterates the Code of Professional Responsibility. Canon 4, DR 4-101(D) provides in part that:

"(D) A lawyer shall exercise reasonable care to prevent his employees, associates, and others whose services are utilized by him from disclosing or using confidences or secrets of a client. . . . "

This obligation is emphasized in EC 4-2 under Canon 4:

". . . It is a matter of common knowledge that the normal operation of a law office exposes confidential professional information to non-lawyer employees of the office, particularly secretaries and those having access to the files; and this obligates a lawyer to exercise care in selecting and training his employees so that the sanctity of all confidences and secrets of his clients may be preserved."

Sub-Rule 5
A lawyer shall not form a partnership with a paralegal if any part of the partnership's activities consists of the practice of law, nor shall a lawyer share on a proportionate basis, legal fees with a paralegal.

Commentary

This Sub-rule is based on the express provisions of DR 3-102(A) and DR 3-103(A) of the Code of Professional Responsibility. In accordance with these provisions, the compensation of a paralegal may not include a percentage of the fees received by his employer, or any remuneration, directly or indirectly, for referring matters of a legal nature to the employer.

DR 3-103(A) provides that: "A lawyer shall not form a partnership with a non-lawyer if any of the activities of the partnership consists of the practice of law." The rationale is found in EC 3-8: "Since a lawyer should not aid or encourage a layman to practice law, he should not practice law in association with a layman. . . . " However, "A lawyer or law firm may include non-lawyer employees in a retirement plan, even though the plan is based in whole or in part on a profit-sharing arrangement." CR 3-102(A)(3).

This Disciplinary Rule also reflects the rationale of EC 3-8:

"Since a layer should not aid or encourage a layman to practice law, he should not. . . share legal fees with a layman."

"Profit-sharing retirement plans of a lawyer or law firm which include nonlawyer office employees are not improper. These limited exceptions to the rule against sharing legal fees with laymen are permissible since they do not aid or encourage laymen to practice law."

Sub-Rule 6
The letterhead of a lawyer may include the name of a paralegal
where the paralegal's status is clearly indicated; A lawyer may
permit his name to be included in a paralegal's business card,
provided that the paralegal's status is clearly indicated.

Commentary

The Code of Professional Responsibility, in particular DR
2-102(A)(4), provides direction concerning the information
which may be provided on a lawyer's letterhead. In keeping with
the spirit of DR 2-102(A)(4), paralegals may be listed on the letterhead if there is a clear indication of their status, i.e., they are
not lawyers. These names should properly be listed under the
separate heading of "Paralegals."

A paralegal may have a business card with the lawyer's name
or law firm's name on it, provided the status of the paralegal is
clearly indicated. It is not necessary that any lawyer's name appear on such business card. The card is designed to identify the
paralegal and to state by whom the paralegal is employed. The
business card of a paralegal shall be approved, in form and substance, by the lawyer-employer.

Sub-Rule 7
A lawyer shall require a paralegal, when dealing with a client, to
disclose at the outset that he is not a lawyer. A lawyer shall also
require such a disclosure when the paralegal is dealing with a
court, administrative agency, attorney or the public, if there is
any reason for their believing that the paralegal is a lawyer or is
associated with a lawyer.

Commentary

A lawyer should instruct a paralegal employee to disclose at
the beginning of any dealings with a client that he is not an attorney. Whenever any person dealing with a paralegal has reason to
believe that the paralegal is a lawyer or associated with a lawyer,
the paralegal shall make clear that he is not a lawyer. Even if a
paralegal appears before an administrative agency or court in
which a lay person is entitled to represent a party, the paralegal
should nevertheless disclose his status to the tribunal. Routine
early disclosure of non-lawyer status is necessary to ensure that
there will be no misunderstanding as to the responsibilities and
role of the paralegal. Disclosure may be made in any way that
avoids confusion. Common sense suggests a routine disclosure at
the outset of communication.

If a paralegal is designated as the individual in the office of
a lawyer or law firm who should be contacted, disclosure of his or

her non-lawyer status should be made at the time of such designation.

Paralegal Supervision

The topic of paralegal supervision appears to be an important issue as indicated in the above Code, in the list of specific paralegal issues raised in the states (p. 55), and in the ABA Model Code and Model Rules (p. 63). We need to examine this topic more closely.

Attorney Grievance Committee of Md. v. Goldberg
292 Md. 650, 441 A.2d 338, 442 (1982)

[T]he public must be protected. Lawyers must be impressed with the fact that at all times they have a responsibility to their clients. This responsibility necessarily includes adequate supervision of their employees.

Statsky, W., *Paraprofessionals: Expanding the Legal Service Delivery Team,* 24 Journal of Legal Education 397, 408 (1972)

A primary requirement of the paralegal-lawyer relationship is the supervision by the lawyer of all delegated work. What is supervision and how do lawyers exercise it? When a lawyer standardizes and specializes his/her practice through the utilization of forms and the hiring of paralegals, what kind of supervision is given? Is it the supervision of an overseer of a system who limits his/her contacts with office personnel to crisis intervention, or is it the supervision of a superintendent who maintains an event-by-event vigilance? There are no definitive answers to these questions that would satisfy the ethical purist. Consequently the paralegal is given a considerable arena in which to roam depending upon his/her employing attorney's conception of supervision.

Illinois State Bar Association, *Report of the Joint Study Committee on Attorney Assistants,* p. 41 (7/21/77)

The lawyer must maintain a "direct relationship with his client," he must supervise the *delegated* work and maintain complete professional responsibility for the work product [according to the three requirements of EC 3-6, p. 63].

As long as these three standards are maintained no problem arises from the use of lay personnel. The employment of secretaries presents few or no problems in terms of unauthorized practice, or in terms of a misled public, because the employment of a secretary does not interfere with any of the three precepts of EC 3-6.

The employment of lay personnel to prepare material for real estate closings, obtain preliminary data perhaps from the client or from other sources, to abstract depositions, and the like, does present problems under this ethical consideration [EC 3-6], unless the lawyer in the administration of the law office is able to establish the guidelines and job descriptions which prevent a transgression of the three standards.

For example, the maintenance of a direct relationship with the client will be jeopardized frequently unless there are clear directions to the lay person as to what he or she may do or not do. We return again to the importance of the precise job description. Whether this be reduced to writing—which appears to be sound management practice anyway—or is delivered by clear oral instructions, the lay person must know in handling the real estate closing, for example, what is within the job and what lies outside the permitted area of delegation. In the absence of such a clear direction, under the normal tensions of a law office, sooner or later the lay employee will in the pressure of time, transgress the bounds. Prevention thereof lies not in generalized directions of what constitutes unauthorized practice; it lies in precise job descriptions and definitions for all lay personnel.

The second precept of EC 3-6 again calls for a management decision. What constitutes "supervising" the "delegated work"? Obviously, the entire purpose of hiring a lay employee is to avoid the necessity of standing over the assistant's shoulder and saying which blank is to be filled in, what document is to be forwarded, to whom, etc. Supervision must imply some generalization of instructions and follow-through to see if the instructions have been carried out accurately. In short, when it is applied to attorney assistants, EC 3-6 basically means that the lawyer must manage his or her law office. The statement of EC 3-6 is not [merely] a statement that the lawyer signs the payroll and therefore is boss.

New Mexico Proposed Guidelines for the Use of Legal Assistant Services, p. 12 (1980)

A lawyer who hires a legal assistant is responsible for carefully evaluating the legal assistant's education and experience to determine if the assistant can competently perform the tasks which it is contemplated will be assigned. Once a legal assistant is in the employ of a lawyer, the lawyer has a continuing obligation to closely supervise the work of the legal assistant. A lawyer may train a legal assistant to perform increasingly complex assignments under the supervision of the lawyer, and a process of gradually escalating the level of difficulty of the type or types of work assigned to the assistant may be used to raise the skill level of a legal assistant. Specialized instruction provided to a legal assistant, whether through the personal efforts of the lawyer who supervises the assistant or through other means such as seminars or classes, may be helpful in

maintaining and raising the assistant's level of competence, but it remains the responsibility of the individual lawyer to determine the extent
of the assistant's skills and to delegate to the assistant accordingly. In addition, a lawyer should explain to the legal assistant that the legal assistant has a duty to inform the lawyer of any assignment which the assistant
regards as being beyond his or her capability.

As a practical matter, it would be impossible for a lawyer to know
everything about what a paralegal is doing all the time. The very concept of delegation assumes the exercise of some responsibility by
nonlawyers.

It is often pointed out that a lawyer's relationship with his/her client must be direct and personal. A "lawyer's relation to his client
should be personal, and the responsibility should be direct to the client." ABA, Formal Opinion No. 303, Nov. 27, 1961. Does this mean
that a paralegal working for the lawyer cannot *also* have a direct relationship with the client? A close reading of EC 3-6, p. 63, does not appear to preclude it. According to a former chairperson of the ABA
Special Committee on Legal Assistants, lawyers "delude themselves by
believing only a lawyer can deal directly with the client."[12] Those
members of the private bar who maintain this position apparently do
so on the theory that it is possible for a paralegal to have direct dealings with clients that do not amount to giving advice. This position is
probably sound, although some might argue that the manner in which
a paralegal interviewer or a paralegal investigator asks a client questions may be interpreted by the client as an indication of what the law
is in his/her case even though on the surface no such interpretation is
intended by the paralegal. This possibility should not change the general rule, however, that the paralegal can directly deal with a client in
addition to the direct and controlling relationship that the lawyer has
with the same client.

Statsky, W., and Lang, P., *The Legal Paraprofessional as Advocate*
and Assistant: Roles, Training Concepts, and Materials,
pp. 47–8 (1971).

The cardinal principle governing the lawyer-lay assistant relationship is that the dynamics of delegation flow primarily from demonstrated ability rather than from ethical codes or statutory practice
norms. Given the time and volume pressures on a practicing attorney,

---

[12] Turner, *Effective Use of Personnel in the Law Office,* Speech before the Section of Legal
Education and Admissions to the Bar and the National Conference of Bar Examiners,
p. 4 (8/12/69).

it is submitted that there is almost nothing, short of actual court appearances, that a lawyer will not delegate to a competent paralegal, and it is further submitted that in such a setting, supervision is sometimes left on a "handle-it-as-best-you-can" basis. Close supervision, case-by-case, step-by-step, of the paralegal is not only impractical but in contradiction to the economy and efficiency motives that originally led the lawyer to hire the paralegal. Lawyers are oriented to advocacy, client interaction, and legal research; they are not always good personnel managers. Consequently, supervision tends to be loose, even though the lawyer retains full responsibility to the client for the final work product. Once the paralegal has gained the confidence of his/her employing attorney, has acquired substantial experience in the areas delegated to him/her, has learned that the boss places a premium on the exercise of ingenuity, and has sensed that even the boss does not always have immediate answers to the day-to-day problems that arise, the paralegal tends to fall back more and more onto his/her own resources and judgment of what should be done. Take, for example, the case of the corporate paralegal doing blue sky work for a lawyer in the firm. A corporate client decides to go public and wants to register in all fifty states. The paralegal is assigned the task of compiling the necessary documents and exhibits for each state. An employee of the state of Oklahoma calls the law firm in reference to a particular question on a submitted registration application that pertains to the stated valuation of designated assets. The paralegal takes the call. Will s/he refer it to a lawyer or will s/he handle it alone? The answer will *not* totally depend on whether the paralegal decides that the question is "legal" or "non-legal," but rather will depend on very practical considerations such as:

- Would the lawyer want me to bother him/her with this call?
- Can I handle it myself?
- Have I answered calls like this before without difficulty?

A survey conducted by the American Bar Association's Special Committee on Legal Assistants dealt with the issue of the supervision a paralegal should receive once s/he is trained and experienced. Of the twenty-one firms addressing the point, seven firms felt that paralegals should be "closely supervised by attorneys," whereas fourteen of the firms indicated that a paralegal should be allowed to "work independently under the general direction of the attorney with only the completed work reviewed." American Bar Association, Special Committee on Legal Assistants, The Training and Use of Legal Assistants: A Status Report, p. 10 (Preliminary Draft, 1973). In this same survey 103 paralegals were also asked to state their opinion on the issue of supervision. All but two of the respondents thought that "they should be allowed to work independently under the general direction of the attorney," again with only their "completed work" checked by their supervisor. Id. at p. 16.

It is also relevant to note that both attorneys and paralegals responding to the survey indicated that the activities of paralegals "could be broadened considerably." Id. at p. 20.

The California Committee on Economics of Law Practice has taken the following position on the supervision of paralegals:

> A legal assistant should act only under the supervision of an active member of the State Bar. Adequacy of supervision will depend on the type of legal matter, including the degree of standardization and repetitiveness of the matter, and the experience of the legal assistant generally and with regard to a particular legal matter. Supervision is a matter of the attorney's professional responsibility and competence. Determination of adequacy of supervision with regard to particular legal matters is best left to the State Bar disciplinary bodies and the courts. Standards for supervision may have to be promulgated in the future.

"Law Economics Committee Reports on Certified Attorney Assistants," 13 State Bar of California Reports 2 (No. 7, July, 1973).

It's easier to define what supervision cannot mean than to define it affirmatively. A lawyer cannot delegate to a paralegal the task of arguing a case in court or of advising clients as to their legal rights in non-agency cases no matter how closely the paralegal is supervised by the lawyer in such undertakings. Supervision cannot authorize what is clearly the unauthorized practice of law.

ASSIGNMENT 12 ✕

Is too much being made about the issue of supervision? Does it make any difference so long as the lawyer is ultimately responsible for what the paralegal does?

4. THE ATTORNEY-CLIENT PRIVILEGE, CONFIDENTIALITY, AND SPECIAL ETHICAL PROBLEMS FACING THE PARALEGAL WHO SWITCHES JOBS AND THE FREE-LANCE PARALEGAL

Dabney v. Investment Corp. of America
82 F.R.D. 464, 465 (E.D. Pa. 1979)

The attorney-client privilege protects from disclosure confidential communications made for the purpose of obtaining a lawyer's professional advice and assistance. *Cohen v. Uniroyal, Inc,* 80 F.R.D. 480, 482 (E.D.Pa.1978). It has long been held that the privilege applies only to members of the bar, of a court, or their subordinates. . . . Examples of such protected subordinates would include any law student, paralegal, investigator or other person acting as the agent of a duly qualified attorney under circumstances that would otherwise be sufficient to invoke the privilege. 8 Wigmore, Evidence § 2301 (McNaughton Rev. 1961).

Communications made in confidence between an attorney and client relating to representation are protected by the attorney-client privilege. If clients knew that what they told their attorney might eventually be revealed to others, the clients would be reluctant to be open with their attorney. As mentioned earlier, the protection of confidential information encourages clients to communicate fully and frankly with the attorney even as to embarrassing or legally damaging topics (p. 59). If a lawyer is called to the witness stand and is questioned or examined concerning such communications, the lawyer can refuse to answer on the ground that the communications are privileged. Paralegals and others employees of the lawyer can also refuse to answer.

Colorado Revised Statutes (1984 Cum. Supp.)
13-90-107. Who may not testify without consent.

(1)(b) An attorney shall not be examined without the consent of his client as to any communication made by the client to him or his advice given thereon in the course of professional employment; nor shall an attorney's secretary, paralegal, legal assistant, stenographer, or clerk be examined without the consent of his employer concerning any fact, the knowledge of which he has acquired in such capacity.

On page 59, we examined the ethical rules on confidentiality in the ABA Model Code (DR 4-101) and in the Model Rules (Rule 1.6). These regulations make it unethical for a lawyer to reveal confidential information. There is also a provision in the Model Code covering nonlawyers:

DR 4-101(D).
A lawyer shall exercise reasonable care to prevent his employees, associates, and others whose services are utilized by him from disclosing or using confidences or secrets of a client, . . .

Similarly, as we have seen, the comments to Rule 5.3 of the Model Rules (p. 64) provide:

A lawyer should give such assistants appropriate instruction and supervision concerning the ethical aspects of their employment, particularly regarding the obligation not to disclose information relating to representation of the client,. . .

The paralegal associations also stress the importance of confidentiality. As we shall see later, the national associations have published ethical standards and rules (p. 110). They include prohibitions against disclosing confidential information. The *Code of Ethics and Professional Responsibility* of the National Associates of Legal Assistants provides:

> Canon 7
> A legal assistant must protect the confidences of a client, and it shall be unethical for a legal assistant to violate any statute now in effect or hereafter to be enacted controlling privileged communications.

The Affirmation of Professional Responsibility of the National Federation of Paralegal Associations provides:

> IV
> A paralegal shall preserve client confidences and privileged communications. Confidential information and privileged communications are a vital part of the attorney, paralegal and client relationship. The importance of preserving confidential and privileged information is understood to be an uncompromising obligation of every paralegal.

An obvious way that a lawyer or paralegal violates such regulations is to tell a stranger something related to a client's case. For example, a paralegal tells his/her spouse that a particular client at the office confessed to a crime during an interview. The spouse has no right to know such information. The paralegal has revealed confidential information. Another example: A lawyer represents Bob Smith on a divorce case and Linda Jackson on an unemployment compensation claim. Bob and Linda happen to know each other. In a conversation with Linda one day, the lawyer tells her that Bob is selling his business at a reduced price in order to try to prevent his wife from interfering with the business in the divorce case. Linda has no right to know such information. The lawyer has revealed confidential information.

Lawyers must be scrupulous in avoiding such breaches of confidentiality. They are under an ethical obligation to avoid even the appearance of impropriety (p. 63).

If there is a danger that a lawyer will breach client confidentiality, the lawyer is *disqualified* from taking or continuing the representation. We will examine this issue from both the lawyer and the paralegal perspective through the following hypothetical:

> Mary is a lawyer in the law firm of Smith & Smith. At the firm, one of her clients is Bill in the negligence case of Bill v. Fred involving an automobile accident. Fred is not represented by counsel.

These facts can give rise to a number of troublesome situations:

> #1: Bill becomes dissatisfied with Mary and dismisses her as his lawyer. *Fred* now tries to hire Mary to represent him in the same negligence case against Bill.

Mary would be disqualified from representing Fred unless Bill consents to such representation. Fred and Bill clearly have adverse interests in the negligence case. If Mary represented Fred, she would surely be using information against Bill that she obtained while she represented Bill. Unless Bill agrees to allow Mary to represent Fred after being fully apprised of the situation, Mary is disqualified from representing Fred.

> #2: Mary decides to leave Smith & Smith in order to become a partner in the firm of Jones & Jones. When she arrives, she discovers that Fred had just retained Jones & Jones in his negligence case against Bill. The firm asks Mary to represent Fred in this case.

To do so would be ethically improper for the same reasons given in situation #1 above. Bill and Fred still have adverse interests. Mary would be using information against Bill that she acquired while representing Bill. This is unethical regardless of the firm for which Mary works— unless Bill consents.

> #3: Bob is a senior attorney at Jones & Jones. The firm asks Bob to represent Fred in the negligence case against Bill.

Again, to do so would be ethically improper. It makes no difference that Bob never represented Bill before. Since Mary is disqualified from representing Bill, *every* member of her new firm is also disqualified if the parties (Bill and Fred) still have adverse interests, and Mary acquired important or material information while she worked at the other firm on the same or substantially same case.

> #4: Assume that Mary does not change jobs; she remains at the firm of Smith & Smith. Assume also that Bill is *not* dissatisfied with Mary's work in the Bill v. Fred negligence case; he does not fire her as his attorney. George is Mary's paralegal at Smith & Smith. He works extensively with Mary on the Bill v. Fred case. Before the case is over, George decides to leave Smith & Smith in order to take a paralegal position with another law firm, Holmes & Holmes. After he arrives, he discovers that Fred has retained Holmes & Holmes to represent him in the Bill v. Fred negligence case.

The ethical question is whether Holmes & Holmes is disqualified from representing Fred because of George's prior work on the Bill v. Fred case while he worked at Smith & Smith. There are no clear answers to this question. The field of paralegalism is still too new. But the problem is not academic in view of the fact that paralegals frequently change jobs.

If no ethical restrictions existed, Holmes & Holmes would be delighted that George once worked on Bill's behalf while George was a paralegal at Smith & Smith. George could tell the attorneys at Holmes & Holmes everything he learned while he was Mary's paralegal. Such information could be quite useful as the firm prepares its defense of Fred. For example, George might know that Bill was not wearing his contact lenses at the time of the accident. The attorneys at Holmes & Holmes may not know this yet. Clearly Smith & Smith could argue that it would be unfair to Bill if Holmes & Holmes had access to such information.

The courts might handle the problem a number of ways. First, a court could treat the case the same way regardless of whether a lawyer or paralegal is involved. If so, Holmes & Holmes would be disqualified from representing Fred because of the paralegal's prior involvement in the case, in the same manner that it would be disqualified if an attorney had switched firms. The critical tests are the presence of adverse interests between the parties on the same or substantially same case, and the acquisition of material information while working on the case in the first firm. A second and less drastic approach would be to require Holmes & Holmes to remove the paralegal from the case. Smith & Smith may not be happy with such a solution. Its preference would probably be to require Holmes & Holmes to fire the paralegal. But dismissing the paralegal would not be necessary so long as the court is convinced that Holmes & Holmes would completely disassociate the paralegal from the Bill v. Fred litigation. Some overly cautious firms, however, may still dismiss the paralegal even if they are not required to do so. They will probably be less concerned with the paralegal's welfare than the risk of losing the right to represent the party because of potential ethical problems.

> #5: Same situation as in #4 above except that this time George is a freelance paralegal. He has his own office and sells his services directly to law firms. For three days in March he worked for Smith & Smith indexing a deposition transcript in the Bill v. Fred negligence case. For six days in May, he undertook some investigation for Holmes & Holmes in the same Bill v. Fred negligence case.

The same problems arise here as in situation #4. It should make no difference whether the paralegal is a salaried employee or an independent free-lancer *if* both kinds of paralegals had the same access to information about the case while they were acting on behalf of Bill at the first firm, Smith & Smith. At one extreme, a court might disqualify Holmes & Holmes from representing Fred, while at the other extreme, it might simply force Holmes & Holmes to stop the paralegal from working on the Bill v. Fred case.

Again, we cannot be sure what a court will do because of the relative newness of the issue and of paralegalism itself.[13]

Finally, a word of advice to the paralegal: keep your own record of case names. Whenever you work on a case, make a note of the names of the parties and of opposing counsel. You do not want to find yourself working on both sides of a case! If you ever change jobs or go into free-lance work, you should refer to this list. Disclose all relevant facts to your supervisors. The most effective way to solve an ethical problem is to avoid it.

> **North Carolina State Bar,** *"Guidelines for Use of Non-Lawyers in Rendering Legal Services,"* *11* Newsletter 6 (Summer, 1986)
>
> A lawyer must insure that no interest or relationship of the assistant impinges upon the services rendered to the client.
>
> A lawyer owes his client utter fidelity. His loyalty must not be diluted by the interest of anyone other than the client, including the legal assistant. In the event that the interest of a legal assistant might materially limit and adversely affect the lawyer's representation of a prospective or current client, . . . the lawyer [must] decline or discontinue representation.
>
> Lawyers should make sure that their assistants clearly understand their professional and ethical responsibilities with respect to conflicts of interest. If a lawyer accepts a matter in which the assistant may have a conflict of interest, the lawyer should exclude the assistant from participation in any services performed in connection with that matter. The lawyer should inform the client that a non-lawyer employee has a conflict of interest which, were it the lawyer's conflict, might prevent further representation of the client in connection with the matter. The nature of the conflict should be disclosed. No interest or loyalty of the assistant may be permitted to interfere with the lawyer's independent exercise of professional judgement.
>
> Quite obviously, the lawyer is better able to insure ethical compliance by assistants who are employees of the lawyer with whom the lawyer is in regular contact. When the assistant is not working as an employee of the lawyer, but instead contracts independently to perform legally related tasks, the lawyer is held responsible for the work product and ethical conduct of the assistant just as if the assistant were an employee of the lawyer. For this reason, special care must be taken by the lawyer before entrusting services to an independent assistant to make sure that the assistant performs both competently and ethically.

[13] See also Marguardt, *Running with the Hares and Chasing with the Hounds: The Emerging Dilemma in Paralegal Mobility,* 2 Journal of Paralegal Education 57 (American Association for Paralegal Education, Oct. 1984).

Quinn v. Lum & Cronin, Fried, Sekiya & Kekina
Civ. No. 81284
Hawaii Court of Appeals

On January 25, 1984, Richard K. Quinn, Attorney at Law, a Law Corporation, filed suit against Rogerlene Lum, a member of the Hawaii Association of Legal Assistants (HALA) and formerly legal secretary with the Quinn firm, for injunctive relief based on the allegation that Mrs. Lum possesses confidential client information from her work as Quinn's legal secretary, which information would be transmitted to the co-defendant, Mrs. Lum's new employer, Cronin, Fried, Sekiya & Kekina, Attorneys at Law, if she were to begin her employment with the Cronin firm as a legal assistant.

On or about January 3, 1984 Mrs. Lum notified Quinn that she had accepted a position as a paralegal with the Cronin firm. Quinn subsequently discussed and corresponded with Mr. Cronin regarding the hiring of Mrs. Lum, who was scheduled to begin work with the Cronin firm on January 30, 1984. Mr. Cronin repeatedly refused Quinn's request that she not be hired by the Cronin firm.

On January 26, a hearing on the application for a temporary restraining order was heard by Judge Philip T. Chun of the Circuit Court of the First Circuit, State of Hawaii. The application was denied.

Quinn alleges in the pleadings filed with the Court in Civil No. 81284 that Mrs. Lum's employment with the Quinn firm from December 1, 1982 to January 17, 1984, and as Mr. Quinn's secretary from April 25, 1983 to January 17, 1984, included attendance at the firm's case review committee meetings. Confidential discussions occurred concerning case evaluation, settlement evaluation, strategy and tactics between Quinn, his associates, and their clients.

Cronin et al. are attorneys of record for the plaintiffs in *Firme v. Honolulu Medical Group and Ronald P. Peroff, M.D.* Quinn's firm represents the defendants. The case was set for trial on March 19, 1984. According to exhibits attached to the records filed in the instant case, Mr. Cronin recognized the *Firme* situation and agreed that Mrs. Lum would not be involved in the *Firme* case in her new employment, nor would his firm "[ever] seek to obtain any information from her concerning cases with which she was involved while in [Quinn's] office, nor would we have her work on any while here." Mr. Cronin goes on to say in his January 24 letter to Quinn that Quinn should consult with his clients on the *Firme* case as to whether Quinn's "attempt. . . to stop Mrs. Lum from working for [the Cronin firm] is with their approval."

Quinn also alleges that while his firm is known in the Honolulu legal community as one which represents hospitals, doctors and other health care providers, the Cronin firm is known as a plaintiff medical malpractice firm. Quinn lists in several pleadings that on more than one occasion, these firms found themselves adversaries in the same cases.

[Quinn contends] that this action was brought not to "bar Lum from working as a legal secretary or even as a paralegal, since that would be ludicrous given the size of Hawaii's legal community." In fact, Quinn states he would have "no objection to Lum's working for any other law firm in Hawaii other than one which specializes in medical malpractice plaintiffs' work, like [Cronin's]."

A subsequent hearing on the original complaint for injunctive relief was then held in Judge Ronald Moon's court on February 6. Plaintiff's motion for a preliminary injunction that would bar such employment "for at least two years" was denied, with the judge noting *Quinn v. Lum* as a case of first impression.

The Court explained its decision in light of the standards to be met before a preliminary injunction could be issued, as dealt with in depth by Mrs. Lum's attorney, David L. Fairbanks, who is also the current President of the Hawaii State Bar Association.

The standards which must be met in order to obtain a preliminary injunction, as listed by Judge Moon, follow:

1. The Court did not feel there was a substantial likelihood that plaintiff would prevail on the merits. If an injunction were to be issued, it would:

"[E]ssentially prevent a paralegal or legal secretary, [or] attorney from joining any law firm that may have had some case in the past, . . . cases pending at the present time, or potential cases which may be worked on in the future" (Transcript of the Hearing, page 82).

2. The evidence is lacking regarding irreparable damage to Richard Quinn's clients.

3. The public interest would not be served by issuing such an injunction.

When an attorney enters practice in the State of Hawaii, he or she agrees to abide and be governed by the Hawaii Code of Professional Responsibility. This code does not attempt to govern the ethical actions of the non-attorneys. While Canon 37 of the American Bar Association's Code of Professional Responsibility, adopted pre-1971, states that a lawyer's employees have the same duty to preserve client confidences as the lawyer, this Canon is not included in the Hawaii code. Compliance, therefore, with the same rules of ethics guiding the Hawaii attorney is currently left to the discretion—and conscience—of the non-attorney.

If an attorney in Hawaii breaches the Code of Professional Responsibility, the office of Disciplinary Counsel may choose to investigate the matter and may pass the matter on to the Disciplinary Board and possibly, to the Hawaii Supreme Court for adjudication.

If an employee of a law office becomes suspect of some breach of ethics or acts of omission, the employing attorney becomes responsible for the employee's deeds. For example, if a legal secretary fails to file the complaint the day the Statute of Limitations expires thinking the next day would suffice, it is the attorney who is responsible to the client. The attorney can fire the secretary "for cause" but the attorney, nevertheless, stands responsible. It appears the only way for an attorney to further censor the employee directly is via a civil suit for tortious damages.

Whether a permanent injunction can or will be granted has yet to be seen in this case. What is clear is that neither the office of Disciplinary Counsel nor the Hawaii Supreme Court would or could become involved; they have no jurisdiction over the non-attorney working in a law office.

_____

See Assignment 33, p. 98 on applying the above opinion.

5. DOING LEGAL RESEARCH ON AN ETHICAL ISSUE

If you were researching an ethical issue in your state, your strategy would be as follows:

- Find the state bar association's canons of ethics, often called the Canons of Professional Responsibility. The canons will probably have been approved by the state's highest court. They may also be printed in the court rules. Check your local bar association and law libraries in your area.
- Determine which bar association committee has jurisdiction over the enforcement of these canons. See Appendix D, p. 174. Call or write the state bar association and ask. Find out if this committee writes ethical opinions applying the canons. If the issue you are researching involves paralegals, determine if another bar committee has special jurisdiction over paralegals. If so, find out what this committee has said. Also check the digest covering your state to locate any court opinions on lawyer ethics.
- If the issues you are researching have never been raised in your state bar association and state courts, check the positions of the ABA in its canons and ethical opinions to determine whether they have covered the issue. In particular, read the ABA Model Code of Professional Responsibility, the more recent ABA Model Rules of Professional Conduct, and ethical opinions interpreting both documents (p. 55). Most large law libraries should have these documents.
- If you find that the ABA has covered your issue, examine the ABA position and then make an argument to your state and local bar association on whether it should adopt the ABA position. Remember, however, that the state and local bar association is not required to accept what the ABA has said. An ABA position can only be persuasive authority.

- You should determine what the bar associations of other states have said about your issue. For example, check the *Code of Professional Responsibility by State* (ABA, National Center for Professional Responsibility, 1980). Also check the *ABA / BNA Lawyer's Manual on Professional Conduct: Current Reports* (BNA, 1984–) and the *National Reporter on Legal Ethics and Professional Responsibility* (University Publications of America, 1983–). Such publications, found in large law libraries, may give you leads to the ethical rules and opinions of other states. Again, your state is not required to adopt what other states have said. They can only be persuasive authority.

ASSIGNMENT 13

Draft your own paralegal code as a class project. First, have a meeting in which you make a list of all the issues that you think should be covered in the code. Divide up the issues by the number of students in the class so that every student has roughly the same number of issues. Each student should draft a proposed rule on each of the issues to which s/he is assigned. Accompany each rule with a brief commentary on why you think the rule should be as stated. Draft alternative versions of the proposed rule if different versions are possible and you want to give the class the chance to examine all of them. The class then meets to vote on each of the proposed rules. Students will make presentations on the proposed rules they have drafted. If the class is not happy with the way in which a particular proposed rule was drafted by a student, the latter will re-draft the rule for later consideration by the class. One member of the class should be designated the "code reporter" who records the rules accepted by the class by majority vote.

After you have completed the code, you should consider inviting lawyers from the local bar association to your class in order to discuss your proposed code. Do the same with officials of the closest paralegal association in your area.

In the following problems, unless otherwise indicated, determine whether any ethical problems exist. If so, state what they are. Use the material on the preceding pages to explain how the problems would be resolved. Also, consult the ethical opinions in Appendix B, p. 159. If there are different ways that have been used to resolve the problems, state the alternative resolutions. Then state what you personally think the resolution of the problems should be.

ASSIGNMENT 14

John Smith is a paralegal who works for the firm of Beard, Butler, and Clark. John's immediate supervisor is Viola Butler, Esq. With the full knowledge and blessing of Viola Butler, John Smith sends a letter to a client of the firm (Mary Anders). Has Viola Butler acted unethically in permitting John to send out this letter? The letter is as follows:

Law Offices of
Beard, Butler, and Clark
310 High St.
Maincity, Ohio 45238
512-663-9410

Attorneys at Law   *Paralegal*

Ronald Beard   John Smith
Viola Butler
Wilma Clark
                                                                    May 14, 1986

Mary Anders
621 S. Randolph Ave.
Maincity, Ohio 45238

Dear Ms. Anders:

   Viola Butler, the attorney in charge of your case, has asked me to let you know that next month's hearing has been postponed. We will let you know the new date as soon as possible. If you have any questions don't hesitate to call me.

Sincerely,

John Smith

JS:wps

ASSIGNMENT 15

Same facts as in Assignment 14 except that the word "Paralegal" and John Smith's name are *not* printed at the top of the law firm's stationery letterhead and the closing of the letter is as follows:

Sincerely,

John Smith
Legal Aide

ASSIGNMENT 16

Suppose that as part of your educational program you were placed in a law firm for an internship period in order to gain some practical experience. While there, you are referred to as a "legal intern." Under what circumstances, if any, could you refer to yourself as a "legal intern," e.g., on the phone, in a letter?

ASSIGNMENT 17

Under what circumstances, if any, would it be appropriate for you to refer to a client of the office where you work as "my client"?

ASSIGNMENT 18

John Smith is a paralegal who works for Beard, Butler, and Clark. He sends out the following letter. Any ethical problems?

John Smith
Paralegal
310 High St.
Maincity, Ohio 45238
512-663-9410

June 1, 1985

State Unemployment Board
1216 Southern Ave.
Maincity, Ohio 45238

Dear Gentlepeople:

    I work for Beard, Butler, and Clark, which represents Mary Anders who has a claim before your agency. A hearing originally scheduled for June 8, 1985 has been postponed. We request that the hearing be held at the earliest time possible after the 8th.

Sincerely,

John Smith

JS:wps

ASSIGNMENT 19

John Jones is a paralegal who works for an attorney named Linda Sunders. Linda is away from the office one day and telephones John who is at the office. She dictates a one-line letter to a client of the office. The letter reads, "I advise you to sue." Linda asks John to sign the letter for her. The bottom of the letter reads as follows:

Linda Sunders
by John Jones

Any ethical problems?

ASSIGNMENT 20

John Jones is a paralegal who works for the XYZ law firm that represents hundreds of corporations throughout the United States. John specializes in corporate law at the firm. One of the corporations makes a request of the firm that it send the corporation certain information on filing requirements with the Secretary of State. The attorney supervising John knows that John has handled such matters often in the past and has handled them well. The attorney says to John, "Here, take care of this request on filing requirements." John calls the corporation and provides it with the correct information.

ASSIGNMENT 21

John Jones is a paralegal working for the XYZ law firm. The firm represents a large number of clients in a class action suit against an insurance company. There are a variety of claims that these clients have against the company. Each claim requires the filling out of a different claim form. John has been trained by his supervising attorney to determine which form to send out to which clients. The clients write to the firm. All letters are routed to John who makes the decision on which form to send out.

ASSIGNMENT 22

John Jones is a paralegal working at the XYZ law firm. The firm is handling a large class action involving potentially thousands of plaintiffs. John has been instructed to screen the potential plaintiffs in the class. Those he screens out by the criteria provided by the firm are told by John, in writing or verbally, that "unfortunately, our firm will not be able to represent you."

ASSIGNMENT 23

a. Read the two New Jersey ethical opinions on paralegals found in Appendix B, p. 160. Tom is a paralegal who works for a single-lawyer firm in New Jersey. The lawyer, Jane Frederickson, is out of town for a month. One of the cases Tom is working on will come to trial in six months, the case of Jones v. Smith. Before Jane left town, she told Tom that if the opposing attorneys on the Jones case try to get in touch with her about obtaining a copy of the investigation report, "it's OK to let them have a copy." Examine the following two situations. Has unethical conduct been committed according to New Jersey standards? Why or why not?

- An opposing attorney on the Jones case writes for a copy of the investigation report. Tom sends the attorney the report. Tom's cover letter is signed "Tom Davis, Paralegal."
- An opposing attorney on the Jones case calls the office where Tom works. Tom answers the phone. The attorney asks for Jane Frederickson. Tom explains that she is out of town, and then says, "I'm Tom Davis, a paralegal working on the case. Can I help you?" The attorney asks for a copy of the investigation report. Tom tells the attorney that he has been instructed to send the report if requested. Tom sends out the report. No cover letter is used.

b. Conduct a debate in class on the merits and demerits of the two New Jersey opinions. One class member will play the role of an attorney who is a member of the New Jersey Advisory Committee on Professional Ethics. Another class member will play the role of the president of the local paralegal association. The setting is a meeting of the paralegal association where the attorney has been invited to speak about the two opinions. The paralegal president begins by explaining what s/he finds objectionable in the two opinions. The attorney then defends the two opinions. Following the two presentations, the rest of the class will be allowed to ask questions of the attorney and the president.

ASSIGNMENT 24

Joan is a paralegal who works for the XYZ law firm that is representing Goff in a suit against Barnard who is represented by the ABC law firm. Joan calls Barnard and says, "Is this the first time that you have ever been sued?" Barnard answers, "Yes it is. Is there anything else that you would like to know?" Joan says "no" and the conversation ends.

ASSIGNMENT 25

John is a paralegal who works for the XYZ law firm that is representing a client against the Today Insurance Company. The Company also employs paralegals who work under the Company's general counsel. One of these paralegals is Mary. In an effort to settle the case, Mary calls John and says, "We offer you $200.00." John says, "We'll let you know."

ASSIGNMENT 26

Viola Butler, Esq., authorizes John Smith (her paralegal) to use the following cards, which John distributes whenever on assignment from Ms. Butler. Has the latter acted unethically in permitting John's use of either of these cards?

Beard, Butler, and Clark
Attorneys at Law
310 High Street
Maincity, Ohio 45238

John Smith   663-9410
Paralegal   X305

John Smith
Paralegal

Beard, Butler, and Clark
Attorneys at Law
310 High Street   663-9410
Maincity, Ohio 45238   X305

ASSIGNMENT 27

Mary Smith is a paralegal who works part time for the ABC law firm. The phone number of the firm is 265-9500. When she is not working for the firm, she represents her own clients before an administrative agency where she is authorized by law to provide this representation.

She does not have a business card that mentions the name, address, or phone number of the ABC firm. For her agency work, however, she does have a card that reads as follows:

```
                    Mary Smith
                    Paralegal

              "The best paralegal in town.
               She'll get results for you."

                    Call Now
                    265-9500
```

ASSIGNMENT 28

Paul is a nonlawyer who works at the Quaker Draft Counseling Center. One of the clients of the Center is Michael Diamond. Paul says the following to Mr. Diamond:

> You don't have anything to worry about. The law says that you cannot be inducted until you have had an administrative hearing on your case. I will represent you at that hearing. If you are inducted before that hearing, I will immediately draft a habeas corpus petition that can be filed at the United States District Court.

ASSIGNMENT 29

Mary is a paralegal who is a senior citizen. She works at the XYZ legal service office. One day she goes to a senior citizens center and makes the following statement:

> All of you should know about and take advantage of the XYZ legal service office where I work. Let me give you just one example why. Down at the office there is an attorney named Armanda Morris. She is an expert on insurance company cases. Some of you may have had trouble with insurance companies that say one thing and do another. Our office is available to serve you.

ASSIGNMENT 30

Mary is a paralegal who works at the XYZ law firm. She specializes in real estate matters at the firm. Mary attends a real estate closing in which her role consists of exchanging documents and acknowledging the receipt of documents. Analyze whether ethical problems exist on the basis of the following variations:

- The closing takes place at the XYZ law firm.
- The closing takes place at a bank.
- Mary's supervising attorney is not present at the closing.
- Mary's supervising attorney is present at the closing.
- Mary's supervising attorney is present at the closing except for thirty minutes when he had to leave, during which time Mary continued to exchange documents and acknowledge the receipt of documents.
- During the closing, the attorney for the other party says to Mary, "I don't know why my client should have to pay that charge." Mary responds: "In this state that charge is always paid in this way."

ASSIGNMENT 31

John Jones is a paralegal at the XYZ law firm. The attorney for whom he works is Joseph Troy. The firm represents the Ace Truck Company against Brown. Brown's attorney is Fay Metz. The next scheduled court date is tomorrow. Due to last minute crises on other cases, Troy cannot go to court tomorrow. Troy calls Metz and they both agree to request a one-week continuance. Troy tells John to go down to court tomorrow and when the case of *Ace Truck Co. v. Brown* is called, to request a one-week continuance. John does so.

ASSIGNMENT 32

Alice is a free-lance paralegal with a specialty in probate law. One of the firms she has worked for is Davis, Ritter & Boggs. Her most recent assignment for this firm has been to identify the assets of Mary Stanton who died six months ago. One of Mary's assets is a 75 percent ownership share in the Domain Corporation. Alice learns a great deal about this company including the fact that four months ago it had difficulty meeting its payroll and expects to have similar difficulties in the coming year.

Alice's free-lance business has continued to grow because of her excellent reputation. She decides to hire an employee with a different specialty so that her office can begin to take different kinds of cases from lawyers. She hires Bob, a paralegal with four years of litigation experience. The firm of Jackson & Jackson hires Alice to digest a series of long deposition documents in the case of Glendale Bank v. Ajax Tire Co. Jackson & Jackson represents Glendale Bank. Peterson, Zuckerman & Morgan represents Ajax Tire Co. Alice assigns Bob to this case. Ajax Tire Co. is a wholly owned subsidiary of the Domain Corporation. Glendale Bank is suing Ajax Tire Co. for fraud in misrepresenting its financial worth when Ajax Tire Co. applied for and obtained a loan from Glendale Bank.

Any ethical problems?

ASSIGNMENT 33

Salem is a factory town of 500 inhabitants in Hawaii. The factory employs 95% of the workers in town. The town has only two private attorneys: Ann Grote and Timothy Farrell. Forty of the employees have decided to sue the factory over a wage dispute. Ann Grote represents all these employees. She works alone except for her only employee, Bob Davis, a paralegal. In this litigation, the factory is represented by Timothy Farrell who has no employees—no secretaries and no paralegals. Grote and Farrell are young attorneys who have just begun their practices. Their only clients are the forty employees and the factory respectively. The litigation has become quite complicated. Several months before the case is scheduled to go to trial, Farrell offers Davis a job as a paralegal at double the salary he is earning with Grote. He accepts the offer. Grote goes to court seeking a preliminary injunction against Davis and Farrell, which would bar them from entering this employment relationship.

Apply *Quinn v. Lum & Cronin, Fried, Sekiya & Kekina,* on p. 87 to the facts of the case of Grote v. Davis and Farrell. (*Quinn* is an actual opinion from a state court Hawaii.)

ASSIGNMENT 34

Mary Smith is a paralegal at the XYZ law firm. One of her tasks is to file a document in court. She negligently forgets to do so. As a result, the client has a default judgment entered against her. What options are available to the client? (See p. 137.)

ASSIGNMENT 35

Joe Mookely is an attorney who represents fifty inmates on a consolidated case in the state court. The inmates are in fourteen different institutions throughout the state. Joe asks the Director of the state prison system to allow his paralegal, Mary Smith, to interview all fifty inmates at a central location. The Director responds as follows:

- He refuses to transport the inmates to one location. The inmates would have to be interviewed at the institutions where they are currently living.

- He refuses to let anyone in any institution unless the individual has either a law degree *or* has been through the prison's two-week orientation program totaling twenty hours in the evenings at the state capital.

Mary Smith has not taken the orientation program and it would be very inconvenient for her to do so since she lives 150 miles from the capital.

ASSIGNMENT 36

Mary Smith is a paralegal at the ABC law firm. She has been working on the case of Jessica Randolph, a client of the office. Mary talks with Ms. Randolph often. Mary receives a subpoena from the attorney of the party that is suing Ms. Randolph. On the witness stand, Mary is asked by this attorney what Ms. Randolph told her at the ABC law office about a particular business transaction related to the suit. Randolph's attorney (Mary's boss) objects to the question. What result?

ASSIGNMENT 37

Before Helen became a paralegal for the firm of Harris & Derkson, she was a chemist for a large corporation. Harris & Derkson is a patent law firm where Helen's technical expertise in chemistry is invaluable. Helen's next-door neighbor is an inventor. On a number of occasions he discussed the chemical make-up of his inventions with Helen. On one of these inventions, the neighbor is being charged by the government with stealing official secrets in order to prepare the invention. Harris & Derkson represent the neighbor on this case. Helen also works directly on the case for the firm. In a prosecution of the neighbor, Helen is called as a witness and is asked to reveal the substance of all her conversations with the neighbor concerning the invention in question. Does Helen have to answer? See *United States v. Kovel,* Appendix B, p. 167.

ASSIGNMENT 38

- What restrictions exist on advertising by lawyers in your state? Give an example of an ad on TV or in the newspaper that would be unethical. On researching an ethical issue, see p. 89.
- In *Bates v. State Bar of Arizona,* 433 U.S. 350 (1970), the United States Supreme Court held that a state could not prohibit all

forms of lawyer advertising. Has *Bates* been cited by state courts in your state on the advertising issue? If so, what impact has the case had in your state? To find out, shepardize *Bates* through Shepard's United States Citations, Case Edition. Read the major cases of your state courts that have applied *Bates* to your state. Shepard's will lead you to the citations of such cases.

5

Bar Association Control
of Paralegal Education

Since the early 1970s, the American Bar Association has been "approving" paralegal training programs after a recommendation is made by its standing Committee on Legal Assistants. There is no requirement that a school be ABA-approved in order to train paralegals. In fact most training programs are not so approved. The approval process is voluntary and the majority of programs have decided *not* to apply for approval. A program will have to meet state government accreditation standards, but it does not have to seek the approval of the ABA. To date, the same is true of state and local bar associations. None of the latter accredit or approve paralegal training programs, although some are moving in this direction.

The ABA approval process has been controversial from its inception. Those who oppose total lawyer control of paralegalism feel that the bar associations are inappropriate mechanisms to regulate training institutions. Nonlawyers cannot be members of bar associations, and even where associate membership status is available for paralegals (p. 107), the ultimate decisions on approval are still left in the hands of the lawyers in the bar associations. Since a major objective of lawyers is to increase their profits by the use of paralegals, critics argue that it is a conflict of interest for lawyers to control the field totally. When regulatory decisions must be made on matters such as the approval of schools, whose interest would the lawyers be protecting in making these decisions? The interest of the paralegals? The interest of the public? Or the profit interest of the lawyer-regulators?

The ABA has been somewhat sensitive to this criticism and, as we will see, at one time considered withdrawing from the approval process. In recent years, challenges have been made to the monopoly that bar associations exercise over the practice of law. In 1975, the United States Supreme Court sent shock waves throughout the legal profession when the Court ruled that lawyers were no longer exempt from the antitrust laws, and that some minimum fee schedules are a violation of these laws. *Goldfarb v. Virginia State Bar,* 421 U.S. 773 (1975). In 1979, an antitrust charge was brought against the ABA on the ground that its paralegal school approval process was designed to eliminate competition from, and restrict entry into, the market for recruitment, training, and placement of paralegals. The ABA won this case. *Paralegal Institute, Inc. v. American Bar Association,* 475 F.Supp. 1123 (E.D.N.Y., 1979). Despite this victory, the ABA remains vulnerable to future challenge.

Note that the ABA uses the word "approval" rather than accreditation in describing its process of exercising control over educational institutions. Yet the process meets the accepted definition of accreditation (p. 4). The use of the more euphemistic word "approval" may be an indication that the ABA is itself not sure whether it should be in the business of regulating paralegal education. Indeed, in 1981, the House of Delegates of the ABA instructed its Committee on Legal Assistants to terminate the ABA involvement in the approval process. Some schools, however, that had already received approval, objected. As a result, the Committee proposed and the House of Delegates accepted an alternative system of approving schools.

The alternative was the creation of an ABA Approval Commission to implement the approval process. The final decision on approval of individual schools is still left in the hands of the ABA. The Commission simply serves the same function that the Committee on Legal Assistants served in making recommendations on approval. The Commission now makes its recommendations to the Committee on Legal Assistants, which in turn makes its recommendations to the House of Delegates of the ABA. The major difference between the Committee and the Commission is that the latter must contain nonlawyer members. There are eleven members of the Commission, all of whom are appointed by the president of the ABA on advice from the Committee:

- Three lawyers (one of whom has taught in a paralegal program).
- One lawyer who represents the ABA Committee on Legal Assistants.
- One paralegal nominated by the National Federation of Paralegal Associations (NFPA).
- One paralegal nominated by the Federation of Paralegal Associations (NFPA).
- Two representatives nominated by the American Association for Paralegal Education (AAfPE).

- One representative nominated by the Association of Legal Administrators (ALA).
- One nonlegal educator.
- One representative of the general public.

The ABA does not view the Commission as a permanent institution. The plan is to phase it out over a period of years and to replace it with an *independent* accrediting body that is equally broad based. It is unclear, however, whether this replacement is feasible. It depends on the willingness of paralegal schools to submit themselves to this still-voluntary approval process. Furthermore, an independent body would be very expensive to run. Its revenues would come from fees paid by the schools that apply for approval and for renewals of approval. If large numbers of schools continue to bypass a national accrediting or approval entity, the process will lose both the political and financial support that is necessary.

ASSIGNMENT 39 *Class Discussion*

Who should control accreditation? Are there too many lawyers on the ABA Approval Commission? Too few paralegals? Could there be too many paralegals on such a body? Do you favor an independent accrediting entity? Who should run it? Should it be voluntary?

What will the ABA do if an independent accrediting body does not materialize? Will it continue with its Approval Commission? It is unclear what the ABA will do but it is unlikely that it will want to continue in its present role.

Only one thing is sure: Change is on the horizon. The legal profession can no longer feel secure in its privileged position as indicated in the following speech.

J. SIMS, "THE LEGAL PROFESSION:
A BOW TO THE PAST—
A GLIMPSE OF THE FUTURE"

(Mr. Sims was the Deputy Assistant Attorney General in the Antitrust Division of the United States Department of Justice. The following are excerpts from a speech he delivered on February 11, 1977, before a conference of the Federation of Insurance Counsel in Arizona.)

Today, in Los Angeles, legal services are being advertised on television. That fact alone gives us some idea of how much change has come to the legal profession in the last few years.

That change has not always come easy, but the fact that it has come so far, so fast, tells us quite a bit about what will happen in the future. We lawyers as a group have grumbled and argued, fought and yelled, struggled and been confused—but there are now lawyers advertising on television. Even a casual observer cannot fail to appreciate the significance of this change.

Competition, slowly but surely, is coming to the legal profession. This opening of traditional doors, the breaking of traditional barriers is the result of many forces—the number of new lawyers, the awakening of consumerism, the growing realization that the complexity of our society requires legal assistance in more and more areas. But one contributing factor has been antitrust litigation and the Department of Justice.

. . .

[T]he Supreme Court fired the shot heard 'round the bar [o]n June 16, 1975. [I]n a unanimous decision, [Goldfarb v. Virginia State Bar, 421 U.S. 773 (1975)] the Court held that the minimum fee schedule challenged by the Goldfarbs violated Section 1 of the Sherman Act. This decision broke the dam and released the flood of change that we see engulfing the profession today. For better or worse, the Goldfarbs had set in motion a series of events that were to change the character of the legal profession forever.

The Court decided several things in *Goldfarb,* but the most important was that the legal profession was subject to the antitrust laws— there was no "professional exemption." The response to *Goldfarb* was fascinating. A large number of private suits were filed challenging various aspects of bar regulation.

. . .

[An] area sure to be controversial in the future is unauthorized practice. There is already at least one antitrust challenge, against the Virginia State Bar, seeking to prohibit the bar from promulgating unauthorized practice opinions. This case, which involves title insurance, is a direct challenge to the extraordinary power that the legal profession now has—in most states—to define the limits of its own monopoly. It would be strange indeed for a state to hand over to, say its steel industry, not only the power to regulate entry into the industry and the conduct of those within it, but also the power to define what the industry was. In many states, that is exactly the power the organized bar now has, and that power is being challenged as inconsistent with the antitrust laws.

The heart of this challenge is that lawyers shouldn't be deciding what is the practice of law—defining the scope of the legal monopoly. The papers filed in that case . . . indicate that the objection is not to such a decision being made; the objection is to the State's delegation of that power to the profession.

In fact, of course, the principle behind this lawsuit could be expanded not only to other subject matter areas, but also to arrangements between the organized bar and other professions which have as their basic result the division of commercial responsibilities.

For example, the American Bar Association has entered into "statements of principles" with respect to the practice of law with a variety of other professions and occupations ranging from accountants to claim adjusters, publishers, social workers, and even professional engineers [p. 14]. These documents generally set forth the joint views of the professions as to which activities fall within the practice of law and which activities are proper for members of the other profession. They nearly all provide that each profession will advise its clients to seek out members of the other profession in appropriate circumstances.

As a general rule, two competitors may not agree with each other to allocate markets, or bids, or even functions; if they do, they violate the antitrust laws. At the least, this traditional antitrust principle raises some questions about the legal effect of such "statements of principles."

. . .

[T]he efforts of the bar to limit the scope of paralegal responsibilities and, in some jurisdictions, to seek a certification requirement for paralegals are seen by many as simply another effort to preserve and protect the legal services monopoly. Many believe that non-lawyers could perform many tasks reserved today for people with law degrees. . . .

These latter issues lead right into a somewhat different focus on bar association activities. While the bar has been reeling from a series of legal setbacks on antitrust and Constitutional grounds, there has been a growing movement in a related area that seems sure to impact upon the legal profession. In a way, this movement can also be traced to a Supreme Court case, the case of Gibson v. Berryhill. [411 U.S. 564 (1973)]

There, the Supreme Court applied the federal due process principle to strike down an attempt by a state optometry board, [which] was dominated by privately practicing optometrists, to halt the corporate practice of optometry. The result of this action would have inured to the pecuniary benefit of each board member and his fellow independent optometrists. The Supreme Court affirmed a District Court's finding that the Board was so biased by its pecuniary interests that it could not Constitutionally conduct hearings designed to discipline corporate optometrists.

Consistent with this decision, there has been a growing concern throughout the country about self-regulation. Perhaps nothing illustrates this trend better than the recent swearing-in, by Governor Brown of California, of 60 new members of state regulatory boards. None of the 60 appointees are certified in the occupation they are to help regulate. This concept of lay members on regulatory boards is a growing one, and will inevitably increase. In fact, in California, lay members have been appointed to 39 regulatory boards, and only those boards in the healing arts, law and accountancy, where membership is prescribed by statute, have no lay members. This privileged status, I am reasonably sure, will not last long.

Lay membership makes sense to a lot of people. Indeed, it may be essential if the legal profession and other similar professions are to retain a measure of self-regulatory ability. As long as the regulators are indistinguishable from those they regulate, it is impossible to tell when the public interest stops and self-interest starts.

ASSIGNMENT 40  Class Discussion

What are the implications of Mr. Sims's remarks on the role of bar associations in regulating paralegal education?

For a series of dramatic proposals to deregulate the legal profession altogether, see the comments of W. Durant, Chairman of the Legal Services Corporation, p. 142.

Should Paralegals Become Part of Bar Associations? =====

At present, no paralegals are full members of any bar associations. In 1981, however, the State Bar of Texas created a Legal Assistant Division of the bar. Its unique aspect is that *all* of its regular members must be paralegals. Hence, while paralegals cannot become members of the bar association, they can become members of a Division of the bar association. The Division is not a mere advisory committee of the bar; it is part of the bar association itself, which means that it is under the ultimate control of the Board of Directors of the State Bar of Texas.

The qualifications for membership in the Division are as follows:

- The applicant must *not* be a Texas attorney.
- The applicant must perform "substantial paralegal services in rendering direct assistance to an attorney" (someone who does occasional paralegal work would not qualify).
- The applicant's supervising attorney must certify that the applicant performs substantial paralegal services for that attorney.

Members pay annual dues of $25.

The bylaws of the Division state its purpose as follows: "to enhance legal assistants' participation in the administration of justice, professional responsibility and public service in cooperation with the State Bar of Texas." All the officers of the Division are paralegals elected by the membership. The budget of the Division, however, must be approved by the State Bar of Texas.

In 1985, the Division began exploring a certification program for Texas legal assistants. This program will be examined later under the general topic of self-regulation. (See p. 122.)

The Legal Assistant Division has been very popular among paralegals in Texas; large numbers have joined. Other bar associations have adopted similar programs. For example, the Columbus Bar Association of Ohio admits paralegals as associate members, and the North Carolina Academy of Trial Lawyers created a new membership category in 1983 called "Legal Assistant Affiliate Member."

Not every bar association, however, has joined the bandwagon. In fact, considerable controversy surrounds the issue. In 1982 the ABA Committee on Legal Assistants proposed that the ABA create a new category of associate membership for paralegals. To become an associate, the person must be a nonlawyer who is "qualified through education, training or certification," and who assists "in the performance of legal services under the direction and supervision of a lawyer who certifies that the assistance is not primarily secretarial or clerical." The National Association of Legal Assistants (NALA) warmly endorsed the proposal, while the National Federation of Paralegal Associations (NFPA) opposed it. The ABA House of Delegates rejected the proposal on the ground that the addition of this nonlawyer membership category would further "dilute" the primary lawyer membership category. The proposal is not dead, however, since its sponsors have asked the House of Delegates to reconsider its opposition.

ASSIGNMENT 41 *Class Discussion*

a. Should paralegals become a formal part of bar associations? What effect do you think associate membership would have on existing paralegal associations? Strengthen them? Destroy them? Is it healthy or unhealthy for paralegals to organize themselves as independent entities? Is it health or unhealthy for them to be able to challenge the organized bar? Do you think there is any validity to the conflict-of-interest argument (p. 101)? What is the relationship between this argument and the issue of whether paralegals should become associate or affiliate members of the bar associations?

b. Should a paralegal association allow *lawyers* to become associate members of the *paralegal* association? Why or why not?

c. If the proposal of the ABA Committee on Legal Assistants to create an associate membership category had been successful, what kinds of paralegals would have been excluded from such membership? Is such exclusion a good idea?

ASSOCIATE MEMBERSHIP v. JOINT EFFORTS
by D. Kuckherman, 10 Update 5
(Cleveland Association of Paralegals, Inc.,
No. 6, Nov., 1984)

Supporters of associate membership for paralegals in bar associations believe that the added recognition accorded to paralegals by the bar will carry through to working situations and reinforce the role of paralegals; that more communication will take place between the two groups, thus encouraging expanded responsibilities and recognition for the paralegal profession; and that the general public will become more familiar with paralegals and their role in the delivery of legal services.

Supporters of associate membership feel that those who oppose associate categories also oppose any type of cooperative effort between paralegal associations and bar associations. These are separate issues.

Opponents of associate membership are generally in favor of joint efforts between paralegal associations and the bar on common goals. It is not necessary for two associations to share membership (or for two professions to share an association) in order for them to effectively work together to their mutual advantage.

Few would dispute that many worthwhile goals can be accomplished by the joint efforts of paralegal associations and bar associations. However, bar associations do not always agree with paralegal associations on what exactly constitutes a "cooperative effort." The definition of this term must be worked out by the associations if they are to work together effectively. Joint efforts by paralegal and bar associations are almost universally supported and should be encouraged. However, joint efforts do not require associate membership categories.

7

Self-Regulation by Paralegals

There are two national organizations of paralegals:

- The National Federation of Paralegal Associations (NFPA). This is an organization of organizations; the membership of NFPA consists of paralegal associations across the country.
- The National Association of Legal Assistants (NALA). This organization is a spin-off from the National Association of Legal Secretaries; NALA is an organization of individual legal assistants plus a number of affiliated local paralegal associations.

National Federation of
Paralegal Associations
104 Wilmot Road
Deerfield, IL 60015
312-940-8800

National Association of
Legal Assistants
1420 S. Utica
Tulsa, OK 74104
918-587-6828

NALA is *not* a member of NFPA. In fact, as we have seen, the two national organizations take very different positions on a number of important issues.

Both, for example, have published ethical standards for paralegals. NALA's is called the Code of Ethics and Professional Responsibility. NFPA's is called the Affirmation of Responsibility. The two documents are printed below.

CODE OF ETHICS AND
PROFESSIONAL RESPONSIBILITY
of the National Association of Legal Assistants, Inc.

NALA

Preamble

It is the responsibility of every legal assistant to adhere strictly to the accepted standards of legal ethics and to live by general principles of proper conduct. The performance of the duties of the legal assistant shall be governed by specific canons as defined herein in order that justice will be served and the goals of the profession attained.

The canons of ethics set forth hereafter are adopted by the National Association of Legal Assistants, Inc., as a general guide, and the enumeration of these rules does not mean there are not others of equal importance although not specifically mentioned.

Canon 1.   A legal assistant shall not perform any of the duties that lawyers only may perform nor do things that lawyers themselves may not do.

Canon 2.   A legal assistant may perform any task delegated and supervised by a lawyer so long as the lawyer is responsible to the client, maintains a direct relationship with the client, and assumes full professional responsibility for the work product.

Canon 3.   A legal assistant shall not engage in the practice of law by giving legal advice, appearing in court, setting fees, or accepting cases.

Canon 4.   A legal assistant shall not act in matters involving professional legal judgment as the services of a lawyer are essential in the public interest whenever the exercise of such judgment is required.

Canon 5.   A legal assistant must act prudently in determining the extent to which a client may be assisted without the presence of a lawyer.

Canon 6.   A legal assistant shall not engage in the unauthorized practice of law and shall assist in preventing the unauthorized practice of law.

Canon 7.   A legal assistant must protect the confidences of a client, and it shall be unethical for a legal assistant to violate any statute now in effect or hereafter to be enacted controlling privileged communications.

Canon 8.   It is the obligation of the legal assistant to avoid conduct which would cause the lawyer to be unethical or even appear to be unethical, and loyalty to the employer is incumbent upon the legal assistant.

Canon 9.   A legal assistant shall work continually to maintain integrity and a high degree of competency throughout the legal profession.

Canon 10.   A legal assistant shall strive for perfection through education in order to better assist the legal profession in fulfilling its duty of making legal services available to clients and the public.

Canon 11.   A legal assistant shall do all other things incidental, necessary, or expedient for the attainment of the ethics and responsibilities imposed by statute or rule of court.

Canon 12.   A legal assistant is governed by the American Bar Association Code of Professional Responsibility.

Adopted May 1, 1975

AFFIRMATION OF RESPONSIBILITY
of the National Federation of Paralegal Associations

Preamble

The National Federation of Paralegal Associations recognizes and accepts its commitment to the realization of the most basic right of a free society, equal justice under the law.

In examining contemporary legal institutions and systems, the members of the paralegal profession recognize that a redefinition of the traditional delivery of legal services is essential in order to meet the needs of the general public. The paralegal profession is committed to increasing the availability and quality of legal services.

The National Federation of Paralegal Associations has adopted this Affirmation of Professional Responsibility to delineate the principals of purpose and conduct toward which paralegals should aspire. Through this Affirmation, the National Federation of Paralegal Associations places upon each paralegal the responsibility to adhere to these standards and encourages dedication to the development of the profession.

I. PROFESSIONAL RESPONSIBILITY

A paralegal shall demonstrate initiative in performing and expanding the paralegal role in the delivery of legal services within the parameters of the unauthorized practice of law statutes.

DISCUSSION: Recognizing the professional and legal responsibility to abide by the unauthorized practice of law statutes, the Federation supports and encourages new interpretations as to what constitutes the practice of law.

II. PROFESSIONAL CONDUCT

A paralegal shall maintain the highest standards of ethical conduct.

[margin notes, handwritten:] more Aggressive in re difining para legalism than NALA

NFPA seems to encourage a stretching of where the limit is.

DISCUSSION: It is the responsibility of a paralegal to avoid conduct which is unethical or appears to be unethical. Ethical principles are aspirational in character and embody the fundamental rules of conduct by which every paralegal should abide. Observance of these standards is essential to uphold respect for the legal system.

III. COMPETENCE AND INTEGRITY

A paralegal shall maintain a high level of competence and shall contribute to the integrity of the paralegal profession.

DISCUSSION: The integrity of the paralegal profession is predicated upon individual competence. Professional competence is each paralegal's responsibility and is achieved through continuing education, awareness of developments in the field of law and aspiring to the highest standards of personal performance.

IV. CLIENT CONFIDENCES

A paralegal shall preserve client confidences and privileged communications.

DISCUSSION: Confidential information and privileged communications are a vital part of the attorney, paralegal and client relationship. The importance of preserving confidential and privileged information is understood to be an uncompromising obligation of every paralegal.

V. SUPPORT OF PUBLIC INTERESTS

A paralegal shall serve the public interests by contributing to the availability and delivery of quality legal services.

DISCUSSION: It is the responsibility of each paralegal to promote the development and implementation of programs that address the legal needs of the public. A paralegal shall strive to maintain a sensitivity to public needs and to educate the public as to the services that paralegals may render.

VI. PROFESSIONAL DEVELOPMENT

A paralegal shall promote the development of the paralegal profession.

DISCUSSION: This Affirmation of Professional Responsibility promulgates a positive attitude through which a paralegal may recognize the importance, responsibility and potential of the paralegal contribution to the delivery of legal services. Participation in professional associations enhances the ability of the individual paralegal to contribute to the quality and growth of the paralegal profession.

ASSIGNMENT 42

(a) Compare these two documents of NALA and NFPA. What differences in content and emphasis do you see?

(b) Earlier it was pointed out that NALA agreed with and NFPA opposed the proposal of the ABA Committee on Legal Assistants to create an associate category membership in the ABA (p. 108). After reading the above two documents, are you surprised that NALA and NFPA took these opposite positions or could you have predicted the split?

The most intense battle between the two national paralegal associations has been over the question of the paralegal certification. NALA favors certification and has its own certification program. NFPA is opposed to certification as premature.

THE CASE FOR CERTIFICATION[14]
by Jane H. Terhune

(Jane H. Terhune is a past president of the National Association of Legal Assistants, Inc. She is employed as a legal assistant for the firm of Hall, Estill, Hardwick, Gable, Collingsworth & Nelson, Tulsa, Oklahoma.)

Professional competence of an *individual* can be assessed by two recognized mechanisms: licensing or certification. Accreditation or approval, on the other hand, examines educational *programs* to determine whether they meet established standards of quality. Although the ABA has an institutional approval process, this paper is concerned only with the assessment of *individual* competence and therefore will not deal with the issue of institutional accreditation or approval.

Since the early 1970s legal assistants have obtained employment by means of formal training, in-house training, or other law office experience. While each method of training has certain advantages, no one method has proven superior to the others. Thus the dilemma: how can prospective employers or clients assess or legal assistants demonstrate paralegal skills and knowledge when there is no standard for performance?

Is licensing the appropriate mechanism to assure professional competence of legal assistants at this time? Several states have recently considered it, but none have yet adopted it. It is generally agreed that re-

---

[14] American Bar Association, Standing Committee on Legal Assistants, *Legal Assistant Update '80* 5–16 (1980). This article has been updated to reflect current positions of NALA and NFPA.

quirements for licensing would either severely limit the growth and development of the still new paralegal field or be so weak as to be meaningless. Licensing, by definition, is a mandatory requirement and is usually administered and controlled by government entities or well-established and strong professional associations. Since the legal assistant concept is still not well understood, it is doubtful that state legislatures can define the profession well enough to regulate it effectively at this time. Therefore, licensing appears to be impractical as well as premature.

Certification, a voluntary professional commitment, appears to be a practical alternative, and the National Association of Legal Assistants believes that one national certification program is preferable to a multitude of possible state programs. Certification is not new or unique. Many professions and paraprofessions have developed and supported certification as an alternative to licensing or other forms of regulation. Certification recognizes expertise and proven ability without limiting entrance into or employment in the field, and the same standards are applied regardless of the individual's background or training. Furthermore, a certification program can help guide educational institutions in developing and evaluating their legal assistant curricula. It is argued that certification would limit the development of the paralegal field, but the CPS (Certified Professional Secretary) program has not thus affected the secretarial field, and the PLS (Professional Legal Secretary) certification of legal secretaries has in no way interfered with their employment. To the contrary, secretaries with the CPS or PLS ratings are regarded as professionals in their respective fields.

In 1974, as part of an effort to set high professional standards for legal assistants while the field was in its early development, the NALA Certifying Board for Legal Assistants was created. It was composed of nine members—five legal assistants (working in different areas of the law), two paralegal educators, and two attorneys. The composition of the Board has remained the same to date, and in number is similar to many certification boards or committees in other fields. During the first year of its existence the Certifying Board acted mainly as a feasibility study group. All known national professional associations with certification programs were contacted for advice and guidance. Paralegal educators were contacted for information about their programs as well as entrance and graduation requirements. Legal assistant duties and responsibilities in various areas of the law were surveyed, and correspondence with the Institute of Legal Executives in England began. Our English counterparts were anxious to share their ten years of experience with NALA. After several months of gathering information, replies were tabulated and summarized and the NALA Certifying Board for Legal Assistants was ready to embark on its task.

Although many legal assistants work in special areas of law rather than as generalists, there are general skills and knowledge which apply to all legal fields and, for this reason, general subjects or topics were selected for inclusion in the examination.

The certification program is a two step process, as follows:

First: successful completion of a two day (eleven hour) comprehensive examination covering the following areas:

Communications—Grammar, vocabulary, correspondence, nonverbal communications, concise writing.

Ethics—Unauthorized practice, ethical rules, practice rules, confidentiality.

Interviewing Techniques—General considerations for interviewing situations, initial roadblocks, manner of questions, special handling situations, use of checklists for specific matters.

Human Relations—Delegation of authority, consequences of delegation, working with people.

Judgment and Analytical Ability—Analyzing and categorizing facts and evidence; legal assistant's relationship with the lawyer, legal secretary, and client, other law firms and the courts; reactions to specific situations; data interpretation.

Legal Research—Principles of legal research, sources of the law, finding tools, court reports, Shepardizing, research procedure.

Legal Terminology—Latin phrases, legal phrases or terms in general, utilization and understanding of common legal terms.

Substantive Law—The American legal system: history, branches of the government, constitution. Applicants must also select and complete four sets of general questions from the areas below:

Real Estate	Corporate	Contracts
Bankruptcy	Litigation	Administrative
Criminal	Federal Tax	Probate and Estate Planning

After passing the examination, a legal assistant may use the CLA (Certified Legal Assistant) designation which signifies certification by the National Association of Legal Assistants, Inc. CLA is a service mark duly registered with the U.S. Patent and Trademark Office (No. 1131999). Any unauthorized use is strictly forbidden.

Second: based on the premise that education, a commitment of all professionals, is a never ending process, Certified Legal Assistants are required to submit evidence of continuing education periodically in order to maintain certified status. The CLA designation is for a period of five years and if the CLA submits proof of continuing education in accordance with the stated requirements, the certificate is renewed for another five years. Lifetime certification is not permitted.

Continuing education units are awarded for attending seminars, workshops or conferences in areas of substantive law or a closely related area. The seminars, etc., do not have to be sponsored by NALA, although all NALA seminars and workshops qualify.

The development of the specific test items was a time consuming and difficult project. Rather than employ professional testing companies unfamiliar with the legal assistant field, it was decided that the Certifying Board, composed of legal assistants, attorneys, and educators from the legal assistant field, were best qualified to prepare the exams. Each member was assigned a topic and asked to prepare sample items, including true-false, multiple-choice, matching, and essay questions. Since it was felt that a legal assistant's ability to communicate was vital to success in the profession, essay items were included in each section of the exam. Then followed a series of meetings to review, refine, and evaluate the proposed exams. The exams were pilot-tested, testing times were noted, results were statistically analyzed, and problems were identified. Every question in each section was carefully scrutinized for "national scope" and questions which did not apply to all states were removed from the exam.

Since legal assistants enter the field through a variety of routes including formal education, in-house training, and law office experience, eligibility to take the exam can be established in a variety of ways. Consequently, the following requirements were set up:

1) Graduation from an ABA approved legal assistant course or from a training school which is institutionally credited;

2) Graduation from an unapproved course or unaccredited school plus two years experience;

3) Bachelor's degree in any field plus one year's experience;

4) Seven years' law related experience under a member of the Bar (this option is available through 12/31/91)

Applicants meeting any one of these criteria may take the exam. Furthermore, they need not be members of the National Association of Legal Assistants to apply for or receive the CLA (Certified Legal Assistant) certification.

The CLA examination was first offered in November, 1976, at regional testing centers. Approximately 50 percent of the first group of applicants passed the entire exam, and the Board was particularly pleased that the passing percentage was uniform throughout the country, a fact which seemed to indicate that the test was free of state or regional bias. Although the passing rate has fluctuated slightly in subsequent testing, the uniformity has been maintained. As of 1980, 300 legal assistants from 35 states successfully completed the CLA examination. As of 1984, the statistics on the examination were as follows:

Number taking the exam: 1,237
Number of times exam was given: 1,722 (includes retakes)
Number who passed: 820
Number who passed on first sitting: 536
Number of states containing legal assistants with CLA status: 44, plus District of Columbia and Virgin Islands
Number of those taking exam who are *not* members of NALA: about 400
Sections of the exam most frequently failed: Substantive Law, Communications, Legal Research

States with the most number of CLAs:

Florida:	202	Michigan:	31
Texas:	130	Alabama:	28
California:	73	Colorado:	26
Arizona:	44	Oklahoma:	25
Kansas:	38	Nebraska:	23

Certification is an ambitious and expensive project for a young professional association. Over $20,000 and thousands of hours were initially invested in the CLA Program, but the National Association of Legal Assistants believes it has been a wise investment. Traditionally, where new professions do not set their own standards, related professions or governments have done so. NALA felt a responsibility to develop a quality national certification program for legal assistants desiring professional recognition. The CLA exam has been in use for a number of years, but work on the project continues. The question bank is continually expanded so that an indefinite number of exam versions can be created, and questions are being reviewed and updated constantly.

Recently, NALA launched a major new component of its CLA program: certification for those who *specialize* in a particular area of the law. In 1983 specialty certification in the areas of Civil Litigation and Probate and Estate Planning was offered for the first time to all CLAs. In 1984, additional specialty examinations were offered in the areas of Corporate and Business Law, and Criminal Law and Procedure. Applicants for the specialty exam sit for a four hour examination to be given during the same time as the regular examination—the third weekend of March and during the July testing session which is held the Friday and Saturday immediately preceding the NALA annual convention.

Legal assistants are becoming more and more specialized—the regular CLA examination tests the broad *general* skills required of *all* legal assistants. Specialty certification is different. It is a goal for those who want to be recognized for achieving significant competence in a *particular* field. Further, a legal assistant may want to take more than one specialty examination if a specialty changes over time.

Conclusion

Although accreditation and/or licensing may become necessary in the future, the National Association of Legal Assistants believes that certification of legal assistants is currently the best device for assessing and assuring professional competence. While no legal assistant must take a test in order to obtain or maintain employment, the NALA certification program offers to legal assistants an opportunity for professional recognition.

THE CASE AGAINST CERTIFICATION
by Judith Current

(Judith Current is a past president of the National Federation of Paralegal Associations. She is employed as a legal assistant in the firm of Holme, Roberts & Owen, Denver, Colorado.)

The National Federation of Paralegal Associations ("the Federation") is a professional organization composed of state and local paralegal associations representing over 11,000 paralegals across the country. The Federation was founded in 1974 and adopted the following purposes in 1975:

- To constitute a unified national voice of the paralegal profession;
- To advance, foster and promote the paralegal concept;
- To monitor and participate in developments in the paralegal profession;
- To maintain a nationwide communications network among paralegal associations and other members of the legal community.

The Federation has continued to foster these goals through its established policies and activities. In 1977 the Federation adopted its Affirmation of Responsibility (p. 112).

The Federation recognizes that certification of paralegals is of national concern, but it feels that there has been insufficient study as to the impact of certification and the means by which certification should be administered. The Federation will only support a certification program which is coordinated by a national, broadly-based, autonomous body in which paralegals have at least equal participation.

The topic of certification of legal assistants has been of concern to the Federation since its inception. It has found every certificate proposal advanced to date to be seriously lacking in the understanding of the true nature of the profession, particularly its diversity, and the proposals have offered a structure that provides little or no representation to the persons most affected, the legal assistants themselves.

Specifically, its reservations fall within the following areas:

NEED/PREMATURITY

The paralegal profession is still a new one and the tremendous diversity in the functions and classifications of its members makes it extremely difficult to create generalized standards that can be fairly applied. This problem may eventually find an acceptable solution; but it will require much study and considerable input from all affected sectors.

No studies have been conducted that have demonstrated a need for certification. A study conducted by the American Bar Association in

1975 concluded that certification was premature. The California State Bar in 1978 rejected a proposal for certification and accreditation after nearly two years of study. Other states have similarly rejected certification. Until a need for certification is clearly demonstrated, certification will be premature.

Premature regulation runs a risk of foreclosing yet unseen avenues of development, as well as creating yet another layer of costly bureaucracy when, in fact, none may be needed. The Federation sees nothing to prevent, and everything to encourage, an extremely cautious approach to the enactment of any program of certification. In the meanwhile, the normal mechanisms of the marketplace, the existing unauthorized practice laws and ethical guidelines, the increasing numbers of legal assistants with demonstrable experience, and the ever growing reputations of various training programs can serve as guidelines for those who seek the sorts of yardsticks that certification might provide.

IMPACT OF CERTIFICATION

No studies have been conducted that satisfactorily assess the potential impact of certification on the delivery of legal services. Some of the possible negative effects include:

1. *The growth, development and diversity of the paralegal profession could be diminished by certification.* The paralegal profession has been developing steadily without a demonstrated need for regulation. Regulating the profession could curtail development into new areas, stifling the potential growth of the field and unnecessarily limiting the role of the paralegals in the delivery of legal services.

2. *Certification could result in a decrease of the availability of legal services to the poor.* Legal aid offices are economically dependent upon paralegals who represent clients at various administrative hearings. Most of these paralegals are in-house trained specialists who are paid lower salaries than private sector paralegals. If certification is implemented, it is conceivable that administrative agencies may initiate a system in which only certified paralegals, or attorneys, would be allowed to represent clients at the hearings. Many paralegals successfully working in this area might not meet the educational or testing requirements imposed by certification, and the legal aid offices would not be able to meet the salary demands that would be made by certified paralegals.

3. *Innovation in paralegal education programs could diminish as a result of certification.* Schools would be forced by necessity to gear their courses to a certification examination rather than to the needs of the legal community and the marketplace. While some standardization of training programs might be desirable in the future, it would be premature at this time because the training programs have not been in existence long enough to determine which types of programs are most effective and because the paralegal profession is still in a dynamic stage of development. Experimentation and variety are currently essential to the field of paralegal education.

4. *Entry into the profession could be curtailed by certification.* At the present time, a paralegal can enter the profession in a variety of ways, including formal education, in-house training, promotion from legal secretary, or a combination thereof. Certification could limit these entry paths by establishing prescribed educational requirements.

5. *Certification could lead to licensing.* Although certification is technically a voluntary program of regulation, certification leads to *de facto* licensing as we have seen in other fields. Until we truly know whom certification would serve, how it would do so, that its value would equal its cost, and, most of all, that it is needed, those involved should be engaging in study and debate, not regulation.

NO ACCEPTABLE MODEL FOR CERTIFICATION

In the Federation's opinion, no acceptable model or program of certification has yet been devised. Oregon is the only state to have adopted a certification program. This bar-controlled program has not been very successful to date, with most paralegals and most lawyers ignoring the certification process. The Federation questions the propriety of the Oregon State Bar controlling the certification of paralegals, and deplores the fact that the paralegals are denied equitable representation on the certifying board. The Oregon program fails adequately to recognize specialization and fails to make any distinctions between the tasks which may be performed by a certified paralegal and those which may be performed by an uncertified paralegal. Thus, certification does not enhance the position of paralegals in Oregon. [Note: The Oregon program has been discontinued.*]

The Federation holds the opinion that the certification program conducted by the National Association of Legal Assistants (NALA) is unacceptable. The examination, in the Federation's opinion, contains questions irrelevant to a practicing paralegal and is not an effective measure of a person's ability to work successfully as a paralegal. The NALA certification program is not officially recognized by a governmental body, and a person certified under this program is not allowed to perform any tasks other than those which may also be performed by uncertified paralegals.

CONTROL AND REPRESENTATION

No certification program will be acceptable to the Federation unless it is developed, implemented and controlled by an autonomous group which is composed of an equal number of attorneys, paralegals, paralegal educators and members of the public. Self-regulation is unacceptable to the Federation since self-regulation can become self-interest and

---

* In January, 1980 a representative of the Oregon State Bar telephoned the ABA Standing Committee on Legal Assistants with the information that the Board of Governors of the State Bar had approved the recommendation of the Legal Assistants Committee to discontinue the certification program (p. 48).

self-interest can conflict with the public interest. The Federation strongly believes that bar control of paralegals is inappropriate in that such regulation may meet the interests of the organized bar and lawyers, but not necessarily the interests of the public or the paralegal profession. The Federation also questions the propriety of the organized bar attempting to regulate another profession. Control of paralegals by the legislative branch of government could create conflict where the practice of law is controlled by the bar and the judicial branch of the government.

NATIONAL COORDINATION

The Federation believes that any program of certification will be most efficient and equitable if it is developed as a national program rather than on a state-by-state basis. A national program would eliminate duplication of effort on the part of each individual state. It would allow for mobility and would avoid a conflict of standards between states.

The Federation recommends that the need for and possible methods of certification be studied in much greater depth, and that this study be conducted by an autonomous group which provides equitable representation to paralegals, attorneys, paralegal educators and members of the public. The Federation also recommends that bar associations work with paralegals and educators to educate lawyers in the proper and effective utilization of paralegals and that paralegals work to promote the growth and the development of the profession through support of and participation in the local and national paralegal associations.

ASSIGNMENT 43

Which side is correct? Conduct a debate in your class on the advantages and disadvantages of certification.

CERTIFICATION IN TEXAS?

Recently the Legal Assistant Division of the State Bar of Texas considered the issue of certification for Texas. As we saw earlier, membership in the Division is limited to legal assistants (p. 107). A survey of these members by the Division revealed a very high interest in launching a voluntary certification program. Over 76 percent indicated that they would take a certification exam if it were offered. As a result, the Division drafted two certification proposals and in 1986 conducted a series of hearings on them. The proposals were as follows:

> *Proposal 1.* The Division would develop and administer its own two-day exam on generic topics (e.g., legal analysis, communications) and on Texas law. To be eligible to take the exam, the

legal assistant must have at least two years actual working experience as a legal assistant.

Proposal 2. The Division would join forces with the National Association of Legal Assistants (NALA) and in effect give two exams. NALA would administer its two-day Certified Legal Assistant (CLA) exam outlined earlier (p. 116). Then the Division would administer its half-day exam designed with a focus on Texas law. Anyone who had previously passed the CLA exam would be required to have worked as a legal assistant in Texas for one year before taking the Division's Texas exam.

These two proposals stirred great controversy in Texas and throughout the country. The National Federation of Paralegal Associations (NFPA) vigorously opposed both proposals, raising many of the same arguments against certification that were discussed earlier (p. 119). The Dallas Association of Legal Assistants (which is a member of NFPA) criticized NFPA for its opposition. The National Association of Legal Assistants (NALA) endorsed the Texas move toward certification. This, of course, is not surprising in view of NALA's history of supporting certification, And, of course, NALA would play a major role if the second proposal were adopted. But some criticized its role. NALA, for example, had to make clear that it "does not stand to profit monetarily" if the proposal were adopted and that NALA would not control the Texas component of the test.

The debate was not limited to NFPA and NALA. Approximately 298 people attended the eight public hearings throughout Texas and 187 submitted written comments. *But no clear consensus emerged from the hearings on the two proposals.* There was considerable confusion about the nature, purpose, and scope of the two proposals, and indeed, about the question of certification itself. Many troublesome questions were raised. For example: Would the proposals limit entry into the profession? Why is certification needed? Are there antitrust implications in a program of certification whether or not the testing is voluntary? Will voluntary certification inevitably lead to mandatory certification and licensing? Many suggested that considerable research and education was needed before concrete proposals could be seriously considered.

Also troublesome is the fact that the State Bar of Texas has taken the position that "the State Bar and the Supreme Court are not the appropriate entities to propose or implement a certification process for Texas legal assistants." But the Legal Assistant Division is a part of the State Bar of Texas and any proposal of the Division will have to be presented to the Board of Governors of the State Bar for approval.

The future of certification in Texas is uncertain. The initial enthusiasm over the two proposals has considerably dampened. Texas, *like the rest of the country,* is not sure what to do about certification. When the topic of certification is raised, Texans, *like the rest of the country,* confront more questions than answers.

POSITION OF THE AMERICAN BAR ASSOCIATION ON CERTIFICATION

The ABA has taken the following positions on paralegal certification:

(1) Certification of *minimal* or entry-level paralegal competence is *not* appropriate.

(2) Voluntary certification of *advanced* paralegal competence or proficiency in specialty areas of the law *might* be appropriate *if* it is administered by the appropriate body.

(3) The ABA is *not* the appropriate body to undertake a program of certifying paralegals in advanced competence or proficiency in specialty areas of the law.

(4) A voluntary program of certifying advanced paralegal competence or proficiency in specialty areas of the law, if undertaken at all, should be undertaken on a national basis by a board that includes lawyers, paralegals, educators, and members of the general public.

(5) Since such a board does not presently exist, there should not be any certification at this time.

According to the ABA, certification of minimal competence does not have the benefits that would justify the time, expense, and effort to implement it. Furthermore, any of the benefits would be outweighed by the potential detriment from it. A major detriment that the ABA sees is that such certification could evolve into licensure which the ABA, and almost everyone else, continues to oppose.

But the ABA does see benefits in certifying paralegals in areas of specialization *after* they have been on the job. This kind of advanced certification would be a way of recognizing "professional" advancement. "Such certification would be a measure of quality of work and experience. Its function would be to demonstrate to employers or prospective employers a high degree of legal assistant competence in a particular area of practice that has already been obtained, rather than just the potential for such competence." ABA Standing Committee on Legal Assistants, "Position Paper on the Question of Legal Assistant Licensure or Certification," 5 *Legal Assistant Update* 167 (1986).

The ABA feels, however, that advanced certification, must be administered by the appropriate body. This body should be broad based in that it includes lawyers, paralegals, educators, and members of the public on it. The ABA recognizes that it is *not* such a body. Nor is the National Association of Legal Assistants and the National Federation of Paralegal Associations. In fact, such a body simply does not exist. It would take a great deal of money, energy, and political skill to create one. Beyond a lot of rhetoric, no one is even trying.

Hence, as a practical consequence, it can be said that the ABA is opposed to *any* certification at this time.

ASSIGNMENT 44

Is it ever possible to have truly *voluntary* certification or *voluntary* regulation of any kind? Do you agree with the following statement of the Legal Services Section of the State Bar of California: "[A] certification. . .program would have significant impact not only on individual paralegals, attorneys and educators but also on the way legal services are delivered to the public." It is possible to propose a *voluntary* program of certification, but the history of certification "demonstrates a tendency for such programs to be so influential that their standards become mandatory even though they are in theory voluntary. Employment standards designed to be guidelines only are followed blindly and become exclusionary. Educators design training to meet testing standards and criteria become uniform and rigid. Individuals somewhat automatically seek status, whether the training standards and testing process are appropriate for them or not." *Economics of Law Practice Committee Proposal for State Bar Certification of Legal Assistants,* p. 4 (Sept. 11, 1978).

MODEL STANDARDS AND GUIDELINES FOR UTILIZATION OF LEGAL ASSISTANTS: THE MOST CURRENT DEBATE BETWEEN NALA AND NFPA

The most recent friction between NALA and NFPA came in 1984 when NALA promulgated its *Model Standards and Guidelines for the Utilization of Legal Assistants.* The goal of NALA in issuing the *Model Standards* was to present one comprehensive document that would address the critical issues of any profession, namely, identification, qualifications, and the role of the individual within the profession. There is nothing to prevent people from calling themselves paralegals regardless of the type of work they do. No one can stop a lawyer, for example, from calling his or her secretary a paralegal even if the duties of this person continue to be 100 percent clerical. The same is true of the law office messenger and the employee who spends all day photocopying legal documents. The *Model Standards* represent the view of one prestigious organization, NALA, on how to combat such chaos. Little did NALA expect, however, the barrage of criticism that the *Model Standards* received.

Members of the ABA Committee on Legal Assistants charged that the *Standards* "may unjustifiably disqualify many present law office employees and others qualified to begin working as legal assistants immediately, under a lawyer's direct supervision." These Committee members acknowledged that the *Standards* present statements that approximate desired conduct by paralegals. But turning "such statements into ethical prescriptions to lawyers and prohibitions placed upon lawyers is both unnecessary and counterproductive. In particular, the stated qualifications and limitations on legal assistant employment are contrary to a lawyer's own professional responsibility for employing non-lawyer staff. They also discourage employment of legal assistants at a time when increased employment is desirable in enabling lawyers to provide legal services most effectively and at reasonable cost."[15]

In order to judge the fairness of this criticism, the *Model Standards* are presented in full below. Following the NALA *Standards*, the reaction of NFPA to them is presented.

MODEL STANDARDS AND GUIDELINES FOR UTILIZATION OF LEGAL ASSISTANTS
proposed by the National Association of Legal Assistants, Inc. (1984)

PREAMBLE

Proper utilization of the services of legal assistants affects the efficient delivery of legal services. Legal assistants and the legal profession should be assured that some measures exist for identifying legal assistants and their role in assisting attorneys in the delivery of legal services. Therefore, the National Association of Legal Assistants, Inc., hereby

---

[15] Littleton & Ulrich, *Comments by the American Bar Association Standing Committee on Legal Assistants Concerning NALA's Model Standards and Guidelines,* 2 Legal Assistant Today 13 (No. 2, Winter, 1985). For NALA's response, see Sanders-West, *The Member Connection,* 11 Facts and Findings 6 (National Association of Legal Assistants, Issue 5, April, 1985).

adopts these Model Standards and Guidelines as an educational document for the benefit of legal assistants and the legal profession.

DEFINITION

Legal assistants* are a distinguishable group of persons who assist attorneys in the delivery of legal services. Through formal education, training, and experience, legal assistants have knowledge and expertise regarding the legal system and substantive and procedural law which qualify them to do work of a legal nature under the supervision of an attorney.

STANDARDS

A legal assistant should meet certain minimum qualifications. The following standards may be used to determine an individual's qualifications as a legal assistant:

1. Successful completion of the Certified Legal Assistant (CLA) examination of the National Association of Legal Assistants, Inc.;
2. Graduation from an ABA approved program of study for legal assistants; _(not practical at this time)_
3. Graduation from a course of study for legal assistants which is institutionally accredited but not ABA approved, and which requires not less than the equivalent of 60 semester hours of classroom study;
4. Graduation from a course of study for legal assistants, other than those set forth in (2) and (3) above, plus not less than six months of in-house training as a legal assistant;
5. A baccalaureate degree in any field, plus not less than six months' in-house training as a legal assistant;
6. A minimum of three years of law-related experience under the supervision of an attorney, including at least six months of in-house training as a legal assistant; or
7. Two years of in-house training as a legal assistant.

For purposes of these standards, "in-house training as a legal assistant" means attorney education of the employee concerning legal assistant duties and these guidelines. In addition to review and analysis of assignments, the legal assistant should receive a reasonable amount of instruction directly related to the duties and obligations of the legal assistant.

GUIDELINES

These guidelines relating to standards of performance and professional responsibility are intended to aid legal assistants and attorneys. The re-

---

* Within this occupational category some individuals are known as paralegals.

sponsibility rests with an attorney who employs legal assistants to educate them with respect to the duties they are assigned and to supervise the manner in which such duties are accomplished.

Legal assistants should:

1. Disclose their status as legal assistants at the outset of any professional relationship with a client, other attorneys, a court or administrative agency or personnel thereof, or members of the general public;
2. Preserve the confidences and secrets of all clients; and
3. Understand the attorney's Code of Professional Responsibility and these guidelines in order to avoid any action which would involve the attorney in a violation of that Code, or give the appearance of professional impropriety.

Legal assistants should not:

1. Establish attorney-client relationships; set legal fees; give legal opinions or advice; or represent a client before a court; nor
2. Engage in, encourage, or contribute to any act which could constitute the unauthorized practice of law.

Legal assistants may perform services for an attorney in the representation of a client, provided:

1. The services performed by the legal assistant do not require the exercise of independent professional legal judgment;
2. The attorney maintains a direct relationship with the client and maintains control of all client matters;
3. The attorney supervises the legal assistant;
4. The attorney remains professionally responsible for all work on behalf of the client, including any actions taken or not taken by the legal assistant in connection therewith; and
5. The services performed supplement, merge with and become the attorney's work product.

In the supervision of a legal assistant, consideration should be given to:

1. Designating work assignments that correspond to the legal assistants' abilities, knowledge, training and experience.
2. Educating and training the legal assistant with respect to professional responsibility, local rules and practices, and firm policies;
3. Monitoring the work and professional conduct of the legal assistant to ensure that the work is substantively correct and timely performed;
4. Providing continuing education for the legal assistant in substantive matters through courses, institutes, workshops, seminars and in-house training; and
5. Encouraging and supporting membership and active participation in professional organizations.

Except as otherwise provided by statute, court rule or decision, administrative rule or regulation, or the attorney's Code of Professional Responsibility; and within the preceding parameters and proscriptions, a legal assistant may perform any function delegated by an attorney, including, but not limited to the following:

1. Conduct client interviews and maintain general contact with the client after the establishment of the attorney-client relationship, so long as the client is aware of the status and function of the legal assistant, and the client contact is under the supervision of the attorney.
2. Locate and interview witnesses, so long as the witnesses are aware of the status and function of the legal assistant.
3. Conduct investigations and statistical and documentary research for review by the attorney.
4. Conduct legal research for review by the attorney.
5. Draft legal documents for review by the attorney.
6. Draft correspondence and pleadings for review by and signature of the attorney.
7. Summarize depositions, interrogatories, and testimony for review by the attorney.
8. Attend executions of wills, real estate closings, depositions, court or administrative hearings and trials with the attorney.
9. Author and sign letters provided the legal assistant's status is clearly indicated and the correspondence does not contain independent legal opinions or legal advice.

POSITION OF THE NATIONAL FEDERATION OF PARALEGAL ASSOCIATIONS (NFPA) ON NALA's MODEL STANDARDS AND GUIDELINES FOR LEGAL ASSISTANTS

Historically, the NFPA has discouraged implementation of guidelines and standards which serve to restrict and limit the growth of the paralegal profession. The parameters of the profession are already defined by the unauthorized practice of law statutes. Rather than further restrict the profession, the NFPA is committed to expanding the paralegal role within the parameters of the unauthorized practice of law statutes, as well as supporting innovative interpretations as to what constitutes the practice of law.

In examining contemporary legal institutions and systems, the members of the NFPA recognize that a re-definition of the traditional delivery of legal services is essential in order to meet the needs of the general public. We are committed to increasing the availability of affordable, quality legal services, a goal which is served by the constant re-evaluation and expansion of the work that paralegals are authorized to perform. Delivery of quality legal services to those portions of our population currently without access to them requires innovation and sensitivity to specific needs of people. Our view is that our future role in the delivery of legal services is almost limitless.

The intent of the guidelines promulgated by the National Association of Legal Assistants ("NALA"), to assure proper utilization of legal assistants to effect efficient delivery of legal services is certainly an admirable goal. However, guidelines should not be adopted without a clear definition of need, a thorough examination of all of the issues involved, and evidence that the program's negative impact would be minimal.

DEFINITION OF NEED

It is unclear who in the legal community needs these guidelines. Is it attorneys, paralegal administrators, educators, paralegals themselves or the public? The guidelines appear to be written to attorneys and therefore perhaps it is assumed that they are the ones that need the guidelines. In any event, it would seem that all of the groups affected by the guidelines should be involved in identifying the need. Once it has been established who needs the guidelines and what their purpose is, we can draft the guidelines to directly correspond to and meet those needs. Guidelines that are too general are ineffective. Since it appears the guidelines are based on already existing ethics opinions again their need becomes a questionable issue.

EXAMINATION OF THE ISSUES INVOLVED

The paralegal profession is still developing. Growth and expansion could be restricted by the requirement that paralegals meet standards and definitions based on current roles rather than allowing paralegals, attorneys and clients the freedom to examine new approaches to the practice of law. The guidelines should recognize the full range of individuals in title companies, corporations, healthcare facilities, governmental agencies, insurance companies, correctional institutions, military service and consumer organizations. Because the profession is evolving at such a rapid pace, definitions, guidelines, or standards should be developed only after a clear need has been established.

Currently employers have the freedom to select paralegals with abilities and backgrounds suited to their individual practice. However, these guidelines may suggest that a single approach will fit the needs of all.

The requirements in the standards portion of the guidelines raise many questions as to what type of education is required to make a paralegal. NFPA has traditionally held the position that accreditation of paralegals should be done by an autonomous group made up of representatives from lawyer, paralegal, paralegal educator, paralegal administration groups and from the public. For that reason, the NFPA would be opposed to a standard which accepted the ABA approval process as the standard.

Additionally, the standards are somewhat vague. What do you call a person who is working to complete the six months of in-house training requirements? Do we create a new position entitled paralegal-in-training?

Use as a criterion for minimum qualifications of the NALA certification exam is another questionable standard. The exam has not been examined in detail by other groups and has not been widely endorsed. The exam fails to recognize the specialized nature of the paralegal profession as it requires in depth knowledge of four specialty areas. For the majority of practicing paralegals, the examination would not be relevant to what their jobs entail. If paralegals are tested on skills that are not applicable to the job they are seeking, firms hiring them would have to train and reeducate them in any event. To impose a test with no relation to improved quality of legal representation is inappropriate and costly. Again NFPA's policy on certification is that if it is determined to be necessary and useful, then it should be done on a nationwide level by an autonomous group representing the various sections within the legal profession so that the public interest and not the self interest of the profession is the prime reason for certifying paralegals.

POSSIBLE NEGATIVE IMPACTS

Employment standards designed to be guidelines only can instead be followed blindly and rigidly and become exclusionary. The NFPA believes the delivery of quality legal services can be better facilitated with the continued expansion of paralegal responsibilities and the development of innovative methods of delivering legal services. The primary reason for the development of the legal assistant concept is to increase the availability of legal services to those who are currently without access to them. Greater access may be hindered by the limitations placed on us by the guidelines.

Educational institutions may design their training to fit into the guidelines, and curriculum could become uniform and rigid. Again, innovation will be hindered by retarding the development both of new roles for paralegals and the diverse types of training that they will need.

How will the guidelines be enforced? In monitoring previously proposed guidelines, the NFPA has noted that guidelines, once adopted, are not usually updated to reflect new developments in the paralegal profession and the practice of law. For example, Guideline VI of the New York State Bar Association's guidelines adopted in 1976 prohibits the inclusion of the name of a non-lawyer on a lawyer's letterhead. However, in light of *Bates v. State Bar of Arizona,* and an informal ABA opinion, the New York State Bar Association Committee Professional Ethics issued Ethical Opinion 500, permitting the inclusion of non-lawyer employees on a firm's letterhead "whenever the inclusion of such name would not be deceptive and might be reasonably expected to supply information relative to the selection of counsel." Years have elapsed since the issuance of Opinion 500, yet, as of this date, Guideline VI has not been revised to reflect the change in the practice of law which is evidenced by this Opinion.

In addition to these more concrete negative impacts, there is a more conceptual problem with the guidelines. Because the guidelines are written for attorneys only and say little to paralegals, the effect is to put paralegals in a very passive position turning control of our profession over to attorneys. The NFPA has always sought to maintain a separate and independent voice that speaks to its members as well as to other groups within the legal community. That independent voice expresses an interest separate from the interests of any other group. The guidelines, by speaking to attorneys and asking that they take control, minimizes the duty of paralegals to take responsibility for their own actions and to take a strong leadership role in educating ourselves in areas such as ethics and unauthorized practice of law. Thus, the guidelines would have the negative effect of weakening the paralegal movement.

CONCLUSION

The need for these guidelines has yet to be determined and should be examined by legal assistants, attorneys, paralegal educators, paralegal administrators and the public. The issues surrounding the guidelines have not been fully discussed and the negative impacts could be prohibitive. All possible ramifications must be thoroughly studied before implementation. If, after study by all affected parties, it is determined that there is sufficient need for guidelines, they must be developed, implemented and controlled by an autonomous group which provokes equitable representation by private and public sector paralegals, attorneys, paralegal educators and consumers of legal services to insure all legitimate interests are represented.

This profession is rooted in the desire to reduce legal fees and demystify the law by creating a pool of lay people who can assist in the delivery of quality legal services. Any guidelines that are adopted should reflect an attempt to meet the needs for legal services of those currently without access to them. The paralegal profession is already restricted by the unauthorized practice of law statutes. Is there a need to further restrict it? We must consider the most important of ramifications; what injury would further restrictions cause in the paralegal fight to assist in the delivery of quality legal services to meet the needs of the general public?

ASSIGNMENT 45

When a new local paralegal association is formed, it is often lobbied by NALA and by NFPA to become a part of one of these national organizations. The local association will usually make one of three decisions: affiliate with NALA; affiliate with NFPA; or remain unaffiliated. In making this decision, the local association will closely examine documents of the two national organizations such as the two ethical codes presented earlier (p. 111), their positions on certification (p. 114), the

Model Standards (p. 126), etc. If you were a member of a local association faced with the decision of whether to join NALA or NFPA, what would your vote be? Why?

ASSIGNMENT 46

Is it a good idea to have two national associations? Why or why not?

Throughout this book the importance of paralegal associations has been stressed. They have had a major impact on the development of paralegalism. For example, it was the vigorous opposition of paralegal organizations that helped defeat the California legislation that tried to control the field in that state. Many other state and local bar associations as well as the ABA have felt the effect of organized paralegal advocacy through the associations.

As soon as possible you should join a paralegal association. If one does not exist in your area, you should form one and decide whether you want to become part of the National Federation of Paralegal Associations or the National Association of Legal Assistants. The paralegal association is your main voice in the continued development of the field. Join one now and become an active member. In addition to the educational benefits of association membership and in addition to the job placement services that many provide, you will experience the satisfaction of helping create the shape of the career in the years to come. Lawyers should not be the sole mechanism of control.

stop!

8

Fair Labor
Standards Act

The Fair Labor Standards Act is a federal statute that requires overtime compensation to be paid to employees.[16] There are, however, exceptions to this requirement. An exemption exists for (and hence no overtime need be paid to) those who are employed in a bona fide executive, administrative, or professional capacity.[17] Can an employer avoid paying overtime to a paralegal?

Although there is no universal answer to this question, most authorities agree that paralegal employees are *not* exempt and hence *are* entitled to the protection of the Act. Phrased another way, they are not considered professionals under the Act and must therefore be paid overtime compensation. If, however, the paralegal is a supervisor with extensive management responsibilities over other employees, the exemption may apply. But this would cover only a small segment of the paralegal population. The following opinion letter explains the position of the government on this issue. As you will see, the criteria used to distinguish exempt from non-exempt employees are the actual job responsibilities of the employee, and not the job title or compensation policy of the office.

Wage and Hour Division
United States Department of Labor
September 27, 1979

This is in further reply to your letter of July 12, 1979,...concerning the exempt status under section 13(a)(1) of the

---

[16] 29 U.S.C. §§201 *et. seq.* (1976).

[17] See 29 C.F.R. (Part 541) (1985).

Fair Labor Standards Act of paralegal employees employed by your organization,. . .

The specific duties of the paralegal employees (all of which occur under an attorney's supervision) are interviewing clients; identifying and refining problems; opening, maintaining, and closing case files; acting as the liaison person between client and attorney; drafting pleadings and petitions, and answering petitions, and interrogatories; filing pleadings and petitions; acting as general litigation assistant during court proceedings; digesting depositions, and preparing file profiles; conducting formal and informal hearings and negotiations; preparing and editing newsletters and leaflets for community development and public relations purposes; performing outreach services; coordinating general activities with relevant local, State, and Federal agencies; assisting in establishing and implementing community legal education programs; and working as a team with other employees to deliver quality legal services. You state that the job requires at least two years of college and/or equivalent experience.

[The Fair Labor Standards] Act provides a complete minimum wage and overtime pay exemption for any employee employed in a bona fide executive, administrative, or professional capacity,. . .An employee will qualify for exemption if all the pertinent tests relating to duties, responsibilities and salary . . . are met. In response to your first question, the paralegal employees you have in mind would not qualify for exemption as bona fide professional employees as discussed in section 541.3 of the regulations, since it is clear that their primary duty does not consist of work requiring knowledge of an advanced type in a field of science or learning customarily acquired by a prolonged course of specialized intellectual instruction and study, as distinguished from a general academic education and from an apprenticeship and from training in the performance of routine mental, manual, or physical processes.

With regard to the status of the paralegal employees as bona fide administrative employees, it is our opinion that their duties do not involve the exercise of discretion and independent judgment of the type required by section 541.2(b) of the regulations. The outline of their duties which you submit actually describes the use of skills rather than discretion and independent judgment. Under section 541.207 of the regulations, this requirement is interpreted as involving the comparison and evaluation of possible courses of conduct and acting or making a decision after the various possibilities have been considered. Furthermore, the term is interpreted to mean that the person has the authority or power to make an independent choice, free from immediate direction or supervision with respect to matters of significance.

The general facts presented about the employees here tend to indicate they do not meet these criteria. Rather, as indicated above, they would appear to fit more appropriately into that category of employees who apply particular skills and knowledge in preparing assignments. Employees who merely apply knowledge in following prescribed procedures or determining whether specified standards have been met are not deemed to be exercising independent judgment, even if they have some leeway in reaching a conclusion. In addition, it should be noted that most jurisdictions have strict prohibitions against the unauthorized practice of law by lay persons. Under the American Bar Association's Code of Professional Responsibility, a delegation of legal tasks to a lay person is proper only if the lawyer maintains a direct relationship with the client, supervises the delegated work and has complete professional responsibility for the work produced. The implication of such strictures is that the paralegal employees you describe would probably not have the amount of authority to exercise independent judgment with regard to legal matters necessary to bring them within the administrative exemption. . . .

With regard to your [other] questions, all nonexempt employees, regardless of the amount of their wages, must be paid overtime premium pay of not less than one and one-half times their regular rates of pay for all hours worked in excess of 40 in a workweek. The fact that an employee did not obtain advanced approval to work the overtime does not relieve the employer from complying with the overtime provisions of the Act.

We hope this satisfactorily responds to your inquiry. However, if you have any further questions concerning the application of the Fair Labor Standards Act to the situation you have in mind please do not hesitate to let us know.

Sincerely,

C. Lamar Johnson
Deputy Administrator

9

The Tort Liability
of Paralegals

Thus far we have discussed a number of ways that paralegal activities are or could be regulated:

- Criminal liability for violating the statutes on the unauthorized practice of law.
- Special authorization rules on practice, e.g., before administrative agencies.
- The ethical rules governing lawyer delegation to paralegals.
- Licensing.
- Bar rules on paralegal education.
- Self-regulation.
- Labor laws.

Finally, we come to the tort liability of paralegals, e.g., for negligence. Tort law also helps define what is and is not permissible.

The governing principle of liability is *respondeat superior*. According to this concept, the paralegal's *employer* is responsible for the torts of his/her employees so long as they were acting in the scope of their employment at the time they did the acts leading to the torts. Hence, if George Rothwell is a paralegal working for Helen Farrell, Esq., and in the course of George's job he does some work negligently that harms the client, Helen Farrell is liable to the client for the negligence because of the doctrine of *respondeat superior*. Helen is vicariously liable. Assume that she did nothing wrong or negligently herself. She is still liable solely because of what someone else has done—her paralegal employee.

An attorney may not escape responsibility to his clients by blithely saying that any shortcomings are solely the fault of his employee. He has a duty to supervise the conduct of his office. *Attorney Grievance Committee of Maryland v. Goldberg,* 292 Md.650, 441 A.2d 338, 341 (1982).

It is important to keep in mind, however, that paralegal employees are *also* responsible for their own torts. The client in the above example could elect to bring a direct action against the paralegal, George Rothwell, for negligence. All employees are also responsible for their own torts.

Respondeat superior is simply a basis upon which liability can be imposed on the employer in the event that the client decides not to sue the employee directly, or in the event that the client decides to sue both the employer and the employee. Of course, the client cannot recover from *both* master (employer) and servant (employee). There can be only one recovery. The point is that the injured party (the client) has a choice. The choice selected is usually to pursue "the deep pocket"—the person who has the most money from which a judgment can be collected. Most often, of course, this is the employer.

INTENTIONAL TORTS AND CRIMINAL ACTIVITY

If a paralegal commits an intentional tort, e.g., deceit, battery, malicious prosecution, the paralegal is *personally* liable to the injured party. If the paralegal commits a crime, the criminal act may also be the basis for a *civil* action against the paralegal. What about the employing attorney? Is s/he *also* liable for the employee's intentional torts or for the civil wrong growing out of the paralegal's criminal act?

The answer depends, in part, on whether the paralegal was attempting to further the "business" of his/her employing lawyer at the time the paralegal committed the tort. If so, then the lawyer is liable to the client under the doctrine of *respondeat superior.* The tortious activity in such cases will be considered within the scope of employment. For example, suppose while trying to collect an unpaid law firm bill, the paralegal assaults or slanders the client. Such activity would probably be considered within the scope of employment since the incident centered around a law firm matter—the client's bill. Quite a different result, however, might be reached if the paralegal happens to meet a law firm client at a bar and assaults or falsely imprisons the client following an argument over a football game.

NEGLIGENCE

It is much easier to establish that the paralegal's negligence was within the scope of employment (making the employer vicariously liable under *respondeat superior*) than it is to prove that intentional torts fall within this scope.

One question that might arise concerns the standard of care. When the paralegal makes a negligent mistake, is s/he held to the standard of care of a lawyer or of a paralegal? The basic standard of care is: reasonableness under the circumstances. If the person is engaged in a trade or profession and thereby possesses greater skills than the average citizen, then the standard of care will be the reasonable person possessing such skills. According to the *Restatement of Torts 2d:*

> **§ 229 A. Undertaking in Profession or Trade.** Unless he represents that he has greater or less skill or knowledge, one who undertakes to render services in the practice of a profession or trade is required to exercise the skill and knowledge normally possessed by members of that profession or trade in good standing in similar communities.

The implication of section 229A is that if the paralegal "represents" or holds him/herself out as having more skill than most paralegals, s/he will be held to the higher skill standard. Suppose, for example, that the paralegal (or secretary or law clerk) deals directly with a client and does not make clear to the client that s/he is not a lawyer. Assume that by the manner in which the paralegal acts, the client justifiably is under the impression that the paralegal is a lawyer. The paralegal then makes a negligent mistake. If the client brings a negligence action against the paralegal and/or against the paralegal's employing lawyer, the standard of care against which the paralegal's conduct will be measured will be that of a lawyer since the paralegal, in effect, represented him/herself to the client as a lawyer. If, on the other hand, the paralegal makes clear to the client that s/he is not a lawyer and that s/he has less training and skill than a lawyer, then the standard of care, under section 229A, may be "the skill and knowledge normally possessed" by paralegals.

Suppose, however, that the paralegal never deals directly with the client. The entire work product of the paralegal in such situations blends or merges into the work product of the lawyer. Therefore, the legal services are represented to the client as the work product of the lawyer. Hence, even though the negligent act about which the client is complaining was committed by the paralegal, the standard of care will be the reasonable *lawyer* under the circumstances since the client had every right to believe s/he was receiving the services of a lawyer.

ASSIGNMENT 47

Go to the *American Digest System.* Give citations to and brief summaries of court cases on the topics listed in (a) and (b) below. Start with the Descriptive Word Index volumes of the most recent Decennial. After you check the appropriate key numbers in that Decennial, check those key numbers in all the General Digest volumes that follow the most recent Decennial. Then check for case law in at least three other recent Decennials. Once you obtain citations to case law in the digest paragraphs, you do not have to go to the reporters to read the full text of the opinions. Simply give the citations you find and brief summaries of the cases as they are printed in the digest paragraphs.

a. Cases, if any, dealing with the negligence of attorneys in the hiring and supervision of legal secretaries, law clerks, investigators, and paralegals.

b. Cases, if any, dealing with the negligence of doctors and/or hospitals in the hiring and supervision of nurses, paramedics, and other medical technicians.

INSURANCE PROTECTION

Most lawyers have liability or malpractice insurance (sometimes called an error and omissions policy) to protect themselves against suits filed against them for professional negligence or other misconduct growing out of the practice of law. The insurance policy will usually cover paralegals and other employees in the office. An employed paralegal should certainly make inquiries at the firm in order to determine whether the firm has a liability insurance policy, whether it covers paralegals, what exclusions exist in the policy, the maximum coverage, etc. At some point, the paralegal should ask for a copy of the policy and read it carefully.

Free-lance or independent paralegals are in a different situation. They are not full-time, salaried employees of an attorney and hence may not be covered by the firm's insurance policy. Assume that a client sues his/her lawyer for negligence. If the client finds out that the lawyer used a free-lance paralegal on the client's case, the client could join this paralegal as a defendant even though, initially, the client may not be sure what role the paralegal had in the case. A common tactic of angry plaintiffs is to sue *anyone* connected with the case (a) who might be partially responsible for the alleged harm, and (b) who may have assets from which a judgment could be collected. The second criteria is critical. Who has resources or assets? Anyone with a separate office or business, such as a free-lance paralegal, is a tempting target. Even if this paralegal can eventually prove that he or she was not negligent in the case, the costs of presenting this defense can be considerable.

Since the free-lance paralegal concept is relatively new, insurance companies may be initially reluctant to issue separate policies to them except at relatively high rates. As more and more free-lance paralegals go into business on their own, however, it is anticipated that standard insurance policies will be developed to cover them.

Post Script

CHANGE: DEREGULATION OF
THE LEGAL PROFESSION?

The rules on the unauthorized practice of law described in this book reflect the legal profession as it exists today. What about the future? It is unlikely that we will soon see any significant change in the essential structure of the system by which the legal profession and paralegals are regulated.

But calls for change will continue to emerge. Some of the proposals for change are nothing short of revolutionary as demonstrated in the following dramatic speech:

W. DURANT, "MAXIMIZING ACCESS TO JUSTICE:
A CHALLENGE TO THE LEGAL PROFESSION"

(Mr. Durant was the Chairman of the Legal Services Corporation, a federal agency that funds programs that provide legal services to the poor. Mr. Durant made the following comments in a speech before the American Bar Association on February 12, 1987.)

The greatest barrier to widely dispersed low cost dispute resolution services for the poor, and for all people, could very well be the laws protecting our profession. They make it a cartel. . . .

The legal monopoly rests on two major pillars. The first are laws that set aside specific work exclusively for lawyers. Anyone else who performs "lawyer's work" may be prosecuted for the Unauthorized Practice of Law [UPL statutes]. The second is a series of restrictions on how one may become a lawyer. These restrictions are really barriers to competition, not guardians of competence.

Stanford Law School Assistant Professor Deborah Rhode concluded an exhaustive study of UPL statutes and practice by observing that "at every level of enforcement, the consumer's need for protection has been proclaimed rather than proven." The use of UPL prosecutions is "inconsistent, incoherent, and, from a policy perspective, indefensible," she says.

We should encourage at every turn the ability of entrepeneurs, para-professionals and lay people to be a part of the delivery of legal services for the poor and for all people. I've met many eligible clients around the country who can quite capably be advocates in resolving disputes if barriers to practice did not exist. How can doors be open to others to participate in this profession? In serving others a private sector deregulated legal profession can deliver a good quality product in much the same way that a good commercial enterprise does. How do some of our most common necessities get most widely distributed, even to the least of our brethren, at the lowest price and best service? We let the free competitive energies of creative and energetic people in the private sector provide and deliver for us. And, for the most part they do. Such people exist for the delivery of legal services but are blocked by UPL statutes and aggressive Bar efforts to halt them.

Peggy Ann Muse in Oregon, Rose Palmer in Pennsylvania, Richard Grimes in Denver, Colorado; Cecile Browning in Kansas, Virginia Cramer in Michigan, Peter Anderson in Wisconsin, Benny Bonanno in Ohio, Phil Lydic in Washington, Barry Wood in New Jersey, Donald Erickson in Missouri and, of course, Rosemary Furman in Florida are just some of the people who are trying to bring lower cost legal services to poor people and others but are or have been aggressively prosecuted by the organized Bar to prevent them from delivering services or "practicing law".

Peggy Muse's firm in Oregon helped arbitrate claims, collect small debts, and service other cases too small to justify hiring an attorney. Her fees were ⅓ or less than those charged by a lawyer. The State Bar, not her clients, complained. The Bar goes after her.

Rose Palmer who founded Legal Advocacy for Women is not a lawyer but she is typical of people harassed by the organized Bar. She goes to court to give encouragement, advice, and help to women, many who are poor, who are trying to get alimony, child support, and just plain fairness in divorce proceedings. She should be a hero. She is; but not to the local Bar in Pittsburgh. She is receiving city funding for her good work but other possible funding was cancelled after an attorney who represents husbands in divorce proceedings filed a UPL complaint against her.

There are many organizations growing up around the country like Rose Palmer's which can help people use the legal system correctly.

Lori Morelock is the product of one. She enforced her court ordered child support without the use of a lawyer. Virginians Organized To Insure Children's Entitlement to Support gave her training and encouragement. Morelock says that several attorneys urged her to accept welfare payments and stop fighting the child support system. She fired her lawyers and tackled the tasks alone. She was discouraged by both judges and lawyers. But in the end she prevailed.

An attorney in Pittsburgh said it simply. "Many in the Bar are afraid of losing control, of people finding ways to do things on their own without their help. If they let women's groups get away with it, other, more lucrative sectors could do the same thing. And then they would lose money."

There are approximately 1.2 million cases handled annually by programs associated with the Legal Services Corporation. A high degree of specialization for these cases seems not to be required. Almost 30 percent are in the Family Law area common to almost any general practice: divorce, separation, annulment, custody, visitation rights, spouse abuse, and support. Housing cases constitute another 19 percent of legal services cases and less than 3 percent involve public housing. Medicaid and Medicare cases that affect the elderly poor represent less than 2 percent of our cases. Further, about one-third of our cases are closed with no more than brief advice being given. These statistics, like all statistics, do not reveal the whole truth. But they do suggest that a broader array of people from all walks of life could be a part of the delivery of legal services.

The second feature of the legal monopoly restricts how one becomes a lawyer and what you can do when you are one.

In all states, you must pass a bar exam to practice law, though the specific tests vary greatly in terms of length, subjects covered and grading standards. The detailed knowledge necessary for someone to answer a question on constitutional law, for example, may be critical for a law professor or a specialized practitioner, but is probably not required for an attorney specializing in the small claims that normally arise in a neighborhood practice. In many states, a Board of Law Examiners can and do vary the pass/fail rate as if operating a medieval drawbridge.

Two-thirds of the state allow someone to sit for the bar exam *only* if he or she has graduated from a school accredited by the ABA; the rest, except for California, require prospective attorneys to attend a school approved by the ABA *or* the state Bar. Law school accreditation by the ABA reduces the number of law schools, the number of law students, and produces students trained in a particular way that may or may not be just what the consumer wants, or needs, in resolving disputes. This is not a quality control issue. It is an issue of control under the pretext of quality. The automotive industry or the Society of Automotive Engineers does not accredit engineering schools. The industry hires the best qualified people from a wide variety of schools. A relevant basic skills test is fine. Let there be many schools which train lawyers or dispute resolvers in their own way, for their own niche in the market. They can probably do it in significantly less time and at less cost.

Think for a moment if you will of the sea of transactions that exist between people. Think of the millions of disputes that will inevitably arise. They can be resolved in almost an infinite number of ways. An entrepeneur sees an opportunity, an opportunity to give and to serve. Perhaps all one wanted to do all his or her life was to provide easier access for people to enforce their rights or to resolve landlord tenant matters, or domestic or consumer claims. Such a person should not have to spend three years in law school, spend so many thousands of dollars to graduate and then pass comprehensive exams on subjects hardly related in order to provide basic service. Competent practitioners who are not looking for Wall Street but simply wish to handle the simpler, less costly cases, cases most often handled for the poor, and the majority of people, are locked out.

In the market place where millions of transactions take place every day, entrepreneurs are coming up with alternatives to the option of high-priced lawyers. High volume, low price legal clinics have prolife-rated; more than 12 million consumers (and the number grows daily) are now served by prepaid legal plans. Alternative Dispute Resolutions (ADR) centers have jumped from 20 a decade ago to some 330 today. Hyatt Legal Services and Jacoby & Meyers are some of the most entre-preneurial lawyers in existence. They have established hundreds of these effective low cost legal clinics throughout the country. Attorney Van O'Steen in Arizona has developed very effective and low cost self-help legal packets on very routine but important legal services. They all perform a wonderful service because they are taking something as im-portant as justice and making it widely available at a low cost to poor and middle class people. Ten years ago, such would not be possible. You could not advertise legal services, hence you could not develop volume, economies of sale, or effectively provide price competition. While price fixing was once the rule and advertising prohibited until a decade ago, solicitation, broader advertising, reciprocity among states, and other normal competitive practices in any other business are still tightly con-trolled. Even membership in the lawyer's guild is mandatory in many states. The ABA is voluntary and look at its strength. State bars should be voluntary.

The overall effect of this system created and operated by lawyers is to limit entry into the profession, to discourage competition, to increase prices, delays and costs and ultimately to deny access to justice for the poor, for all of us. The legal cartel's heaviest burden falls on the poor. They are denied choices and access. They are denied advocates and opportunities.

State Unauthorized Practice of Law statutes simply should be re-pealed. The legal business should be like any other business subject to the usual consumer protections.

On a federal level, Congress and the President can initiate legisla-tion or executive orders to make it possible for lay people to appear in administrative hearings before administrative boards, and agencies, to prepare necessary documents and advise clients in such matters.

The most effective method for change is the power of a shared vi-sion. Here, it is simply a vision to unleash the tremendous energies of a free and creative people to bring about an open and competitive system of resolving disputes and providing access to justice for all people. It is a vision that offers to entrepreneurs, eligible clients, teachers, ministers, paralegals, social workers, legal secretaries, and so many others a chance to be involved in opening up our profession to develop a broader array of service mechanisms for resolving disputes between people and for providing access to justice. It is a vision to empower communities, individuals and local associations of all sorts, . . . to be involved in the resolution and reconciliation of disputes and people.

The question is really whether we truly want to maximize access to justice and in what ways. Shakespeare is wrong. We need not kill all the lawyers. We simply need to de-regulate them. Open up the profession. Broaden the base. Let more people, let more institutions deliver the services. Costs will come down, services will be expanded and alternatives in resolving disputes will be developed. Deregulation in the trucking, airline, and railroad industries, and even, to some extent the accounting profession, to name but a few, all reflect this positive development for consumers. Justice likewise is too important to be left bottled up by laws protecting the legal profession.

Review Questions

When you complete this book you should:

1. Be able to define (a) accreditation, (b) certification, (c) licensure, (d) registration, (e) approval, (f) code, (g) guideline, and (h) regulation.
2. Know how states use the criminal law to enforce laws against the unauthorized practice of law.
3. Be able to give a definition of the practice of law. Know the main categories of tasks that often fall within a definition of the practice of law.
4. Know why there are laws against the unauthorized practice of law.
5. Know when helping someone fill out forms might constitute the unauthorized practice of law.
6. Know why the Florida Bar Association wanted to have Rosemary Furman prosecuted.
7. Know what an "inter-occupational treaty" is between the legal profession and other occupations. Know what a statement of principle is.
8. Know the names of some of the main occupations that have entered such "treaties" with the legal profession.
9. Be able to state another method by which occupations acquire the right to perform tasks that would otherwise constitute the unauthorized practice of law.
10. Know the difference between saying, "paralegals cannot practice law," and "paralegals cannot engage in the unauthorized practice of law."
11. Know whether lawyers are solely interested in protecting the public when they support the enforcement of laws on the unauthorized practice of law.
12. Know why lawyers have not been able to maintain an exclusive monopoly over the practice of law.
13. Be able to give examples of where a paralegal is allowed to represent clients in court.
14. Know the role of nonlawyers in Tribal Courts.

15. Know the role of nonlawyer probation officers and social workers in the courts of some states.

16. Know whether it is the unauthorized practice of law for a paralegal to answer a calendar or motion call in the courts of most states.

17. Be able to describe the "paralegal rules of practice" program in the Allen County Bar Association of Indiana.

18. Be able to compare this Indiana program with that of several counties in Washington state, e.g., Tacoma-Pierce County.

19. Know what a jailhouse lawyer is.

20. Know what *Johnson v. Avery* decided.

21. Know how the rationale of the *Johnson* opinion might be expanded to legitimize other nonlawyer activities that are now within the exclusive domain of lawyers.

22. Know what *Procunier v. Martinez* decided.

23. Know what *Bounds v. Smith* decided.

24. Know what Justice Douglas thinks about rules on the unauthorized practice of law.

25. Know how Justice Douglas would describe a legal problem of the poor.

26. Know what the Administrative Procedure Act says about agency representation by nonlawyers.

27. Know the different ways that agencies authorize nonlawyer representation.

28. Be able to describe the role of (a) registered agents in the United States Patent Office, (b) nonlawyer practitioners at the Interstate Commerce Commission, and (c) enrolled agents or enrolled actuaries at the Internal Revenue Service.

29. Be able to describe laws governing paralegal practice before the Social Security Administration.

30. Know the name of the case holding that federal laws allowing paralegal practice at federal agencies take precedence or supremacy over state laws that prohibit such practice.

31. Know when a state agency's authorization of paralegal practice is valid.

32. Know why some lawyers are reluctant to allow paralegals to represent clients at agencies even where the latter authorize it.

33. Know whether any state now licenses paralegals.

34. Be able to give a brief description of licensing proposals in (a) Michigan, (b) Arizona, (c) Oregon, and (d) California.

35. Know why most lawyers are opposed to the licensing of paralegals.

36. Know whether it is a conflict of interest for lawyers to control paralegal regulation.

37. Know whether it is a conflict of interest for paralegals to control paralegal regulation.
38. Know the major steps that should be taken when a licensing bill is proposed in your state.
39. Know how lawyers are regulated. Know the process by which a lawyer can be disciplined.
40. Know why a paralegal cannot be disciplined by a bar association.
41. Be able to describe the relationship between the American Bar Association and state bar associations.
42. Distinguish between (a) the ABA Model Code of Professional Responsibility, and (b) the ABA Model Rules of Professional Conduct.
43. Be able to define (a) a canon, (b) a disciplinary rule—DR, and (c) an ethical consideration—EC.
44. Know why paralegals must understand the ethical obligations of lawyers.
45. Be able to describe the ethical rules governing lawyers on (a) competence, (b) client crimes and fraud, (c) candor and honesty, (d) communication with the client, (e) fees, (f) confidentiality, (g) conflict of interest, (h) gifts from clients, (i) property of the client, (j) withdrawal from a case, (k) frivolous claims (l) communicating with the opposing party, (m) advertising, (n) solicitation, (o) reporting professional misconduct, and (p) the appearance of impropriety.
46. Be able to state the essence of the following documents that directly pertain to the use of paralegals: (a) DR-101, (b) EC 3-6, (c) ABA Formal Opinion 316, and (d) ABA Model Rule 5.3.
47. Be able to identify ethical problems, if any, concerning the title of this new career in law.
48. Be able to identify ethical problems, if any, concerning signing letters on law firm stationery.
49. Be able to identify ethical problems, if any, concerning a paralegal's name printed on law firm stationery.
50. Be able to identify ethical problems, if any, concerning business cards for paralegals.
51. Be able to identify ethical problems, if any, concerning oral communication of a paralegal's nonlawyer status.
52. Be able to identify ethical problems, if any, concerning a paralegal's name printed (a) on a door, or, (b) in a document submitted to a court.
53. Be able to identify ethical problems, if any, concerning a lawyer and paralegal forming a partnership.

54. Be able to identify ethical problems, if any, concerning a lawyer and paralegal sharing fees.
55. Be able to identify ethical problems, if any, concerning a paralegal's participation in the retirement program of a firm.
56. Be able to identify ethical problems, if any, concerning paralegal communication with the client of the opposing side.
57. Be able to identify ethical problems, if any, concerning paralegal communication with opposing counsel.
58. Be able to identify ethical problems, if any, concerning paralegal attendance at a real estate closing.
59. Be able to identify ethical problems, if any, concerning a paralegal asking questions at a deposition.
60. Be able to identify ethical problems, if any, concerning paralegal interviewing clients.
61. Know the broad and narrow interpretations of Sub-Rule 2 in the Kentucky Paralegal Code.
62. Know the major ways that a lawyer fulfills his/her ethical obligation to supervise a paralegal.
63. Know whether a paralegal can have a direct relationship with a client.
64. Know the purpose of the attorney-client privilege.
65. Know whether paralegals or any other nonlawyers are protected by the attorney-client privilege.
66. Be able to state the rule on confidentiality as expressed by the National Association of Legal Assistants and by the National Federation of Paralegal Associations.
67. Be able to give examples of paralegal violation of the rule on confidentiality.
68. Be able to identify the ethical problems that might exist when a paralegal moves from one job to another.
69. Be able to identify the ethical problems that might exist in a freelance paralegal business.
70. Be able to list the main sets of books that you would use to research an ethical issue.
71. Be able to explain the ABA school approval process, including the role of the ABA Approval Commission, the ABA Committee on Legal Assistants, and the ABA House of Delegates.
72. Know the antitrust argument that was made against the ABA in *Paralegal Institute, Inc. v. American Bar Association.*
73. Be able to describe the proposal for an independent accrediting body.
74. Be able to state the holding in *Goldfarb v. Virginia State Bar.*
75. Know the conflict-of-interest argument against lawyer control of the education approval process or of any other aspect of paralegal regulation.

76. Be able to describe the operation of the Legal Assistant Division of the State Bar of Texas.
77. Know the arguments for and against paralegal membership in bar associations.
78. Know the difference in structure between NALA and NFPA.
79. Be able to describe some of the major similarities and differences in (a) NALA's Code of Ethics and Professional Responsibility, and (b) NFPA's Affirmation of Responsibility.
80. Be able to describe NALA's (a) basic CLA certification process, and (b) NALA's specialty certification process.
81. Be able to describe NALA's main arguments in favor of paralegal certification.
82. Be able to describe NFPA's main arguments in opposition to the paralegal certification program of NALA.
83. Be able to state the reason why NALA proposed the Model Standards for the Utilization of Legal Assistants.
84. Know the reasons why NFPA opposes the Model Standards.
85. Be able to state when paralegals are and are not entitled to overtime compensation under the Fair Labor Standards Act.
86. Be able to state the basic principle of respondeat superior.
87. Know when a paralegal is responsible for his/her own intentional torts.
88. Know when an employer is responsible for the intentional torts of his/her paralegals.
89. Be able to state the basic standard of care in a negligence case involving a trade or profession.
90. Know when a paralegal is responsible for his/her own negligence.
91. Know when an employer is responsible for the negligence of his/her paralegals.
92. Know what insurance protection might govern a paralegal in a law office.

Appendix A

State Bar Associations
Local Bar Associations

ALABAMA

Alabama State Bar
P.O. Box 671
Montgomery, AL 36101
205-269-1515

Birmingham Bar Association
109 N. 20th St.
Birmingham, AL 35203
205-251-8006

ALASKA

Alaska Bar Association
P.O. Box 279
Anchorage, AK 99510
907-272-7469

ARIZONA

State Bar of Arizona
363 N. 1st Ave.
Phoenix, AZ 85004
602-252-4804

Maricopa County Bar Association
3033 N. Central Ave.
Phoenix, AZ 85012
602-277-2366

ARKANSAS

Arkansas Bar Association
400 W. Markham
Little Rock, AR 72201
501-375-4605

CALIFORNIA

State Bar of California
555 Franklin St.
San Francisco, CA 94102
415-561-8200

Alameda County Bar Association
405 14th St.
Oakland, CA 94611
415-893-7160

Bar Association of San Francisco
220 Bush St.
San Francisco, CA 94102
415-392-3960

Beverly Hills Bar Association
300 S. Beverly Dr.
Beverly Hills, CA 90212
213-533-6644

Lawyers Club of Los Angeles
P.O. Box 58525
Los Angeles, CA 90058
213-624-2525

Lawyers Club of San Francisco
870 Market St.
San Francisco, CA 94102
415-433-2133

Los Angeles County Bar
P.O. Box 55020
Los Angeles, CA 90055
213-627-2727

Orange County Bar Association
601 Civic Center Dr. W.
Santa Ana, CA 92701
714-541-6222

San Diego County Bar Association
1434 Fifth Ave.
San Diego, CA 92101
619-231-0781

Santa Clara County Bar
   Association
111 N. Market St.
San Jose, CA 95115
408-288-8840

COLORADO

Colorado Bar Association
1900 Grant St., #950
Denver, CO 80203
303-860-1112

Denver Bar Association
1900 Grant St.
Denver, CO 80203
303-860-1112

CONNECTICUT

Connecticut Bar Association
101 Corporate Place
Rocky Hill, CT 06067
203-721-0025

DELAWARE

Delaware State Bar Association
820 N. French St.
Wilmington, DE 19801
302-658-5278

DISTRICT OF COLUMBIA

The District of Columbia Bar
1426 H. St. NW
Washington, D.C. 20005
202-638-1500

Bar Association of the District of
   Columbia
1819 H. St. NW
Suite 300
Washington, D.C. 20006
202-223-1480

FLORIDA

The Florida Bar
The Florida Bar Center
Tallahassee, FL 32301
904-222-5286

Dade County Bar Association
111 N.W. First Ave.
Miami, FL 33128
305-379-0641

GEORGIA

State Bar of Georgia
84 Peachtree St.
Atlanta, GA 30303
404-522-6255

Atlanta Bar Association
606 Equitable Bldg.
Atlanta, GA 30303
404-521-0781

HAWAII

Hawaii State Bar
P.O. Box 26
Honolulu, HI 96810
808-537-1868

IDAHO

Idaho State Bar
P.O. Box 895
Boise, ID 83701
208-342-8958

ILLINOIS

Illinois State Bar Association
Illinois Bar Center
Springfield, IL 62701
217-525-1760

The Chicago Bar Association
29 S. LaSalle St.
Chicago, IL 60603
312-782-7348

Chicago Council of Lawyers
220 S. State St.
Chicago, IL 60604
312-427-0710

INDIANA

Indiana State Bar Association
230 East Ohio St.
Indianapolis, IN 46204
317-639-5465

Indianapolis Bar Association
One Indiana Sq.
Indianapolis, IN 46204
317-632-8240

IOWA

Iowa State Bar Association
1101 Fleming Bldg.
Des Moines, IA 50309
515-243-3179

KANSAS

Kansas Bar Association
1200 Harrison St.
P.O. Box 1037
Topeka, KS 66601
913-234-5696

KENTUCKY

Kentucky Bar Association
West Main at Kentucky River
Frankfort, KY 40601
502-564-3795

Louisville Bar Association
717 W. Main St.
Louisville, KY 40202
502-583-5314

LOUISIANA

Louisiana State Bar Association
210 O'Keefe Ave.
No. 600
New Orleans, LA 70112
504-566-1600

MAINE

Maine State Bar Association
124 State St.
P.O. Box 788
August, ME 04330
207-622-7523

MARYLAND

Maryland State Bar Association
207 E. Redwood St.
Baltimore, MD 21202
301-685-7878

Bar Association of Baltimore City
627 Courthouse East
111 N. Calvert St.
Baltimore, MD 21202
301-539-5936

MASSACHUSETTS

Massachusetts Bar Association
20 West St.
Boston, MA 02111
617-542-3602

Boston Bar Association
16 Beacon St.
Boston, MA 02108
617-742-0615

MICHIGAN

State Bar of Michigan
306 Townsend St.
Lansing, MI 48933
517-372-9030

Detroit Bar Association
2380 Penobscot Bldg.
Detroit, MI 48226
313-961-6120

Oakland County Bar Association
1200 N. Telegraph Rd.
Pontiac, MI 48053
313-338-2100

MINNESOTA

Minnesota State Bar Association
430 Marquette Ave.
Minneapolis, MN 55401
612-335-1183

Hennepin County Bar Association
430 Marquette Ave.
Minneapolis, MN 55402
612-340-0022

MISSISSIPPI

Mississippi State Bar
P.O. Box 2168
Jackson, MS 39205
601-948-4471

MISSOURI

The Missouri Bar
P.O. Box 119
Jefferson City, MO 65102
314-635-4128

Kansas City Bar Association
P.O. Box 26276
Kansas City, MO 64196
816-474-4322

Bar Association of Metropolitan
  St. Louis
One Mercantile Center
St. Louis, MO 63101
314-421-4134

MONTANA

State Bar of Montana
P.O. Box 4669
Helena, MT 59604
406-442-7660

NEBRASKA

Nebraska State Bar Association
635 South 14th St.
Lincoln, NB 68508
402-475-7091

NEVADA

State Bar of Nevada
834 Willow St.
Reno, NV 89502
702-329-4100

NEW HAMPSHIRE

New Hampshire Bar Association
18 Centre St.
Concord, NH 03301
603-224-6942

NEW JERSEY

New Jersey State Bar Association
172 W. State St.
Trenton, NJ 08608
609-394-1101

Essex County Bar Association
24 Commerce St.
Newark, NJ 07102
201-622-6207

NEW MEXICO

State Bar of New Mexico
P.O. Box 25883
Albuquerque, NM 87125
505-842-6132

NEW YORK

New York State Bar Association
One Elk St.
Albany, NY 12207
518-445-1211

Association of the Bar of the City
of New York
42 W. 44th St.
New York, NY 10036
212-382-6600

New York County Lawyers
Association
14 Vesey St.
New York, NY 10007
212-267-6646

NORTH CAROLINA

North Carolina State Bar
P.O. Box 25908
Raleigh, NC 27611
919-828-4620

North Carolina Bar Association
P.O. Box 12806
Raleigh, NC 27605
919-828-0561

NORTH DAKOTA

State Bar Association of North
Dakota
P.O. Box 2136
Bismarck, ND 58502
701-255-1404

OHIO

Ohio State Bar Association
33 W. 11th Ave.
Columbus, OH 43201
614-421-2121

The Bar Association of Greater
Cleveland
118 St. Clair Ave.
Cleveland, OH 44114
216-696-3525

Cincinnati Bar Association
26 E. 6th St.
Cincinnati, OH 45202
513-381-8213

Columbus Bar Association
66 S. Third St.
Columbus, OH 43215
614-221-4112

Cuyahoga County Bar
Association
850 Euclid Ave.
Cleveland, OH 44114
216-621-5112

OKLAHOMA

Oklahoma Bar Association
P.O. Box 53036
Oklahoma City, OK 73152
405-524-2365

Oklahoma County Bar
Association
500 W. Maine
Oklahoma City, OK 73102
405-236-8421

Tulsa County Bar Association
1446 S. Boston
Tulsa, OK 74119
918-584-5243

OREGON

Oregon State Bar
1776 S.W. Madison
Portland, OR 97205
503-224-4280

Multnomah Bar Association
711 S.W. Alder
Portland, OR 97205
503-222-3275

PENNSYLVANIA

Pennsylvania Bar Association
100 South St.
P.O. Box 186
Harrisburg, PA 17108
717-238-6715

Allegheny County Bar Association
920 City-Cty. Bldg.
Pittsburgh, PA 15219
412-261-0518

Philadelphia Bar Association
1339 Chestnut St.
Philadelphia, PA 19107
215-686-5686

PUERTO RICO

Puerto Rico Bar Association
Box 1900
San Juan, PR 00903
809-721-3358

RHODE ISLAND

Rhode Island Bar Association
91 Friendship St.
Providence, RI 02903
401-421-5740

SOUTH CAROLINA

South Carolina Bar Association
P.O. Box 11039
Columbia, SC 29211
803-799-6653

SOUTH DAKOTA

State Bar of South Dakota
222 E. Capitol
Pierre, SD 57501
605-224-7554

TENNESSEE

Tennessee Bar Association
3622 W. End Ave.
Nashville, TN 37205
615-383-7421

TEXAS

State Bar of Texas
P.O. Box 12487
Austin, TX 78711
512-475-4200

Dallas Bar Association
2101 Ross Ave.
Dallas, TX 75201
214-969-7066

Houston Bar Association
707 Travis St.
Houston, TX 77002
713-222-1441

UTAH

Utah State Bar
425 E. First South
Salt Lake City, UT 84111
801-531-9077

VERMONT

Vermont Bar Association
P.O. Box 100
Montpelier, VT 05602
802-223-2020

VIRGINIA

Virginia State Bar
Suite 1622, 700 Bldg.
700 East Main St.
Richmond, VA 23219
804-786-2061

Virginia Bar Association
701 Franklin Bldg.
Richmond, VA 23219
804-664-0041

WASHINGTON

Washington State Bar Association
505 Madison
Seattle, WA 98104
206-622-6054

Seattle-King County Bar
  Association
320 Central Bldg.
Seattle, WA 98104
206-624-9365

WASHINGTON D.C.

See District of Columbia

WEST VIRGINIA

West Virginia State Bar
State Capitol, E-400
Charleston, WV 25305
304-346-8414

West Virginia Bar Association
P.O. Box 346
Charleston, WV 25322
304-342-1474

WISCONSIN

State Bar of Wisconsin
P.O. Box 7158
Madison, WI 53707
608-257-3838

Milwaukee Bar Association
610 E. Wisconsin Ave.
Milwaukee, WI 53202
414-274-6760

WYOMING

Wyoming State Bar
P.O. Box 109
Cheyenne, WY 82003
307-632-9061

Appendix B

Bar Association and
Court Opinions
on Paralegals

Chicago Bar Association
Real Property Law Committee Recommendations
4/5/83

THE USE OF PARALEGALS IN
REAL ESTATE TRANSACTIONS

The paralegal may perform such tasks in connection with a real estate transaction as are assigned by the employing attorney, provided that the tasks are performed under the direction and supervision of, and are reviewed by, the attorney and do not involve the giving of legal advice. The paralegal may attend a closing with the employing attorney. A paralegal may close a real estate transaction, unaccompanied by the employing attorney, only (i) if all documents have been prepared and approved by all parties in advance of the closing, (ii) with prior consent of other counsel, and (iii) with the employing attorney being available for consultation and instructions by telephone. Within the foregoing limitations, the use of a paralegal to close a real estate transaction, unaccompanied by the employing attorney, should be approached with caution, having regard to the skill and experience of the paralegal, the complexity of the transaction and the client-attorney relationship, and bearing in mind that the employing attorney retains ultimate responsibility for the transaction.

Florida Bar Association
Committee on Professional Ethics
Advisory Opinion No. 73-43

. . . .

2. Whether the employee may attend closings of sales of condominium units to be held in the firm's office but without any attorneys in the firm being present. She will give no legal advice.

. . . .

Cannot Act without lawyer

We answer the second question in the negative. The question itself recognizes that the employee may not give legal advice or perform any acts that would amount to practicing law. The committee, one member dissenting in part, is of the opinion that there is no reason for the employee to attend the closings except to give legal advice and that her presence could be construed as answering unasked questions about the propriety or legality of documents. One committeeman is of the opinion that the employee may properly attend such closings provided she does nothing more than distribute documents for signature.

Below you will find two opinions of the New Jersey Bar Association and one of the New York State Bar Association. Note the differences in the approaches taken by the two bar associations. New Jersey is quite restrictive. New York was also once restrictive, but became considerably less so when the U.S. Supreme Court decided *Bates v. State of Arizona,* 433 U.S. 350 (1977). The *Bates* opinion sent shock waves throughout the legal profession. It struck down laws that prohibited all forms of lawyer advertising. One effect of *Bates* was to cause some bar associations, such as New York, to allow paralegals to have their names printed on law firm stationery. Before *Bates,* this practice was frowned upon as a practice that was contrary to professional dignity and etiquette. It also suggested commercialization and a form of publicity for the firm. Once advertising was permitted after *Bates,* however, the practice was no longer considered unacceptable. Some states, however, such as New Jersey, still adhere to the more conservative position.

New Jersey Bar Association
Supreme Court of New Jersey's Advisory Committee
on Professional Ethics, Opinion 296
(98 N.J.L.J. 105, Feb. 6, 1975)

PARALEGAL EMPLOYEES—IDENTIFICATION WITH LAW FIRMS

Three inquiries have been submitted to this Committee relating to investigators and paralegal employees of a law firm.

Question One

Is it ethically proper for an attorney or firm to permit an investigator-paralegal full-time employee to sign correspondence on the attorney's or firm's letterhead where he identifies himself as a nonlawyer?

A paralegal employee is a lay person employed by an attorney to perform certain law office functions for which legal training and bar admission are not required.

Disciplinary Rule 3–101(A) reads as follows:

"A lawyer shall not aid a non-lawyer in the unauthorized practice of law."

Attorneys should avoid not only unprofessional conduct but also the appearance of such conduct. Our *Opinion* 8, 86 N.J.L.J. 718 (1963) and 9, 86 N.J.L.J. 617 (1963).

If a staff investigator were permitted to sign correspondence on the firm letterhead, such a seemingly innocent practice could foster myriad abuses, not the least of which might be the unauthorized practice of law in violation of *DR* 3–101(A). Such signed correspondence, even accompanied by an identification of the investigatory position of the signatory, might be taken as a representation that the layman is involved in the firm's practice in a manner contrary to *DR* 3–101(A) and *DR* 3-103(A). Given such a possible consequence, it is our conclusion that such practice cannot be sanctioned.

Question Two

May a firm include on its letterhead the name of a full-time investigative employee along with his title as staff investigator?

The American Bar Association, Standing Committee on Professional Ethics, *Informal Opinion* 619 (1962), quoting *Drinker, Legal Ethics* (1953) 228, refused to allow a secretary's name to appear on a lawyer's letterhead stating:

"A lawyer's letterhead may not carry the name of a client or of a patent agent associate, non-lawyer, notary or engineer or clerk or student or other layman, or give the names of references, or state that a layman's association is associated with him in handling collections. . . . "

Similarly, ABA *Informal Opinion* 845 (1965) held that the inclusion of a name on a letterhead with the designation "office manager" would be improper. Likewise, ABA *Informal Opinion* 1000 (1967), citing both *Informal Opinions* 619 and 845, supra held:

". . . that it would be improper to list your salaried investigator on your firm letterhead as 'Staff Investigator' or in any other manner."

Disciplinary Rule 2–102(A)(4) stipulates that an attorney or firm can use no letterhead except one of a prescribed content and dignified form. Additionally *DR* 2–101 inveighs generally against self-laudation, an inescapable effect should we allow the inclusion of a staff investigator's name and title on the letterhead. In ABA *Informal Opinion* 845, supra, it was stated that use of such a letterhead would:

> ". . . impress upon those seeing the letterhead the size, importance and efficiency of the firm. . . ."

Clearly, such a letterhead would have a self-laudatory effect, contravening the spirit of *DR* 2–101 in addition to offending the letter of *DR* 2–102(A)(4), and therefore it cannot be permitted.

Question Three

We are also called upon to consider whether the use by such an investigator-paralegal employee of a business card in the following form would be ethically proper:

John Doe
Investigator
Firm Name & Address Tel. No. 123–4567

We considered this question in our *Opinion* 9, supra, and answered it in the negative. Parenthetically, it might be added, that we maintain this position in full cognizance of the American Bar Association Committee on Professional Ethics, *Informal Opinion* 909 (1966) which saw fit to sanction such cards, though the committee admitted:

> ". . . It is true, of course, that the card is a physical article and that possibilities of its improper use or effect are far greater than in the case of an oral identification. . . ."

As was stated in *Opinion* 9, supra, of this Committee:

> "There are, of course, other ways of identification besides the suggested means, without any possible abuse or misrepresentation."

Therefore, such cards may not be used as they are in possible derogation of the general integrity of the legal profession.

**Supreme Court of New Jersey's Advisory Committee on
Professional Ethics, Opinion 296 (Supplement)
(99 N.J.L.J. 113, Feb. 12, 1976)**

PARALEGAL EMPLOYEES—
IDENTIFICATION WITH LAW FIRMS

The Professional Economics Committee of the New Jersey State Bar Association and several law firms of this State have petitioned that we reconsider *Opinion* 296, 98 N.J.L.J. 105 (1975), relating to the use of paralegals in law offices.

The original opinion dealt with three inquiries. The petition for reconsideration was limited to Question One.

In response to Questions Two and Three, we had held that the names of nonlawyers may not be included on a firm letterhead and the use of the firm business card identifying a nonlawyer was improper.

For convenience we repeat Question One in full:

> "Is it ethically proper for an attorney or firm to permit an investigator-paralegal full-time employee to sign correspondence on the attorney's or firm's letterhead where he identifies himself as a non-lawyer?"

The inquiry as posed called for the approval of the unrestricted right of a paralegal employee to sign correspondence on the attorney's or firm's letterhead.

A hearing was held before this Committee on the petition for review to decide the propriety of our determination and whether it should be modified. The use of paraprofessionals was described as being in a state of development, a development which the petitioners urged as being in the best interests of the public and practicing lawyers.

The American Bar Association has recently concluded extensive hearings concerning the use of paraprofessionals and the subject is still under discussion.

There are two kinds of legal paraprofessionals:

1. Those who assist lawyers on behalf of clients, performing a variety of tasks, such as investigation, drafting, tax return preparation and research, which are performed under the supervision of a lawyer who is completely responsible for that work to a client. See American Bar Association, Committee on Professional Ethics, *Opinion* 316 (1967) and Code of Professional Responsibility *EC* 3–6. These paralegals cannot counsel clients, interpret the law, or represent people in adversary proceedings.

2. Individuals involved in the management of law firms who are not involved in the rendition of legal services, but who assist the partners in the conduct of their practice.

As noted, the original inquiry was unrestricted and made no differentiation between the kinds of paraprofessionals. As to the latter, the ministerial or office-type matters not involving the practice of law, we see no objection to the paralegal's signing such correspondence, since it does not in any way involve the practice of law. As to the former, we believe that routine requests for documents from officials, court stenographers, and the like would not constitute the practice of law and should be permitted.

However, we believe that any interaction with other attorneys, law firms, parties, or agents of parties would tend to aid in the practice of law by laymen. Parenthetically, in the course of the hearings, one of the firms described its use of paraprofessionals in "adjusting" property claims. Whether that would constitute the unauthorized practice of law is a point which we need not decide here, but it is an apt illustration of the difficulty in permitting the unrestricted use of paraprofessional assistance.

It is not the function of this Committee to undertake to designate every particular act or function of lay employees which would constitute the unauthorized practice of law. Whenever any question might reasonably arise, it seems to us that the profession's duty to the public and the recognition of the need to preserve the dignity of the profession suggest that correspondence ought to be signed by the responsible lawyer in the firm. Since the ultimate responsibility must reside with the attorney in the firm, the burden of signing the correspondence ought not to be intolerable.

. . .

In summary, we conclude that *Opinion* 296 should be modified by amending the answer to Question One, to permit the paraprofessional to sign the letter if his identity is clearly stated and under the guidelines noted in this opinion.

We reiterate that a paralegal should never perform services which involve the exercise of the professional judgment of a lawyer, nor should he advise clients with respect to their legal rights, nor should the activities of a paralegal in any way modify or interfere with direct attorney-client relationships or those between an attorney and his opposing attorney.

Our modification of *Opinion* 296 does not extend to Questions Two and Three which are not being amended by this opinion. Accordingly, we would modify our original opinion as follows:

> 1. A lay assistant may sign letterhead stationery of a law firm involving administrative communications not involving the practice of law to ministerial officials, vendors, and others.
>
> 2. A lay assistant may sign letterhead stationery of the law firm addressed to other administrative personnel, such as court printers, stenographers, court clerks, record custodians, and the like.

New York State Bar Association

New York State Bar Association, Committee on Professional Ethics, Opinion #500 (12/6/78) (52–78)

Question

May the letterhead of a law firm list certain non-lawyer employees such as registered patent agents and paralegals?

Opinion

Prior to the recent amendment of our Code of Professional Responsibility, DR 2–102(A)(4) rigidly circumscribed the information that could be disclosed on a lawyer's professional letterhead. The former Disciplinary Rule did far more than prohibit the inclusion of untruthful or misleading information. It was intended to set a standard of professional dignity which standard was, in turn, thought to encourage public confidence in both the profession and the administration of justice. See, *e.g.,* former EC 2–9 and EC 2–10.

Under this standard, as well as those of former Canon 27, the listing of all non-lawyer employees on a lawyer's letterhead was prohibited. See, *e.g.,* N.Y. State 261 (1972) (paralegals), N.Y. County 589 (1971) (patent agents), N.Y. City 545 (1940) (non-lawyer patent attorney), N.Y. City 829 (1937) (patent agents), ABA Inf. 1367 (1976) (paralegals), ABA Inf. 845 (1965) (office manager), ABA Inf. 619 (1962) (lawyer's secretary); *cf.,* N.Y. State 85 (1968) and ABA Inf. 571(b) (1962) (involving potentially misleading information concerning lawyers).

The Supreme Court's decision in *Bates* v. *State of Arizona,* 433 U.S. 350 (1977), led to the adoption in this State of major amendments to the Ethical Considerations and Disciplinary Rules under Canon 2. These amendments not only incorporated the court adopted uniform rules governing lawyer advertising and publicity, but included a number of other court authorized liberalizing amendments permitting the free flow of reliable and useful information about lawyers and their services. See, N.Y. State 487 (1978).

The basic impact of these amendments was to bring about a revolutionary shift of emphasis in favor of the dissemination of information "designed to educate the public to an awareness of legal needs and to provide information relevant to the selection of the most appropriate counsel." DR 2–101(D), as amended. Disciplinary Rules which had seemed to interfere with the dissemination of such information primarily for reasons of professional dignity and etiquette were either repealed or substantially modified. In place of the former broad prohibitions on publicity and commercial advertising, the amendments essentially narrowed the ambit of proscription to specified practices which in themselves were thought to be injurious to both the profession and the public. See, amended DR 2–101(A) and (B); see also, amended EC 2–10.

The only explicit references to professional letterheads contained in the amended Code are now set forth in DR 2–102(A)(4) and (D)* Except for the requirements of DR 2–102(D) relating to lawyers not admit-

---

* As amended, DR 2–102 now provides in relevant part:

A. A lawyer or law firm may use professional cards, professional announcement cards, office signs, letterheads or similar professional notices or devices, provided the same do not violate any statute or court rule, and are in accordance with DR 2–101, including the following:

* * *

(Footnote continued on page 166.)

ted to practice in all jurisdictions listed on a firm's letterhead, the only limitation on information appearing on letterheads is that the information be "in accordance with DR 2–101." The most important of the standards established by amended DR 2–101 are set forth in subdivisions (A), (B) and (D) which now provide:

> A. A lawyer on behalf of himself or herself or partners or associates, shall not use or disseminate or participate in the preparation or dissemination of any public communication containing statements or claims that are false, deceptive, misleading or cast reflection on the legal profession as a whole.

> B. Advertising or other publicity by lawyers, including participation in public functions, shall not contain puffery, self-laudation, claims regarding the quality of the lawyers' legal services, or claims that cannot be measured or verified.

> * * *

> D. Advertising and publicity shall be designed to educate the public to an awareness of legal needs and to provide information relevant to the selection of the most appropriate counsel. Information other than that specifically authorized in subdivision (C) that is consistent with these purposes may be disseminated providing that it does not violate any other provisions of this rule."

The effect of these amendments is to permit lawyers to include on their letterheads the names of their non-lawyer employees whenever the inclusion of such names would not be deceptive and might reasonably be expected to supply information relevant to the selection of counsel.

While non-lawyer status will no longer preclude the use of a person's name on a firm's letterhead, his name should be accompanied by language that makes clear his non-lawyer status. *Cf.,* DR 2–102(D) (requiring a clear statement concerning the "jurisdictional limitations" of a firm's "members and associates" who appear on its letterhead). Thus, for example, the term "registered patent agent" should be qualified by a designation such as "nonlawyer." Even then, to avoid deception, such persons should only be listed when their non-lawyer status is relevant to the work of the firm. See, DR 2–101(A) and DR 2–102(A).

(Unlike the term "registered patent agent," the term "paralegal," albeit somewhat imprecise, is sufficient without further qualification to

4. A letterhead identifying the lawyer by name and as a lawyer, and giving the addresses, telephone numbers, the name of the law firm, associates and any information permitted under DR 2–105. A letterhead of a law firm may also give the names of members and associates, and names and dates relating to deceased and retired members. A lawyer may be designated 'Of Counsel' on a letterhead if there is a continuing relationship with a lawyer or law firm, other than as a partner or associate. A lawyer or law firm may be designated as 'General Counsel' or by similar professional reference on stationery of a client if the lawyer or the firm devotes a substantial amount of professional time in the

(Continued)

make clear the employee's non-lawyer status. Whether use of the term "paralegal" is appropriate to the actual status enjoyed by the employee is another question to be determined under the standards established by DR 2–101(A).)

Our prior opinion in N.Y. State 261, *supra,* is overruled to the extent that the same is inconsistent with the foregoing.

For the reasons stated, and subject to the qualifications hereinabove set forth, the question posed is answered in the affirmative.

United States v. Kovel

United States Court of Appeals, Second Circuit, 1961
296 F.2d 918.

FRIENDLY, Circuit Judge.

This appeal from a sentence for criminal contempt for refusing to answer a question asked in the course of an inquiry by a grand jury raises an important issue as to the application of the attorney-client privilege to a non-lawyer employed by a law firm.

Kovel is a former Internal Revenue agent having accounting skills. Since 1943 he has been employed by Kamerman & Kamerman, a law firm specializing in tax law. A grand jury in the Southern District of New York was investigating alleged Federal income tax violations by Hopps, a client of the law firm; Kovel was subpoenaed to appear on September 6, 1961. The law firm advised the Assistant United States Attorney that since Kovel was an employee under the direct supervision of the partners, Kovel could not disclose any communications by the client or the result of any work done for the client, unless the latter consented; the Assistant answered that the attorney-client privilege did not apply to one who was not an attorney.

On September 7, the grand jury appeared before Judge Cashin. The Assistant United States Attorney informed the judge that Kovel had refused to answer "several questions * * * on the grounds of attorney-client privilege"; he proffered "respectable authority * * * that an accountant, even if he is retained or employed by a firm of attorneys, cannot take the privilege." The judge answered "You don't have to give me any authority on that." A court reporter testified that Kovel, after an initial claim of privilege had admitted receiving a statement of Hopps' assets and liabilities, but that, when asked "what was the purpose of your receiving that," had declined to answer on the ground of privilege "Be-

representation of that client. The letterhead of a law firm may give the names and dates of predecessor firms in a continuing line of succession.

Amended DR 2–102(D) provides:

D. A partnership shall not be formed or continued between or among lawyers licensed in different jurisdictions unless all enumerations of the members and associates of the firm on its letterhead and in other permissible listings makes clear the jurisdictional limitations on those members and associates of the firm not licensed to practice in all jurisdictions; however, the same firm name may be used in each jurisdiction.

cause the communication was received with a purpose, as stated by the client"; later questions and answers indicated the communication was a letter addressed to Kovel. After verifying that Kovel was not a lawyer, the judge directed him to answer, saying "You have no privilege as such." The reporter then read another question Kovel had refused to answer, "Did you ever discuss with Mr. Hopps or give Mr. Hopps any information with regard to treatment for capital gains purposes of the Atlantic Beverage Corporation sale by him?" The judge again directed Kovel to answer reaffirming "There is no privilege—you are entitled to no privilege, as I understand the law."

Later on September 7, they and Kovel's employer, Jerome Kamerman, now acting as his counsel, appeared again before Judge Cashin. The Assistant told the judge that Kovel had "refused to answer some of the questions which you had directed him to answer." A reporter reread so much of the transcript heretofore summarized as contained the first two refusals. The judge offered Kovel another opportunity to answer, reiterating the view, "There is no privilege to this man at all." Counsel referred to New York Civil Practice Act, § 353, which we quote in the margin.*

Counsel reiterated that an employee "who sits with the client of the law firm * * * occupies the same status * * * as a clerk or stenographer or any other lawyer * * *"; the judge was equally clear that the privilege was never "extended beyond the attorney." The court held [Kovel] in contempt, sentenced him to a year's imprisonment, ordered immediate commitment and denied bail. Later in the day, the grand jury having indicted, Kovel was released until September 12, at which time, without opposition from the Government, I granted bail pending determination of this appeal.

Here the parties continue to take generally the same positions as below—Kovel, that his status as an employee of a law firm automatically made all communications to him from clients privileged; the Government, that under no circumstances could there be privilege with respect to communications to an accountant. The New York County Lawyers' Association as *amicus curiae* has filed a brief generally supporting appellant's position.

Decision under what circumstances, if any, the attorney-client privilege may include a communication to a nonlawyer by the lawyer's client is the resultant of two conflicting forces. One is the general teaching that "The investigation of truth and the enforcement of testimonial duty demand the restriction, not the expansion, of these privileges," 8 Wigmore, Evidence (McNaughton Rev. 1961), § 2192, p. 73. The other is the more particular lesson "That as, by reason of the complexity and

* "An attorney or counselor at law shall not disclose, or be allowed to disclose, a communication, made by his client to him, or his advice given thereon, in the course of his professional employment, nor shall any clerk, stenographer or other person employed by such attorney or counselor * * * disclose, or be allowed to disclose any such communication or advice."

difficulty of our law, litigation can only be properly conducted by professional men, it is absolutely necessary that a man * * * should have recourse to the assistance of professional lawyers, and * * * it is equally necessary * * * that he should be able to place unrestricted and unbounded confidence in the professional agent, and that the communications he so makes to him should be kept secret * * *," Jessel, M.R. in Anderson v. Bank, 2 Ch.D. 644, 649 (1876). Nothing in the policy of the privilege suggests that attorneys, simply by placing accountants, scientists or investigators on their payrolls and maintaining them in their offices, should be able to invest all communications by clients to such persons with a privilege the law has not seen fit to extend when the latter are operating under their own steam. On the other hand, in contrast to the Tudor times when the privilege was first recognized, the complexities of modern existence prevent attorneys from effectively handling clients' affairs without the help of others; few lawyers could now practice without the assistance of secretaries, file clerks, telephone operators, messengers, clerks not yet admitted to the bar, and aides of other sorts. "The assistance of these agents being indispensable to his work and the communications of the client being often necessarily committed to them by the attorney or by the client himself, the privilege must include all the persons who act as the attorney's agents." 8 Wigmore, Evidence, § 2301; Annot., 53 A.L.R. 369 (1928).

Indeed, the Government does not here dispute that the privilege covers communications to non-lawyer employees with "a menial or ministerial responsibility that involves relating communications *to an attorney.*" We cannot regard the privilege as confined to "menial or ministerial" employees. Thus, we can see no significant difference between a case where the attorney sends a client speaking a foreign language to an interpreter to make a literal translation of the client's story; a second where the attorney, himself having some little knowledge of the foreign tongue, has a more knowledgeable non-lawyer employee in the room to help out; a third where someone to perform that same function has been brought along by the client; and a fourth where the attorney, ignorant of the foreign language, sends the client to a non-lawyer proficient in it, with instructions to interview the client on the attorney's behalf and then render his own summary of the situation, perhaps drawing on his own knowledge in the process, so that the attorney can give the client proper legal advice. All four cases meet every element of Wigmore's famous formulation, § 2292, "(1) Where legal advice of any kind is sought (2) from a professional legal advisor in his capacity as such, (3) the communications relating to that purpose, (4) made in confidence (5) by the client, (6) are at his instance permanently protected (7) from disclosure by himself or by the legal advisor, (8) except the protection be waived,". . . § 2301 of Wigmore would clearly recognize the privilege in the first case and the Government goes along to that extent; § 2301 would also recognize the privilege in the second case and § 2301 in the third unless the circumstances negated confidentiality. We find no valid policy reason for a different result in the fourth case, and we do not read

Wigmore as thinking there is. Laymen consulting lawyers should not be expected to anticipate niceties perceptible only to judges—and not even to all of them.

This analogy of the client speaking a foreign language is by no means irrelevant to the appeal at hand. Accounting concepts are a foreign language to some lawyers in almost all cases, and to almost all lawyers in some cases. Hence the presence of an accountant, whether hired by the lawyer or by the client, while the client is relating a complicated tax story to the lawyer, ought not destroy the privilege, any more than would that of the linguist in the second or third variations of the foreign language theme discussed above; the presence of the accountant is necessary, or at least highly useful, for the effective consultation between the client and the lawyer which the privilege is designed to permit. By the same token, if the lawyer has directed the client, either in the specific case or generally, to tell his story in the first instance to an accountant engaged by the lawyer, who is then to interpret it so that the lawyer may better give legal advice, communications by the client reasonably related to that purpose ought fall within the privilege; there can be no more virtue in requiring the lawyer to sit by while the client pursues these possibly tedious preliminary conversations with the accountant than in insisting on the lawyer's physical presence while the client dictates a statement to the lawyer's secretary or is interviewed by a clerk not yet admitted to practice. What is vital to the privilege is that the communication be made *in confidence* for the purpose of obtaining *legal* advice *from the lawyer*. If what is sought is not legal advice but only accounting service, or if the advice sought is the accountant's rather than the lawyer's, no privilege exists. We recognize this draws what may seem to some a rather arbitrary line between a case where the client communicates first to his own accountant (no privilege as to such communications, even though he later consults his lawyers on the same matter, Gariepy v. United States, 189 F.2d 459, 463 (6 Cir. 1951)),‡ and others, where the client in the first instance consults a lawyer who retains an accountant as a listening post, or consults the lawyer with his own accountant present. But that is the inevitable consequence of having to reconcile the absence of a privilege for accountants and the effective operation of the privilege of client and lawyer under conditions where the lawyer needs outside help. We realize also that the line we have drawn will not be so easy to apply as the simpler positions urged on us by the parties—the district judges will scarcely be able to leave the decision of such cases to computers; but the distinction has to be made if the privilege is neither to be unduly expanded nor to become a trap.

The judgment is vacated and the cause remanded for further proceedings consistent with this opinion.

---

‡ We do not deal in this opinion with the question under what circumstances, if any, such communications could be deemed privileged on the basis that they were being made to the accountant as the client's agent for the purpose of subsequent communication by the accountant to the lawyer; communications by the client's agent to the attorney are privileged, 8 Wigmore, Evidence, § 2317–1.

UNITED STATES v. CABRA

United States Court of Appeals, Fifth Circuit, 1980.
622 F.2d 182.

AINSWORTH, Circuit Judge:

This appeal raises the novel question whether a district judge can impound notes taken during a criminal trial by a paralegal employed by defense counsel to assist in preparation of the defense. We hold that in this case, the district judge acted improperly in impounding the notes.

Appellants Edwin L. Cabra and Claude "Buddy" Leach were tried in district court on charges of vote buying in connection with the November 7, 1978 general election. After three weeks of trial, appellants were acquitted on all counts. Other charges against Leach alleging illegal receipt of campaign contributions are still pending.

During the trial, the district judge, on his own motion, called a bench conference to ask defense counsel if anyone associated with the defense was taking notes on the proceedings. Defense counsel informed the court that Ms. Mary Jane Marcantel, a paralegal employed by the defense, was taking shorthand notes of portions of the testimony. Counsel stated that the purpose of the note-taking was to assist in the preparation of cross-examination, to provide summaries of testimony, and to aid in the preparation of the defense in anticipated criminal prosecutions in related cases. Ms. Marcantel was not present during the entirety of the trial and thus her notes did not reflect a complete account of the proceedings. The shorthand notes were not verbatim, but merely reflected, as accurately as possible, the substance of the testimony.

After ascertaining the character of the notes, the district judge, over defense counsel's objection, ordered that Ms. Marcantel could continue to take notes but that at the completion of the trial the notes were to be submitted to the court and sealed. After trial, the district judge sent a letter requesting compliance with the order. Appellants moved to vacate the order and filed a memorandum of law supporting their position. The district judge denied the motion, but stayed the order pending this appeal.

The district judge based the order on the court's duty "to insure the orderly process of a case." He stated that since the notes could be considered as an unofficial transcript the validity of the official transcript was at stake. "The court feels that there should only be one official transcript and that such unofficial transcripts should not be allowed. The court by this does not mean that these particular defendants would make any improper use of these notes. Rather this order is required to protect the integrity of the official court reporter's transcript." (R. 1140)

A district judge has the power to issue appropriate orders regulating conduct in the courtroom in order to assure an orderly trial. *See, e.g., United States v. Columbia Broadcasting System, Inc.,* 497 F.2d 102, 104 (5th Cir. 1974); *Seymour v. United States,* 373 F.2d 629 (5th Cir. 1967). *See also United States v. Dinitz,* 538 F.2d 1214, 1223–24 (5th Cir. 1976), *cert. denied,* 429 U.S. 1104, 97 S.Ct. 1133, 51 L.Ed.2d 556 (1977). Often the basis of the power is the need to insure that a defendant obtains a fair trial free from unnecessary disruption. *See United States v. Schiavo,* 504 F.2d 1, 6 (3rd Cir.) *(en banc)* ("The Sixth Amendment imposes a duty on the district courts. . . to take reasonable measures to ensure defendants fair trials, free of prejudice and disruption"), *cert. denied sub. nom. Ditter v. Philadelphia Newspapers, Inc.,* 419 U.S. 1096, 95 S.Ct. 690, 42 L.Ed.2d 688 (1974). *See generally Sheppard v. Maxwell,* 384 U.S. 333, 349–51, 86 S.Ct. 1507, 1515–16, 16 L.Ed.2d 600 (1966).

This case is similar to the facts presented in *Columbia Broadcasting System.* There, the district court issued an order prohibiting any sketching of the proceedings. Sketches were made by artists employed by the media for subsequent showing on television news programs. This court, while acknowledging the district court's power to control its proceedings, rejected the order as overly broad. "We are unwilling. . . to condone a sweeping prohibition of in-court sketching when there has been no showing whatsoever that sketching is in any way obtrusive or disruptive." *Columbia Broadcasting System, supra,* 497 F.2d at 107 (footnote omitted). As in *Columbia Broadcasting System,* we cannot understand how Ms. Marcantel's note-taking resulted in any disruption of the courtroom proceedings. There is no evidence that her work had any disturbing or disruptive effect. It appeared that her actions did not differ from the note-taking activities of the press covering the trial or of opposing counsel. Certainly, the note-taking did not interfere with or infringe appellants' rights to a fair trial as the task was performed on their behalf.

The district court placed great weight on the fact that Ms. Marcantel's notes were verbatim. There is no evidence, however, that this was true. Defense counsel stated that the notes were incomplete and that while Ms. Marcantel strived for accuracy, the notes were not always taken in question and answer form. Even assuming that the notes were verbatim, however, we do not believe that the district judge's action was proper. Note-taking at trial is an acknowledged function of paralegals, *see* W.P. Statsky, *Introduction to Paralegalism,* 356 (West 1974). [First edition] A court should not penalize a party on account of the proficiency of its paralegal's performance. The district court's concern for the sanctity of the official transcript is misplaced. While it is the court's responsibility to assure that the official transcript is prepared in accordance with the Court Reporter's Act, 28 U.S.C § 753, *see United States v. Garner,* 581 F.2d 481, 488 (5th Cir. 1978), the Act explicitly states that "[n]o transcripts of the proceedings of the court shall be considered as official except those made from the records taken by the reporter." Moreover, defense counsel stated that they had no intention of relying on the notes as an official summary of the testimony. Thus, the district court was operating under the mistaken assumption that the paralegal's notes challenged the validity of the official transcript.

Since the district court's reasons for impounding the notes were based on unwarranted concerns, the order was an improper exercise of the court's discretionary authority to control courtroom proceedings. Accordingly, the order is reversed.

REVERSED.

Appendix C

Example of Law Firm Stationery that Prints Paralegal Names

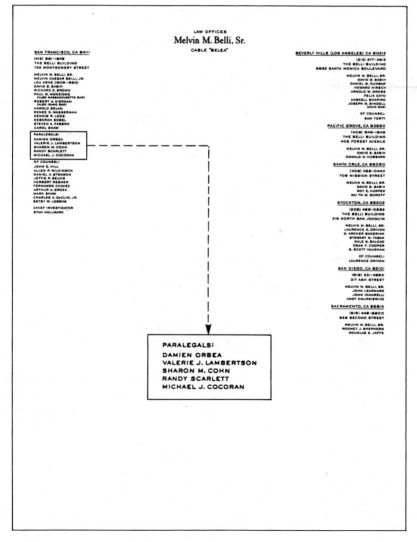

LAW OFFICES
Melvin M. Belli, Sr.
CABLE "BELEA"

SAN FRANCISCO, CA 94111
(415) 981-1849
THE BELLI BUILDING
722 MONTGOMERY STREET

MELVIN M. BELLI, SR.
MELVIN CAESAR BELLI, JR.
LOU ASHE (1908-1980)
DAVID S. SABIH
RICHARD E. BROWN
PAUL M. MONZIONE
(ALSO MASSACHUSETTS BAR)
ROBERT A. KIERNAN
(ALSO IDAHO BAR)
HAROLD BELAN
RENEE D. WASSERMAN
DENNIS R. LOOS
DEBORAH SOBEL
STEVEN A. FABBRO
CAROL SHAW

PARALEGALS:
DAMIEN ORBEA
VALERIE J. LAMBERTSON
SHARON M. COHN
RANDY SCARLETT
MICHAEL J. COCORAN

OF COUNSEL:
JOHN E. HILL
ALLEN P. WILKINSON
DANIEL A. STENSON
JETTIE P. SELVIG
HERBERT RESHNER
FERNANDO CHAVEZ
ARTHUR A. GROZA
MARK BRANK
CHARLES A. DeCUIR, JR.
BETSY W. LEBBOS

CHIEF INVESTIGATOR
STAN HALLMARK

BEVERLY HILLS (LOS ANGELES) CA 90212
(213) 277-3612
THE BELLI BUILDING
9952 SANTA MONICA BOULEVARD

MELVIN M. BELLI, SR.
DAVID S. SABIH
DANIEL W. DUNBAR
HOWARD HIRSCH
ARNOLD W. GROSS
FELIX CAYO
HASKELL SHAPIRO
JOSEPH H. BINDELL
(OHIO BAR)

OF COUNSEL:
SAM YORTY

PACIFIC GROVE, CA 93950
(408) 649-1849
THE BELLI BUILDING
405 FOREST AVENUE

MELVIN M. BELLI, SR.
DAVID S. SABIH
DONALD H. HUBBARD

SANTA CRUZ, CA 95060
(408) 458-0440
709 MISSION STREET

MELVIN M. BELLI, SR.
DAVID S. SABIH
ROY E. HARPER
RAI "H" W. BOROFF

STOCKTON, CA 95202
(209) 466-0992
THE BELLI BUILDING
215 NORTH SAN JOAQUIN

MELVIN M. BELLI, SR.
LAURENCE E. DRIVON
G. ARCHER BAKERINK
STEWART M. TABAK
DALE S. BALCAO
DEAN F. COOPER
S. SCOTT VAUGHAN

OF COUNSEL:
LAURENCE DRIVON

SAN DIEGO, CA 92101
(619) 231-4890
317 ASH STREET

MELVIN M. BELLI, SR.
JOHN LEARNARD
JOHN VAMARELLI
ANDY ZMURKIEWICZ

SACRAMENTO, CA 95814
(916) 448-8600
928 SECOND STREET

MELVIN M. BELLI, SR.
RODNEY J. SHEPHERD
DOUGLAS E. JAFFE

PARALEGALS:
DAMIEN ORBEA
VALERIE J. LAMBERTSON
SHARON M. COHN
RANDY SCARLETT
MICHAEL J. COCORAN

————— *Appendix D*

Who Disciplines
Attorneys? —————————

Who disciplines attorneys for violating ethical canons or rules of professional responsibility? In every state the ultimate authority over attorney discipline is in the highest state court. Before a final decision is made by such a court, the state bar association or some other agency usually has a role to play.

The following is a state-by-state survey* of the disciplinary process:

Alabama

The state bar is responsible for the discipline process through the supervision of the bar's Board of Commissioners.

Alaska

The state bar is responsible for the discipline process. The Supreme Court must approve bar disciplinary rule revision proposals.

Arizona

The state bar is responsible for the discipline process through a panel comprised of lawyer members appointed by the bar and public members appointed by the Supreme Court. The Supreme Court also must approve disciplinary rule revisions proposed by the bar's Board of Governors.

---

*"Bars Disciplinary Role Varies Across the Nation," CAL BAR VIEW, The State Bar of California, pp. 1-3 (June, 1980).

Arkansas

The Supreme Court Committee on Professional Conduct Agency is responsible for the discipline process. The committee, in association with a committee of The Arkansas Bar Association, proposes disciplinary rule revisions to the Supreme Court.

California

The state bar's Offices of Trial Counsel, Investigation and State Bar Court are responsible for the discipline process, under the supervision of the bar's Board of Governors.

Colorado

A state Grievance Commission is responsible for investigating and adjudicating disciplinary cases, while a state Disciplinary Prosecutor prosecutes the cases.

Connecticut

A state Grievance Commission Agency adjudicates discipline cases and can impose private reprimands. The commission may prosecute attorneys in Superior Court.

Delaware

The Supreme Court, through separate adjudicating and prosecutorial agencies, is responsible for the discipline process.

District of Columbia

A Board on Professional Responsibility is responsible for the discipline process.

Florida

The state bar's Grievance Committee, Referees, Staff Counsel and Bar Counsel share responsibility for the discipline process, under the supervision of the bar's Board of Governors.

Georgia

The state bar's Disciplinary Board, appointed by the president and approved by the Board of Governors, is responsible for the discipline process. The board also proposes disciplinary rule changes to the Supreme Court.

Hawaii

The state Office of Disciplinary Counsel investigates and prosecutes attorneys in disciplinary matters, while the state Disciplinary Board adjudicates.

Idaho

The state bar's Board of Commissioners appoints a disciplinary board and oversees the board's activities. The Board of Commissioners also is empowered to make and amend disciplinary rules.

Illinois

A state Attorney Registration and Disciplinary Commission is responsible for the discipline process.

Indiana

A state Disciplinary Commission is responsible for the discipline process. The state bar assists in the investigation and prosecution when requested by the commission.

Iowa

A state Committee on Professional Ethics and Conduct and a state Grievance Commission share responsibility for initiating and processing disciplinary complaints.

Kansas

A state Disciplinary Board is responsible for the prosecution and adjudication of attorneys in disciplinary matters and proposes disciplinary rule revisions to the Supreme Court. Local bar associations also may investigate.

Kentucky

The state bar's Inquiry Tribunal investigates complaints and decides whether to pursue disciplinary action against attorneys. Bar counsel investigates and prosecutes, and the bar's Board of Governors reviews disciplinary cases and makes recommendations to the Supreme Court.

Louisiana

The state bar's Committee on Professional Responsibility is responsible for the discipline process. The committee also proposes rules to the bar's Board of Governors and House of Delegates, subject to Supreme Court approval.

Maine

A state Board of Overseers of the Bar Adjudicative and Prosecutorial Functions is responsible for the discipline process.

Maryland

A state Attorney Grievance Commission, cooperating with lawyer members of the state bar's Inquiry Committee and a Review Board selected by the bar's Board of Governors, is responsible for the discipline process.

Massachusetts

A state Board of Bar Overseers is responsible for the discipline process.

Michigan

A state Attorney Grievance Commission is responsible for investigating and prosecuting attorney discipline cases, while a state Attorney Discipline Board adjucates the cases.

Minnesota

A state Lawyers Professional Responsibility Board is responsible for the discipline process. The state bar may nominate six of the 21 Supreme Court-appointed members.

Mississippi

The state bar's Complaints Committee, appointed by the president, is responsible for the discipline process.

Missouri

A state Advisory Commission is responsible for the discipline process.

Montana

A state Commission on Practice is responsible for the discipline process.

Nebraska

The state bar appoints a Disciplinary Counsel, which is responsible to a Supreme Court Disciplinary Board.

Nevada

The state bar's Disciplinary Agency is responsible for the discipline process, subject to review by the bar's Board of Governors. The Supreme Court must approve any disciplinary rule changes.

New Hampshire

The Supreme Court's Disciplinary Agency is responsible for the discipline process.

New Jersey

The Supreme Court's Disciplinary Agency is responsible for the discipline process.

New Mexico

A state Disciplinary Board, appointed by the Supreme Court, investigates and prosecutes disciplinary cases after a Hearing Committee conducts hearings and makes recommendations to the board. The state bar nominates board members to the Supreme Court.

New York

Four state Judicial Department Disciplinary Committees are responsible for the discipline process.

North Carolina
Three state bar entities share responsibility for the discipline process. The Grievance Committee is responsible for conducting hearings. The Office of Counsel is responsible for prosecuting cases, and the Hearing Commission adjucates disciplinary cases.

North Dakota
A state Disciplinary Board is responsible for the discipline process. A state bar Hearing Committee, appointed by the president, participates in proceedings.

Ohio
A state Office of Disciplinary Counsel, under Supreme Court supervision, investigates and prosecutes disciplinary cases. The Board of Commissioners on Grievance and Discipline adjudicates cases. Local bar grievance committees investigate complaints and report to The Board of Commissioners.

Oklahoma
The state bar Professional Responsibility Tribunal investigates disciplinary cases and makes recommendations to the Supreme Court.

Oregon
The state bar's Disciplinary Committee, appointed and supervised by the Board of Governors, is responsible for the discipline process. Rules of Procedure are adopted by the board, subject to Supreme Court approval.

Pennsylvania
The Supreme Court's Disciplinary Board prosecutes and adjudicates cases.

Rhode Island
A state Disciplinary Board is responsible for the discipline process.

South Carolina
A state Board of Commissioners on Grievances and Discipline is responsible for the discipline process. The State Attorney General's Office prosecutes cases.

South Dakota
The state bar's Disciplinary Board is responsible for the discipline process and proposes changes in the Rules of Procedure to the Supreme Court.

Tennessee

A state Board of Professional Responsibility prosecutes and adjudicates disciplinary cases.

Texas

State bar Volunteer Grievance Committees, appointed by the president, investigate and decide if a case can be prosecuted. The committees may not take disciplinary action without attorney concurrence. Disciplinary sanctions without the consent of the attorney are allowed only after a civil trial.

Utah

State bar Hearing Committees, under the supervision of the Board of Bar Commissioners and Bar Counsel, are responsible for the discipline process.

Vermont

The State Attorney General investigates disciplinary cases and makes recommendations to the Supreme Court.

Virginia

The state bar's Disciplinary Board is responsible for the discipline process. The bar's Office of Bar Counsel manages the progress of cases, while complaints are investigated by the District Committee of the Bar.

Washington

The state bar's Bar Counsel, Review Committee and Disciplinary Board are responsible for the discipline process, under the supervision of the bar's Board of Governors.

West Virginia

The state bar's Disciplinary Committee is responsible for the discipline process.

Wisconsin

A state Board of Attorneys Professional Competence prosecutes and adjudicates disciplinary cases. The state bar may nominate members to the board.

Wyoming

A state Grievance Committee prosecutes and adjudicates disciplinary cases. The state bar nominates members of the committee.

————— *Appendix E*

Survey of Nonlawyer
Practice before Federal
Administrative Agencies —————

STANDING COMMITTEE ON LAWYERS' RESPONSIBILITY
FOR CLIENT PROTECTION AND THE AMERICAN BAR
ASSOCIATION CENTER FOR PROFESSIONAL
RESPONSIBILITY

February, 1985

I. BACKGROUND

The American Bar Association Standing Committee on Lawyers' Responsibility for Client Protection disseminated this survey to thirty-three (33) federal administrative agencies in late August, 1984. The survey was intended to provide background information on the experiences of agencies permitting nonlawyer practice (other than for purposes of self-representation). During September and October ninety-seven percent (97%) of the agencies responded either over the phone or by mail following initial contact with their Offices of General Counsel. The ABA Center for Professional Responsibility tabulated the results in October, 1984.

II. BRIEF ANALYSIS AND CONCLUSIONS

We found that the overwhelming majority of agencies studied permit nonlawyer representation in both adversarial and nonadversarial proceedings. However, most of them seem to encounter lay practice very infrequently (in less than 5% of adjudications), while only a few encounter lay practice as often as lawyer practice. Thus, although universally permitted, lay practice before federal agencies rarely occurs.

Few of the responding agencies comprehensively monitor or control the lay practice that does occur. Only about twenty percent (20%) require nonlawyers to register with the agency before permitting them to practice. Registration procedures may range from simply listing nonlawyers' names to more formalized certifying or licensing procedures which may include testing and character reviews. Proceedings in most of these agencies tend to require highly technical or specialized knowledge. Registration insures that lay representation meets an appropriate level of quality and competence. In at least one agency, registration insures that nonlawyer representatives will charge only nominal fees or no fees at all.

No agencies indicated that they would discipline nonlawyers differently from lawyers, although they clearly have an additional ability to pursue sanctions against lawyers through external disciplinary mechanisms. Only a few agencies indicated any special need for nonlawyer discipline. Most reported they had not encountered any problems with misconduct by nonlawyers or any inability of nonlawyers to meet appropriate ethical standards (though fewer than a third of the agencies studied have actually defined any specific ethical standards). Of those that voiced complaints about nonlawyers' skills in representation, most indicated that the problem they encounter most frequently is nonlawyers' lack of familiarity with procedural rules and tactics. The majority of responses suggest that nonlawyers do not pose any special practice problems, nor do they receive any special disciplinary consideration. Overall, the concern for nonlawyers' competence and ethical conduct seems limited, perhaps because nonlawyer practice is not widespread.

III. METHODOLOGY

Throughout the survey our questions focused on lay representation (other than self-representation) occurring in adjudicatory proceedings. In question 1, in which we asked whether agencies permitted nonlawyer representation, we attempted to distinguish between adversarial and nonadversarial proceedings. Our distinction did not prove particularly informative because all agencies permitting nonlawer practice (97%) allow such practice in both arenas.

Question 2 sought the methods by which agencies control or limit those practicing before them. The responses vary considerably from agency to agency. Questions 3 and 4 requested statistics concerning the frequency of nonlawyer practice. Many of the agencies indicated that statistics were unavailable. These responses also vary considerably. The results of questions 1 through 4 are tabulated in Chart I.

CHART I

REGULATIONS GOVERNING NONLAWYER
REPRESENTATION, FREQUENCY, AND TYPE OF PRACTICE

Agency	Statute/ Regulation Permitting Appearance	Permits Nonlawyer Adversarial Representation	Permits Nonlawyer Nonadversarial Representation	Provisions Limiting or Governing Practice	Frequency of Nonlawyer Representation	Change in Frequency of Nonlawyer Rep. w/in Past 6 Years	Most Common Type(s) of Nonlawyer Representation
Bd. of Immigration Appeals: Immigration and Naturalization Serv.	8 CFR § 292.1-3	Yes	Yes	"Accredited representative"[1] working for "recognized organization"[2] may charge only nominal fees. "Reputable individual"[3] may not charge fees	No statistics available	No statistics available	One time only by family member/friend; charitable, religious or social service organization
Civil Aeronautics Bd.	14 CFR § 300.1-6 14 CFR § 302.11	Yes	Yes	None	Fewer than 6 appearances per yr., less than 1% of appearances[4]	None	Economic consultants for corporations

[1] May become accredited by the Department of Immigration Appeals (D.I.A.) by submitting an application through a recognized organization for review of character and fitness and experience with and knowledge of immigration law. No formal testing requirement or licensing fee.

[2] Typically a religious, charitable or social service organization becomes recognized by submitting an application for approval to the D.I.A. assuring that it will charge only nominal fees and assess no representation charges.

[3] Typically a family member or friend submits declaration that he or she charges no fee, has a preexisting relationship with immigrant-applicant, and appears only on individual basis at request of immigrant-applicant.

[4] Although nonlawyer practice not discouraged, complexity of agency proceedings tends to require specialized legal practice. Typical parties, large corporations or businesses, tend to hire lawyers.

CHART I
REGULATIONS GOVERNING NONLAWYER
REPRESENTATION, FREQUENCY, AND TYPE OF PRACTICE—Continued.

Agency	Statute/Regulation Permitting Appearance	Permits Nonlawyer Adversarial Representation	Permits Nonlawyer Nonadversarial Representation	Provisions Limiting or Governing Practice	Frequency of Nonlawyer Representation	Change in Frequency of Nonlawyer Rep. w/in Past 6 Years	Most Common Type(s) of Nonlawyer Representation
Comptroller of the Currency	12 CFR § 19.3	Yes[5]	Yes	Nonlawyer may be required to file a power of attorney or show to the satisfaction of the Comptroller the possession of requisite qualifications	None	None	None
Consumer Product Safety Comm'n	16 CFR § 1025.61 et. seq.	Yes	Yes	Filing and approval of proof of qualifications. See 16 CFR § 1025.65	Very infrequent, 2–5% of appearances	None	Non-fee by industry rep., consultant, or private service agency
Dep't of Agric., Agricultural Marketing Serv.	7 CFR § 50.27	Yes	Yes	None	Fewer than 3 appearances per yr., less than 1% of appearances	Decreased,[6] no statistics available	Economist/accountant providing assistance prior to appearance

[5] Permitted but lay representation rare because of complex proceedings and substantial rights or amounts of money involved.

[6] In agency's early history, economists provided a substantial amount of representation because of the economic nature of agency proceedings. As proceedings became more sophisticated, economists began aiding lawyers rather than assuming primary responsibility for legal representation. Representation by economists is now rare, and lawyers handle the bulk of representation.

CHART I
REGULATIONS GOVERNING NONLAWYER
REPRESENTATION, FREQUENCY, AND TYPE OF PRACTICE—Continued.

Agency	Statute/ Regulation Permitting Appearance	Permits Nonlawyer Adversarial Representation	Permits Nonlawyer Nonadversarial Representation	Provisions Limiting or Governing Practice	Frequency of Nonlawyer Representation	Change in Frequency of Nonlawyer Rep. w/in Past 6 Years	Most Common Type(s) of Nonlawyer Representation
Dep't of Commerce, Office of Secretary	Those of other agencies governing appearances before administrative bodies, e.g., MSPB, 5 CFR Part 1201	Yes	Yes	Reasonable atty's fees for litigated matters set by agency; maximum atty's fees for settlement set at $75./hr.; government pays fees to winning atty.	No statistics available	No statistics available	Non-fee by union reps.
Dep't of Commerce, Patent and Trademark Office	35 U.S.C. §§ 31-33	Yes	Yes	Only registered[7] practitioners permitted to practice	Less than 16% of appearances[8]	None	Repeated practice for a fee by registered agents

[7] Nonlawyers become registered by passing a character and fitness review and an examination. Nonlawyers having served four years in the examining corps of the Patent and Trademark Office (P.T.O.) may waive the exam. *See* 57 CFR § 1.341.

[8] Nonlawyers comprise about 16% of registered practitioners, but not all registered practitioners appear before P.T.O., so that nonlawyers probably appear in less than 16% of patent applications filed with P.T.O.

CHART I
REGULATIONS GOVERNING NONLAWYER
REPRESENTATION, FREQUENCY, AND TYPE OF PRACTICE—Continued.

Agency	Statute/ Regulation Permitting Appearance	Permits Nonlawyer Adversarial Representation	Permits Nonlawyer Nonadversarial Representation	Provisions Limiting or Governing Practice	Frequency of Nonlawyer Representation	Change in Frequency of Nonlawyer Rep. w/in Past 6 Years	Most Common Type(s) of Nonlawyer Representation
Dep't of Health and Human Services, Food and Drug Admin.	21 CFR §§ 12.40, 12.45	Yes	Yes	None	No appearances in recent years	None	None
Dep't of Justice, Drug Enforcement Admin.	21 CFR § 1316.50	Yes	N/A, all proceedings adversarial	None	2 to 3 appearances per yr., 5% of appearances[9]	None	One time only by officer/employee of small family-owned business
Dep't of Justice, Foreign Claims Settlement Comm'n	45 CFR § 500.1-6	No	No[10]	Lawyers' fees set by statute at 10% of claim award and deducted from award	N/A[11]	N/A[11]	Family member providing assistance prior to appearance

[9] Appearances are by the employees or officers of small family-owned businesses, analogous to pro se appearances.

[10] The agency only allows "representation" by bar members. Family members may sometimes assist in preparation of claims or at oral hearings, typically where elderly parent has language barrier problems.

[11] No nonlawyer representation allowed.

CHART I

REGULATIONS GOVERNING NONLAWYER
REPRESENTATION, FREQUENCY, AND TYPE OF PRACTICE—Continued.

Agency	Statute/ Regulation Permitting Appearance	Permits Nonlawyer Adversarial Representation	Permits Nonlawyer Nonadversarial Representation	Provisions Limiting or Governing Practice	Frequency of Nonlawyer Representation	Change in Frequency of Nonlawyer Rep. w/in Past 6 Years	Most Common Type(s) of Nonlawyer Representation
Dep't of Labor, Benefits Review Bd.	20 CFR § 802.201(b) 20 CFR § 802.202	Yes	N/A, all proceedings adversarial	Employer pays fee for successful claimant represented by lawyer; claimant pays fee when represented by nonlawyer; lawyer may acquire lien against award; nonlawyers may not.[12] Professional status is criterion for determining fee.[13]	2–4% of appearances	None	Repeated practice for fee
Dep't of Labor, Employees Compensation Appeals Bd.	20 CFR § 501.11	Yes	N/A, all proceedings adversarial	All fees approved by board	Appear as frequently as lawyers	None	One time only by family member/friend; repeated practice for a fee

[12] These policies may tend to discourage lay representation.

[13] Typically approved rates for nonlawyers are less than half of those attorneys receive.

CHART I
REGULATIONS GOVERNING NONLAWYER
REPRESENTATION, FREQUENCY, AND TYPE OF PRACTICE—Continued.

Agency	Statute/Regulation Permitting Appearance	Permits Nonlawyer Adversarial Representation	Permits Nonlawyer Nonadversarial Representation	Provisions Limiting or Governing Practice	Frequency of Nonlawyer Representation	Change in Frequency of Nonlawyer Rep. w/in Past 6 Years	Most Common Type(s) of Nonlawyer Representation
Dep't of Labor, National Railroad Adjustment Bd.	45 U.S.C. § 3153	Yes	N/A	Only entities identified in 45 U.S.C. § 151 allowed to practice	Almost 100% of appearances	None	Industry employees
Dep't of Labor, Wage and Appeals Bd.	20 CFR § 725.362(a) 20 CFR § 725.365 20 CFR § 725.366(b)	Yes	N/A	Fees must be reasonably commensurate with services performed[14]; attorney's fee deducted from award; employer pays fee for successful claimant represented by lawyer; claimant prep fee when represented by nonlawyer; lawyer may require lien against award, nonlawyers may not.[15]	3% of appearances; as in 180 case/yr.	Decrease due to investigations by Office of Inspector General into unauthorized receipt of fees	One time only by family member or friend; repeated practice for fee; assistance prior to appearance

[14] *See* 20 CFR § 725.366(b) (black lung) and 20 CFR § 702.132 (longshore).

[15] These policies may tend to discourage lay representation.

CHART I

REGULATIONS GOVERNING NONLAWYER
REPRESENTATION, FREQUENCY, AND TYPE OF PRACTICE—Continued.

Agency	Statute/ Regulation Permitting Appearance	Permits Nonlawyer Adversarial Representation	Permits Nonlawyer Nonadversarial Representation	Provisions Limiting or Governing Practice	Frequency of Nonlawyer Representation	Change in Frequency of Nonlawyer Rep. w/in Past 6 Years	Most Common Type(s) of Nonlawyer Representation
Dep't of Transportation, Maritime Admin.	46 CFR § 201.21	Yes	Yes	Only registered nonlawyers permitted to practice	Very infrequent	None	
Federal Deposit Ins. Corp.	12 CFR § 308.04	Yes	Yes	Only qualified nonlawyers permitted to represent	10 to 20 appearances per yr., 5% of appearances	50% decrease	One time only by family member/friend; nonlawyer assistance prior to appearance
Federal Energy Regulatory Comm'n	18 CFR § 385.2101	Yes	Yes	None	1 or 2 per yr.	None	Engineering firm assisting in technical nonadversarial proceeding
Federal Maritime Comm'n	46 CFR § 502.30	Yes	Yes	Only registered nonlawyers permitted to appear[16]	.5 to 1% of appearances	None	One time only by family member/friend; non-fee by industry rep., consultant or private service agency

[16] Certificates of registration are issued on payment of $13.00 processing fee and completion of application form indicating sufficient educational qualifications and recommendations. There is no testing or formal licensing.

CHART I

REGULATIONS GOVERNING NONLAWYER
REPRESENTATION, FREQUENCY, AND TYPE OF PRACTICE—Continued.

Agency	Statute/ Regulation Permitting Appearance	Permits Nonlawyer Adversarial Representation	Permits Nonlawyer Nonadversarial Representation	Provisions Limiting or Governing Practice	Frequency of Nonlawyer Representation	Change in Frequency of Nonlawyer Rep. w/in Past 6 Years	Most Common Type(s) of Nonlawyer Representation
Federal Mine Safety & Health Review Comm'n	29 CFR § 2700.3(b)	Yes, at trial hearings before A.L.J.'s; at appellate reviews before commissioners (A.L.J. = Administrative Law Judge.)	N/A	Nonlawyer may practice only if party, "representative of miners,"[17] or owner, partner, full time officer or employee of party-business entity; otherwise permitted to appear for limited purpose in special proceedings.	5–10% of appearances	None	Non-fee by industry rep., consultant or private service agency
General Accounting Office	31 U.S.C. § 731-732; 4 CFR §§ 11 and 28; GAO Orders 2713.2, 2752.1, and 2777.1	Yes, in adverse actions, grievance proceedings, and discrimination complaints	Yes	Nonlawyers not permitted fees; government pays fees to winning representatives.[18]	Very infrequent	Not aware of any	

[17] *See generally* 30 CFR § 40.1(b).

[18] As provided in discrimination statutes, backpay act, and appeals authorized by law.

CHART I
REGULATIONS GOVERNING NONLAWYER
REPRESENTATION, FREQUENCY, AND TYPE OF PRACTICE—Continued.

Agency	Statute/ Regulation Permitting Appearance	Permits Nonlawyer Adversarial Representation	Permits Nonlawyer Nonadversarial Representation	Provisions Limiting or Governing Practice	Frequency of Nonlawyer Representation	Change in Frequency of Nonlawyer Rep. w/in Past 6 Years	Most Common Type(s) of Nonlawyer Representation
Internal Revenue Serv.	13 CFR Part 10; 31 U.S.C. § 330; Treasury Dept. Circular 230	Yes	Yes	Non-certified public accountant and nonlawyer must become enrolled agent[19] to practice	As frequent as lawyer representation[20]	Increased, no statistics available	Repeated practice for fee by certified public accountant or enrolled agent
Interstate Commerce Comm'n	49 CFR § 1103	Yes	Yes	Fee limitations[21]; only registered nonlawyer permitted to practice,[22] however, self-representation is allowed without registration	1,600 nonlawyers now registered and account for 5% of appearances.[23]	Decreased,[24] no statistics available	Repeated practice for a fee

[19] Nonlawyers and noncertified public accountants become enrolled agents by 1) passing a character and fitness review, and 2) successful completion of special enrollment examination testing on federal taxation and related matters, or 3) former employment with the IRS, provided duties qualify the individual. Lawyers and certified public accountants may practice without enrollment.

[20] Includes representation by certified public accountants as well as enrolled agents.

[21] Practitioners may not overestimate the value of services, accept compensation from party other than client, make contingent fee arrangements or divide fees with laypersons. *See* 49 CFR § 1103.70.

[22] To become registered applicant must 1) meet educational and experience requirements, 2) undergo character and fitness review, 3) pass exam administered by the agency testing knowledge in the field of transportation, and 4) take an oath. *See* 49 CFR § 1103.3.

[23] Figure includes appearances in rulemaking as well as adjudicatory proceedings.

[24] Deregulation has reduced the caseload while proceedings have become more complex, creating a greater need for legal expertise.

CHART I
REGULATIONS GOVERNING NONLAWYER
REPRESENTATION, FREQUENCY, AND TYPE OF PRACTICE—Continued.

Agency	Statute/ Regulation Permitting Appearance	Permits Nonlawyer Adversarial Representation	Permits Nonlawyer Nonadversarial Representation	Provisions Limiting or Governing Practice	Frequency of Nonlawyer Representation	Change in Frequency of Nonlawyer Rep. w/in Past 6 Years	Most Common Type(s) of Nonlawyer Representation
National Credit Union Admin.	12 CFR § 747	Yes	Yes	None	No statistics available	Decreased, no statistics available	Credit union representatives
National Labor Relations Bd.		Yes	Yes	None	Infrequent	None	
National Mediation Bd.	None, agency governed by 29 CFR § 1200 et seq.	N/A, all proceedings adversarial	Yes	None	200 appearances per yr., appear twice as frequently as lawyers	Decreased, no statistics available	Union representatives
National Transportation Safety Bd.	49 CFR § 821 49 CFR § 831 49 CFR § 845	Yes	Yes	In adjudication lawyer representation encouraged; in investigation lawyer participation discouraged because technical expertise required; parties[25] participate in investigations	Very infrequent except at investigatory levels	None	Manufacturers at investigatory levels

[25] "Parties" includes manufacturers, unions, operators and other regulatory agencies.

CHART I

REGULATIONS GOVERNING NONLAWYER
REPRESENTATION, FREQUENCY, AND TYPE OF PRACTICE—Continued.

Agency	Statute/ Regulation Permitting Appearance	Permits Nonlawyer Adversarial Representation	Permits Nonlawyer Nonadversarial Representation	Provisions Limiting or Governing Practice	Frequency of Nonlawyer Representation	Change in Frequency of Nonlawyer Rep. w/in Past 6 Years	Most Common Type(s) of Nonlawyer Representation
Occupational Safety and Health Review Comm'n	29 CFR § 2200.22	Yes	N/A, all proceedings adversarial	Optional simplified procedures to encourage self-representation by small businesses	20% of appearances[26]	20% decrease[27]	Nonlegal employee representing employer; union representative
Small Business Admin.	13 CFR § 121.11 13 CFR § 134.16	Yes	N/A, all proceedings adversarial	None	Less than 1% of appearances[28]	None	

[26] Statistic includes pro se representation.

[27] Nonlawyer practice accounted in 1980 for 40% of the agency's caseload but decreased in 1982–83 to 20%. Decrease may result from increasing complexity in cases causing claimants to seek legal representation.

[28] Figure excludes pro se appearances in size and Standard Industrial Classification (SIC) Appeals. Approximately 50% of size and SIC appeals are conducted pro se by nonlawyers.

CHART I
REGULATIONS GOVERNING NONLAWYER
REPRESENTATION, FREQUENCY, AND TYPE OF PRACTICE—Continued.

Agency	Statute/Regulation Permitting Appearance	Permits Nonlawyer Adversarial Representation	Permits Nonlawyer Nonadversarial Representation	Provisions Limiting or Governing Practice	Frequency of Nonlawyer Representation	Change in Frequency of Nonlawyer Rep. w/in Past 6 Years	Most Common Type(s) of Nonlawyer Representation
Social Security Admin.	42 USC § 406(a) 29 CFR	Yes, tentatively as part of experiment; generally agency has no adversarial proceedings	Yes	Claimants advised of advantages of representation at hearing level[29]; fees set by agency[30]; attorneys' fees withheld from awards[31]	Appear in 13% of total hearings or in 25–30% of hearings with representation	None, although lawyer representation increased by 56% since 1978[32]	One time only by family member/friend; repeated practice for fee; non-fee rep. by legal services paralegal

[29] When hearing request filed, agency sends a letter to unrepresented claimant describing advantages of representation. Attached to letter is a list of organizations which may provide representation. The list includes lawyer referral services, legal aid groups, law schools, etc.

[30] The agency sets all fees based on criteria listed in 20 CFR § 404.1725(b), including extent and type of services, complexity of case, level of skill and competence required in performing services, time spent, results achieved, level at which representative became involved, and amount requested.

[31] When decision is entered in favor of a claimant represented by a lawyer in a Title II or Black Lung case, normally 25% of the benefits awarded are withheld. After agency has set the fee it forwards fee directly to the lawyer from the amount withheld. If attorney's fees exceed the amount withheld, the lawyer must seek the remainder from the claimant. If the attorney's fees are less than the amount withheld, the claimant receives the remainder. Nonlawyer representatives do not have this withholding benefit.

[32] In fiscal year 1978 lawyers appeared in 32% of hearings; nonlawyers in 12%. In fiscal year 1983 lawyers appeared in 50% of hearings; nonlawyers in 13%. Though the letter discussed in footnote 29 does not exclusively reference lawyers' services, this list may attribute to the increase in lawyer representation. Lawyers also have a high success rate before the agency as well as the advantage of award withholdings to secure fees in Title II and Black Lung cases (see footnote 31).

CHART I

REGULATIONS GOVERNING NONLAWYER

REPRESENTATION, FREQUENCY, AND TYPE OF PRACTICE—Continued.

Agency	Statute/ Regulation Permitting Appearance	Permits Nonlawyer Adversarial Representation	Permits Nonlawyer Nonadversarial Representation	Provisions Limiting or Governing Practice	Frequency of Nonlawyer Representation	Change in Frequency of Nonlawyer Rep. w/in Past 6 Years	Most Common Type(s) of Nonlawyer Representation
U.S. Customs Serv.	None	Yes	Yes	None	5 to 15% of caseload volume	None	Repeated practice for fee by licensed customs brokers and former customs officials
U.S. Environmental Protection Agency	40 CFR § 124 40 CFR § 164.30 40 CFR § 22.10	Yes	N/A	None	No appearances	None	None

Index ━━━━━━━━━━━━━━━━━━━━━━